THE RUSSIAN CHURCH

AND

RUSSIAN DISSENT

COMPRISING

ORTHODOXY, DISSENT, AND ERRATIC SECTS

BY

ALBERT F. HEARD

FORMERLY CONSUL-GENERAL FOR RUSSIA AT SHANGHAI

NEW YORK
HARPER & BROTHERS, FRANKLIN SQUARE
1887

Copyright, 1887, by HARPER & BROTHERS.

All rights reserved.

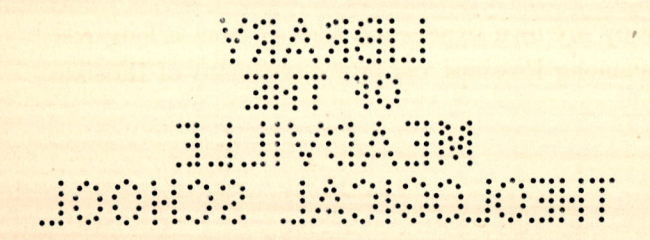

PREFACE.

In the following pages I have given a consecutive account of the Orthodox Church of Russia, commencing with its origin and history, then investigating its present condition and that of its clergy, tracing the causes and consequences of the schism which arose in the seventeenth century, and still continues, and finally examining the innumerable sects springing from the schismatic movement, or from the inherent devotional character of the people. A work of this nature, without any pretence of theological erudition, and intended for the general reader, does not, so far as I have been able to ascertain, exist, and I have endeavored to supply the deficiency. I have been compelled to seek information from many sources, and a list of the authorities I have consulted is appended; but for a view of the Church and the clergy, and of the various sects, as they are at present known, I have followed and borrowed freely from the interesting and able articles of M. Anatole Leroy-Beaulieu, in the *Revue des Deux Mondes*. This distinguished writer has treated, in a thoroughly philosophic spirit, the complex institutions of Russia; and, if I may judge by my own experience, derived from a long residence among Russians, and by the testimony of Russians of eminence, he is entitled to rank highest among foreign authorities on the subject.

I speak advisedly above of the *present* state of information upon the religious question, especially as regards the masses of the people, among whom, chiefly, devotional feeling and sectarianism flourish. They are frequently unable to give intelligible explanations of their religious beliefs, even when willing to do so; and generally, with Asiatic dislike of strangers, or with suspicious distrust of their own superiors, generated by centuries of serfdom, they evade every attempt at inquiry. Moreover, it is only in recent years that the internal condition of the Russian Empire has received from Russians themselves the investigation and study which its importance demands, and it may yet be long before it can be safely averred that the religious question, any more than others of a political nature, is fully understood and appreciated.

Loyalty to the Tsar, and aptitude for organization, are universal among the people, but religious devotion is their strongest and most general characteristic; in no country is it so universally and so intimately interwoven in the daily life of every individual. Wars against the infidel Turk excite the same enthusiasm as the crusades of the Middle Ages; and the intensity of this feeling, together with the pious credulity of the people, are a prodigious power in the hands of the government, that may be easily directed in furtherance of political ends.

"It is for Christ that we are to fight," a peasant was heard to say to a fellow-conscript in 1877. "He suffered on the cross for us, and it is but right that we should suffer, in our turn, for Him."

CONTENTS.

CHAPTER I.
The Separation of the Churches of the East and the West; the Causes, Political and Ecclesiastical. — Differences between the Churches, External and Internal.................................. Page 1

CHAPTER II.
Introduction of Christianity into Russia........................ 13

CHAPTER III.
The Russian Church from its Establishment to its Independence of Constantinople.—The Unia and the Orthodox Church in Poland; Separation of the Latter from the Church in Russia............ 22

CHAPTER IV.
The Church in the Fifteenth Century.—Effect of Tatar Occupation.—Liberation of Russia from the Tatars.—Attempted Reforms in the Church.—The Orthodox Church in Poland.—Establishment of the Patriarchate in Russia....................................... 39

CHAPTER V.
Boris Godounov.—The Church in Poland.—Peter Mogila.—Liberation of Russia from the Poles.—Philaret.—Alexis.—Nikon and his Reforms.—Dissent... 65

CHAPTER VI.
Reunion of the Polish to the Russian Church.—Dissent.—Peter the Great and his Successors.—Substitution of the Holy Synod for the Patriarchate.—Absorption of the Unia by the Russian Church.—Reforms.. 111

CHAPTER VII.

Influence of the Religious Element; its Development. — National Character of the Church; its Isolation.—Differences from Catholic and Protestant Churches.—Popes.—Development of Church and State in Russia.—Church Government.................. Page 137

CHAPTER VIII.

The Clergy, Black and White.—Monasticism and Monasteries.—Parish Priests 160

CHAPTER IX.

The Raskol.—Early Heresies.—Attempted Reforms in Church.—Nikon. —Peter the Great.—The Popovtsi and the Bezpopovtsi.—Political Aspect of the Raskol 179

CHAPTER X.

The Raskol, Socially and Politically.—Praobrajenski and Rogojski.— Organization of Popovtsism and Bezpopovtsism.—Attempts at Reconciliation with the Church.—The Edinovertsi.—Modification of the Raskol; its Extreme Sects 208

CHAPTER XI.

Sects not belonging to the Raskol.—Mystical and Rationalistic Sects. —Erratic Sects.—Recent Sects.—Vitality of Sectarian Spirit.—Attitude of Government towards Dissent........................ 250

INDEX.. 299

LIST OF BOOKS CONSULTED.

Barry, H.................Russia in 1870. London, 1871.
Burnet, G...............History of His Own Times. London, 1809.
Castera, J.............. { History of Catherine II., Empress of Russia. London, 1800.
Coxe, W................ { Account of Russian Discoveries, etc. London, 1803.
Custine, A., Marquis de...La Russie en 1839. Bruxelles, 1843.
Delaveau, H.............In *La Revue des Deux Mondes.* Paris, 1858.
Dixon, W. H............Free Russia. New York, 1870.
Fleury, C., et Fabre, J. C..Histoire Ecclésiastique. Paris, 1722–1738.
Fletcher, Giles, and } { A Treatise on the Russian Commonwealth. 1588.
Horsey, Sir Jerome } { Travels of. 1591.
                  Two books in one, entitled "Russia at the Close of the XVI. Century," edited by E. A. Bond for the Hakluyt Society. London, 1856.
Foy de la Neufville.......An Account of Muscovy as it was in 1689.
Freeman, E. A...........In *Edinburgh Review,* vol. cvii.
Gagarin, Father J...... { The Russian Clergy, translated by C. du G. Makepeace. London, 1872.
Gibbon, E.............. { The History of the Decline and Fall of the Roman Empire. London, 1797.
Gurowski, A. G. de.......Russia as it is. New York, 1854.
Hapgood, I. F...........The Epic Songs of Russia. New York, 1886.
Hare, A. J. C...........Studies in Russia. London, 1885.
Hakluyt, R..............Collection of Voyages. London, 1809–1812.
Haxthausen, A. von.... { The Russian Empire, translated by R. Farie. London, 1856.
Karamsin, N. M........ { Histoire de L'Empire de Russie traduite par M. M. St. Thomas et Jauffret. Paris, 1819–1826.
Kelly, W. K.............History of Russia. London, 1854.

LIST OF BOOKS CONSULTED.

King, J. G............... { The Rites and Ceremonies of the Greek Church in Russia. London, 1772.
Kohl, J. G............... Russia and the Russians. London, 1842.
Lea, H. C............... { Studies in Church History. Philadelphia, 1869.
Leger, L............... { Cyrille et Méthode. Etude sur la Conversion des Slaves. Paris, 1868.
Leroy-Beaulieu, A...... { In *La Revue des Deux Mondes*. Paris, 1873–1880.
Levesque, P. C........... Histoire de la Russie. Paris, 1812.
Macarius (Patriarch).... { Travels Written by Paul of Aleppo, translated by F. C. Balfour. London, 1829.
Mérimée, P............. Les Faux Démétrius. Paris, 1853.
Michelet, J............. { Louis XI. et Charles le Téméraire. Paris, 1854.
Mogila, Peter........... { Exposition of the Orthodox Faith of the Eastern Church. Published about 1750.
Mosheim, J. L.......... { Ecclesiastical History, translated by A. Maclaire. London, 1774.
Mouravief, A. N........ { History of the Church of Russia, translated by R. W. Blackmore. Oxford, 1842.
Neale, J. M............. { History of the Holy Eastern Church. London, 1850–1857.
Neander, A............. { General History of the Christian Religion and the Church, translated by J. W. Torrey. London, 1853.
Nestor................. { La Chronique de, traduite par L. Paris. Paris, 1834.
Noble, E................ The Russian Revolt. Boston, 1885.
Palmer, W............. { The Patriarch and the Tsar; the Replies of Nikon translated by W. Palmer. London, 1871.
"   " .... { Dissertations on the Orthodox or Eastern Communions. London, 1853.
Pears, E............... { The Fall of Constantinople. New York, 1886.
Platon, L.............. { Present State of the Greek Church in Russia, translated by R. Pinkerton. New York, 1815.
"   " .... Histoire de L'Eglise Russe.
Ralston, W. R. S......... Songs of the Russian People. London, 1872.
Rambaud, A............ Histoire de la Russie. Paris, 1878.

LIST OF BOOKS CONSULTED.

Raskol, Le	Anonyme. Essai sur les Sectes religieuses en Russie. Paris, 1878.
Romanof, H. C.	Sketches of the Rites and Ceremonies of the Greco-Russian Church. London, 1868.
Schnitzler, J. H.	Les Institutions de la Russie. Paris, 1856.
" "	Secret History of the Court of Russia. London, 1847.
Schuyler, E.	Peter the Great, Emperor of Russia. New York, 1884.
Stanley, A. P.	Lectures on the History of the Eastern Church. London, 1861.
Stepniak (Pseudonym)	Russia under the Tsars. New York, 1885.
" "	The Russian Storm-Cloud. London, 1886.
Strahl, P., and Herman, E.	Geschichte des Russischen Staates. Hamburg, 1832–1866.
Ternaux-Compans	Archives des Voyages, vol. ii. Paris, 1840–41.
Theiner, A.	Vicissitudes de L'Eglise Catholique des Deux Rites en Pologne et en Russie. Paris, 1843.
Tooke, W.	History of Russia. London, 1800.
Vogué, E. M. de	In *La Revue des Deux Mondes*. Paris, 1879.
Voltaire	Œuvres et Correspondence. 1785.
Waddington, G.	History of the Church. London, 1831–1833.
" "	Condition and Prospects of the Greek Church. London, 1854.
Wallace, D. McK.	Russia. London, 1877.

THE
RUSSIAN CHURCH AND RUSSIAN DISSENT.

CHAPTER I.

The Separation of the Churches of the East and the West; its Causes, Political and Ecclesiastical. — Differences between the Churches, External and Internal.

THE immediate causes of the great schism between the churches of the East and the West, in A.D. 1054, were ecclesiastical in their nature, but political events had material influence in preparing the way for the separation.

The partition of the world, in A.D. 395, between Honorius and Arcadius, aroused diverse and conflicting interests which had slumbered while the empire was united.

The transfer of the capital from Rome to Ravenna, the conquest of the West by the barbarians, and its final severance from the East, resulted in the rise of papacy to temporal as well as spiritual power. It obtained ascendancy over half the world, and claimed jurisdiction over the whole.

The foundation of Constantinople, the dismemberment of the empire, and the complete separation, in a political sense, of the East from the West, exalted the pride of the patriarch, and raised his see to an equality with that of Rome. He as indignantly resented the pope's pretensions to supremacy as they were vehemently asserted.

During these centuries of incessant struggle great changes supervened in the character and constitution of the two Churches.

In the West the theocratic element became predominant; the Church, left to its own resources, learned to suffice for itself. It gave, instead of asking, protection, grasped the sceptre of absent emperors, and successfully established its dominion over kings and princes.

In the East the Church, shielded from harm by the State, remained subservient to civil authority, rarely interfered in political affairs, and was content with its own spiritual jurisdiction.

The persistent pretensions of Rome, the constant antagonism, the frequent wars, the incessant conflicts to which they gave rise, were accompanied by differences of dogma and of discipline. These served to further embitter the struggle, to render the contest more implacable, and to make reconciliation or harmony impossible.

Disputes arose in the second and third centuries as to the date and celebration of Easter. The heresy of Arius, at first, and for a time, accepted in the East, but condemned in the West, followed in the fourth century. In the seventh, discussion as to the double or single nature of Christ convulsed the Christian world. The monotheletian patriarchs and the dyotheletian popes mutually anathematized each other, until unity was restored by the Sixth Œcumenical Council, A.D. 680 to 691. Then came the great controversy on the subject of image worship, which raged with intense virulence for a century and a half.

Meanwhile another grave subject of dispute arose, which still constitutes the essential dogmatical difference between the Churches. The doctrine of the Double Procession of the Holy Ghost originated in Spain during the fifth century. From Spain it spread into France, was accepted by Charlemagne and the Council of Aix-la-Chapelle in A.D. 809, and finally, approved at Rome, became an obligatory article of belief throughout the West. The Greek Church obstinately adhered to the old faith and letter of the creed. It absolutely rejected the Double Procession, and both parties appealed to the records of œcumenical councils. The interpolation of the words "filio-que," in the creed established by the Council of Constantinople in A.D. 381, was detected. Nevertheless the Latin Church maintained the dogma, while the Greek persisted in denying it.

The seventh general council, convened at Nicæa in A.D. 787, is, in the estimation of the Eastern Church, the last œcumenical council. It completed, by its decrees, the entire body of doctrine of the Universal Church of Christ. By it unity was apparently restored, and in outward appearance the ecclesiastical fabric was then one and indivisible. The innumerable shades and differences of opinion within it were indiscriminately distributed through the whole mass. Sects and denominations abounded, with mutual denunciations and revilings; but no schism, properly so called, arrayed any great geographical division of the world in open religious hostility to the others.

In the middle of the ninth century the emperor, Michael III., deposed the patriarch Ignatius for daring to rebuke the licentiousness of the court, and named Photius in his stead. The new prelate was a man of unimpeachable character, commanding genius, and vast ambition. He excelled in theological erudition, but, as he was a layman, his appointment was irregular. Ignatius appealed to Nicholas I., Pope of Rome, who was glad of the opportunity to assert his right of interference. He anathematized Photius, and endeavored to reinstate

Ignatius. Photius, undisturbed, retaliated upon Nicholas his sentence of deposition and excommunication, and widened the field of controversy by making appeal to the whole Christian world. In a circular letter, addressed to his brother patriarchs, he formally charged the Roman Church with five distinct heresies, and formulated the differences dividing the Churches. He declared:

That the Romish Church erroneously fasted on the Sabbath, or seventh day of the week.

That in the first week of Lent it wrongfully permitted the use of milk and of food prepared from milk.

That, contrary to Scripture, it prohibited priests from marrying, and separated from their wives such as were married when they took orders.

That it uncanonically authorized bishops, only, to anoint baptized persons with the Holy Chrism, withholding that authority from presbyters.

That it had sacrilegiously interpolated the words "filioque" in the creed of the Council of Constantinople, and held the heretical doctrine of the Procession of the Holy Ghost from the Son and from the Father.

To arid discussions, characterized by the bitterness and rancor of religious fanaticism, were added fierce contentions on either side for increased jurisdiction, aroused by the addition to the see of Constantinople of Bulgaria and other provinces, conquered by Greek armies and converted by Greek missionaries.

That the final schism should have been delayed must be attributed, not merely to the pious horror which so direful an event would have inspired, but to the peculiar condition of the Greek Empire and Church. There was, within the empire, a continual struggle for power, with constantly fluctuating success, between contending parties, and which, from the intimate connection of State

SEPARATION OF THE CHURCHES—EAST AND WEST.

and Church, affected both. Photius and Ignatius were alternately deposed and reinstated. A submissive clergy bent to the nod of the sovereign, and venal bishops hailed or condemned one prelate after another at command. The pope was appealed to in turn by the contending factions, and flattered by delusive hopes; in reality his pretensions were hateful to them all, and he was but a tool in the hands of the astute Greeks, to be availed of when needed, and to be denied when he claimed his reward.

Amid these internal dissensions, these alternate appeals to, and rejection of, Romish intervention, a species of armed neutrality, of impending, yet deferred hostility, seemed to pervade the Churches, and the final catastrophe, though ever threatening, was ever postponed.

A fresh subject of theological discussion arose early in the eleventh century, regarding the use of leavened or unleavened bread in the Eucharist. The Greeks adhered to the custom of the primitive Church and condemned the Latins, who, in the eighth century, had substituted unleavened for leavened bread.

Michael Cerularius, the patriarch, was a prelate as bigoted as he was zealous. Chafing against the pretensions of the pope, and resenting his oft-renewed assumption of superiority, he seized upon this occasion to make a violent attack upon the Latin Church and its chief. He proclaimed their apostasy from the true faith, ordered their churches and monasteries in Constantinople to be closed, and prohibited the celebration of their service. Retaliatory measures followed in the West. A final effort was made by the emperor, Constantine Monomachus, to restore harmony. At his request, Pope Leo IX. sent delegates to Constantinople with power to adjust all matters of controversy; but the haughty patriarch, incensed at the lofty tone assumed by them as ambassadors of Rome, refused to admit them to his presence. The papal legates, filled with a sense of the august authority of their chief, boldly resented the indignity offered him in their persons. Resorting to the great Church of St. Sophia, they publicly excommunicated the patriarch and his adherents, and reverently deposited the written declaration of anathema upon the grand altar. By this solemn act the schism between the Churches was finally consummated on the 10th of June, A.D. 1054.

The points of difference, besides minor matters of practice and discipline, may be summarized as being those stated in the circular letter of Photius, to which are to be added the use of leavened or unleavened bread in the Eucharist and the question of papal supremacy. The most important, as involving fundamental principles, was that concerning the Double Procession of the Holy Ghost. The most potent and wide-spread in its influence was that regarding Rome's pretension to universal jurisdiction. It has ever been the chief obstacle at every attempt to restore unity. This point the popular mind, however bewildered on theological controversies, has always been able to appreciate, and by it popular indignation has always been easily aroused to support clerical or state authority.

The divergence of the two Churches was greater in reality than it appears to be from a superficial view. It was based on essential variations in the character and disposition of the people in the East and in the West, on the nature of their civilization, and on the different, almost antagonistic, development of the Christian idea in one Church and in the other.

These influences, profoundly affecting the character and constitution of the Greek Church, merit consideration from the consequences which have ensued and which are still perceptible. They aid in appreciating the attitude of the Russian Church, as chief exponent and representative of the Greek communion, towards other Christian denominations; and they also help to explain the dissensions which, in Russia, have arisen within its bosom.

The natural bent of the Greek mind was to speculative inquiry; it was more active and acute, more lively and less practical, easily swayed by and interested in scholastic disquisition and controversy, fond of argument for argument's sake, skilled in disputation, nice in definitions and distinctions. The East was the home and fountain-head of science and literature; the cultivation of letters was there carried to a far greater extent and held in higher estimation than in the West. The Greeks were vain of their superior learning and more polite culture; they looked down with supercilious contempt upon the outer world as mere barbarians; they felt pride in their inheritance of the wisdom and intellect of ancient Greece, and gloried in their language, formed and fashioned by sages and philosophers, as the only competent vehicle of elevated refined thought; in it Christ taught, the apostles and early fathers preached and wrote; the first heads of the Church were Greek, and the name of pope was Greek. The Eastern Church rejoiced in its direct affiliation with apostolic times, in its careful preservation of traditions, and was convinced of its especial right to be considered the true heir and successor of Christ.

Intellectual and moral progress in the East was, however, stifled by political and spiritual despotism when the seat of empire was established at Constantinople, and the Church came under the immediate protection and control of the State. With Christian emperors on the throne it no longer feared persecution, and, relying on the temporal power, it gradually fell into subjection and tutelage, a condition fatal to its true development: it submitted to the encroachments of imperial authority; human passions proved stronger than religious convictions, and its patriarchs and prelates, eager for advancement, appealed to the emperor in their mutual quarrels and contentions, striving by subserviency and compliance to conciliate his favor. The theocratic theory of its independence of principalities and powers gradually yielded to servility and dependence; civil authority became paramount over the Church, influenced or dictated its decrees, and was the supreme judge and arbiter of its destinies. Spiritual life within it became dead, and its religion degenerated to scholastic investigation and metaphysical disquisition on barren points of doctrinal belief; its intellectual activity, though great and in constant exercise, wasted its ingenuity and energy on the study of the historical, exegetical, dogmatical side of Christianity, and neglected the practical application of its precepts to the daily life and conduct of men. The fathers were busy in establishing precise definitions, in collecting and transmitting to posterity the lore and learning of the past, augmented and explained by their comments, rather than in endeavoring to improve humanity in the present; nor was this disputatious spirit peculiar to dignitaries of the Church, it pervaded all classes of society; in the words of Gregory Nazianzen, "this city is full of mechanics and slaves, who are all of them profound theologians, and preach in the shops and in the streets. If you ask a man to change a piece of silver, he informs you wherein the Son differs from the Father; if you demand the price of a loaf, you are told by way of reply that the Son is inferior to the Father; and if you inquire whether the bath is ready, the answer is that the Son was made out of nothing."[1]

The letter of the law superseded the spirit; religion stiffened into formalism; piety consisted in strict observance of ceremonial rites; external holiness replaced sincere and heartfelt devotion.

The Church eagerly embraced the idea of monastic discipline, and monasticism exercised profound influence upon its destinies; but in this element of Christian life the tendency was the same: convents became the seats of mystical theology, of refined speculations on abstruse points of doctrine; penances, mortification of the flesh, worship of images and symbols, were spiritualized and raised far above the comprehension of the ignorant, who could grasp only the outward and material expression, and, blindly following their teachers, were plunged into the grossest, most superstitious, and idolatrous practices.

Delight in discussion, fondness for dialectic controversy and mental gymnastics, led to the development of inherent weaknesses of the Greek character—insincerity, fickleness, and disregard of truth. In keen but unscrupulous emulation sophistry became a justifiable weapon when reason failed; falsehood and deception were plied without hesitation to compass success. Amid the general degradation manly virtues disappeared from among the people. Instead of courageously resisting invasion, the empire purchased safety from barbarians, whom it despised, but with whom it dared not cope; the Church, in common with the community, suffered from these debasing influences, and sank into spiritual apathy. It became stationary, or, as it claimed, and still pretends to be, immutable and orthodox.

---

[1] Gibbon, vol. v., p. 17.

Throughout the West the tendency was in a contrary direction—towards the practical application of the religious idea. The effete, worn-out civilization of the past was there renovated by contact and admixture with young and vigorous races, and gained new strength and vitality in the struggle for existence. The Church, freed from control, became independent and self-asserting; the responsibility of government, the preservation of social order, devolved upon it, and it rose proudly to the task; it subdued and conquered by the Word the fierce Northern tribes whom the State was powerless to resist; by its spiritual dominion over them it exalted its station and increased its influence; popes grasped the sceptre of absent emperors, and assumed their authority; they had no rival prelates to dispute their claims, and the Western Church was united under their sway. What imperial Rome lost, papal Rome gained; it was willing and able to protect itself and the people who gathered around it; its independence of the civil power fostered and encouraged the theocratic element which had disappeared from the Eastern Church; the assertion of its divine origin and prerogatives raised it to be a judge and arbiter between princes, and established its superiority over temporal rulers; its army of priests and monks, filled with devotional zeal, instead of resting content with spiritual abstractions and contemplative self-communion, went forth boldly as a Church militant, trusting in their sacred mission to overcome by preaching and example the enemies of the faith. Mere learning, polemical discussions, scholastic and theological controversies, were secondary considerations amid the dislocations of a falling empire and the reconstruction of new states, and in the struggle for existence. The monastic establishments of the Church were organized to fight error, to propagate the truth, and to enlarge its domain, not for indulgence in polite ease or literary culture, nor for the satisfaction of individual aspirations towards an ideal life by asceticism and mortification of the flesh; they undertook works of active piety, benevolence, and charity, and their inmates were inspired by the desire to accomplish good for others rather than for themselves. The religious orders were instituted for divers ends, with definite and varying purpose. A spirit of rivalry and emulation among them grew with increase of power and wealth, and, while acknowledging a single head and pursuing a common object, the keen struggle for pre-eminence kept alive within them the fervor of religious enthusiasm. From the supreme pontiff to the mendicant friar action and progress were the characteristics of the Church, and blind adoration for the past was forgotten in anxiety for the present and hope for the future; while recognizing ancient authority and tradition, it believed in a constantly increasing and more thorough comprehension of Christ's teachings, and of the essential nature of Christian doctrines to be attained by study and gradually revealed. Its restless activity, exercised in this direction, saved it from the formalism of the East, and preserved the energy of its spiritual life; from progressive it became aggressive; victorious over the West, its ambition was insatiable, and it looked for other worlds to conquer; it aimed at universal dominion, and claimed to be, not merely orthodox, but catholic.

CHAPTER II.

Introduction of Christianity into Russia.

THE power and dignity of the Church in the East were doomed to dwindle and decrease with the waning glories of the lower empire. Its patriarchs were to become mere puppets of court favor, nominees and sycophants of an infidel sovereign; but brighter destinies and renewed splendor awaited it in other climes. From the dwarfed and puny shoulders of the effeminate Greek its mantle was to fall on the strong and stalwart frame of the Barbarian; enervated and lifeless in its ancient home, it was to be rejuvenated by the bracing atmosphere of the North, and spring again into fresh and youthful life in the rude, inhospitable regions of its later conquests.

But little is positively known regarding the first introduction of Christianity into Russia, although legends and traditions abound.

In popular belief, the city of Novgorod was founded by Japhet, son of Noah, and thither St. Andrew came to preach the gospel. The wild and barbarous natives ridiculed teachings so contrary to their fierce and savage habits. They found amusement in tormenting the apostle and mocking his simplicity; they plunged him, bound with cords, into a bath heated to the utmost, and the saint, distressed and suffocated by the vapor, exclaimed, "$ἵδρωσα$" ("I sweat"); hence, it is said, came the name of Roussa, or Russia. Moved by his patience and meekness, his rough hosts released him, listened to his words, and believed. They glory over all the rest of the people of Muscovy for being rooted in the faith from ancient times, and having been the first to receive it.

Novgorod is a city of great antiquity, and its religious edifices are held in deepest veneration by the people. In popular tradition its celebrated monastery of St. Anthony the Great, or "the Roman," was founded by a monk of Rome, who, during the persecution for image worship, was miraculously borne upon a rock from the Tiber, over seas and rivers, to Novgorod on Lake Ilmen. The treasures of his convent, which he had consigned to the waters, followed him on his voyage. At Novgorod he found a Christian church, of which St. Nikita was metropolitan; with him Anthony joined in prayer, and immediately a knowledge of each other's tongue was imparted to them both. The ruler of the city gave him land for a convent; and his treasures, fished up from the lake, provided sacred furniture for the altars. The boat of stone still excites the devotion of the worshippers, and the palm branches in the chapel are still as green as when brought from Rome by Anthony.

Of St. Nikita it is related that he shut up Satan in a jar, and released him upon condition that he would carry him to Jerusalem and back. Thus the saint visited the holy places of the East in a single night.

These pious legends generally bear impress of the Oriental origin of the Church.

The Russian monk, Nestor, who died in 1116, relates in his chronicle that St. Andrew the Apostle, journeying by the river Dnieper, on his way from Asia Minor to Rome, came to the hills surmounting the site of the city of Kiev, and on their summit, after kneeling in prayer, he exclaimed to his companions: "Behold this mountain, for it is here that the grace of God shall shine forth. A great city shall arise on this spot, and in it the Lord shall have many temples to His name."[1]

Byzantine annalists record the labors of St. Peter of Kiev, a Greek monk sent thither by the Emperor Basil, the Macedonian, and who was, according to them, the first metropolitan of Russia. The heathen inhabitants demanded proof of the divine nature of his teachings; to convince them he passed, uninjured, with the Gospel in his hands, through a great fire kindled by them, whereupon they all embraced the faith. He repeated the same miracle among the Muscovites, and they also were converted.

The patriarch Photius, in a circular letter addressed to the Eastern bishops in A.D. 866, speaks of the Russians as having renounced their pagan superstitions and professed the faith of Jesus Christ, and adds that he has sent them a bishop and priests.

In the same year Oskold and Dir, companions of Ruric and rulers of Kiev, pursuing their quest for booty and plunder, descended the Dnieper and appeared before Constantinople; the city was saved by the miraculous interposition of the Virgin; her robe, a relic of the Church of Blacherne, was bathed in the sea, whereon a furious tempest arose which dispersed the hostile fleet. According to Greek chroniclers the Russian princes, struck with awe, abjured their heathen gods and embraced Christianity. These chroniclers also enumerate Russia as the seventieth archbishopric depending on the see of Constantinople.

The recruitment of the imperial body-guard from the Varagians along and beyond the Dnieper, bringing many from those regions under Christian influences, and the

---

[1] La Chronique de Nestor, vol. i., p. 6.

intercourse between Russians and Greeks, arising from trade and from frequent predatory excursions of the former against the empire, doubtless combined to spread among them some knowledge of Christianity. Efforts for their conversion, attempted by emperors preceding Basil I., were continued by him and by his successors, stimulated by their desire, during the struggles of the Greek Church with Rome, to extend its sway. A treaty, concluded in 945, between Igur of Kiev and Constantine VII., distinguishes Russians who had been baptized from those who were yet pagans, and makes mention of a church at Kiev, dedicated to St. Elias.

From these scanty and confused historical data it would appear that Christianity had penetrated into Russia prior to the middle of the tenth century.

The conversion of the savage tribes who occupied the vast deserts of Dacia and Sarmatia was preceded, and the way for it prepared, by the missionary labors of the Greek Church along the Danube and in the Chersonesus. Slavonic tribes, who had heard of Christ, applied to Constantinople for teachers. Constantine Cypharas, a monk better known as St. Cyril, was sent to them by Michael III. in 860. He called to his assistance his brother Methodius, and they both, animated by true apostolic zeal, extended their mission to the surrounding pagans. They invented a Slavonic alphabet, translated the Scriptures and the Liturgy, and celebrated religious services in the language of the people, according to the rites of the Greek Church. Their lives were devoted with single-hearted earnestness to the conversion of the heathen, and the results of their missionary efforts spread far beyond the sphere of their labors. They had great influence upon the growth and destinies of the Church in Russia, where their translations of the Bible and the Liturgy into Slavonic were subsequently adopted, and their practice of celebrating the service in a language familiar to the people was followed.

In 955 Olga, wife of Igur, ruler of Kiev, mother of Sviatoslav, and whom Nestor calls "the dawn and morning-star of salvation for Russia," journeyed to Constantinople in search of knowledge of the true God, and was there baptized by the name of Helena, in memory of the sainted mother of Constantine the Great. The humble creed and self-denying precepts of her new religion were repugnant to the rude barbarian, her son, a proud and haughty chief of fierce warriors; but he respected the genius and virtues of his mother, who, venerated and loved by his people, was surnamed by them "the Wise." He tolerated and protected the belief she professed, and confided his children to her care. His son, Vladimir, was a kindred spirit to his own—enterprising and ambitious, of fiery passions, strong and enthusiastic temperament, imbued with the superstitions and addicted to the gross and sensual indulgences of his race, fit leader of hardy and rapacious tribes, whose only occupation was war, and whose pastimes were revelry and the chase. A zealous worshipper of idols, Vladimir erected a huge image of Peroun, the God of Thunder, and offered to it human sacrifices. To celebrate a victory over a neighboring tribe, lots were cast for a victim, and fell on Feodor, son of Ivan, a Christian Varagian; the father refused to yield him up, mocked the heathen deities of wood and stone, and declared the God of the Greeks to be the true and only God; whereon the people massacred them both—the first and the only martyrs of the Church at Kiev. Vladimir's success in war spread his renown abroad; his alliance was courted, and his conversion became an object of solicitude to nations near and remote. Emissaries came to him from the Mahometan Bulgarians and the Khorazian Jews, from the Latin Christians of Germany and Rome, and from the Greeks of Constantinople. To each of them he returned a characteristic reply. The pleasures of Mahomet's paradise were tempting, but he refused to be circumcised or to abstain from pork or from wine, "for drinking," said he, "is the delight of Russians, nor can we live without it." Of the Jews he asked: "Where is your country?" and when they acknowledged that for their sins God had driven them forth and scattered them over the earth, he indignantly rejoined, "Do you, whom your God has forsaken and dispersed, pretend to teach others, and would you have us share your fate?" The Western doctors were dismissed with scant courtesy, as coming from troublesome neighbors; "Our fathers have never believed in your religion," said he. He listened more attentively to the Greek, who alternately aroused and soothed his superstitious fears by eloquently depicting the future torments of the wicked and the reward of the righteous, enforcing his words by pictures representing the Judgment Day. "Tell me more," said Vladimir, "happy are those seated on the right, wretched the sinners on the left." All the mysteries of the Orthodox faith were explained; he was deeply moved, and perhaps recalled the teaching of his grandmother Olga. In the succeeding year, 987, by the advice of his boyars, he sent trusty counsellors to examine in different countries the religion of each. At Constantinople the importance of their mission was more seriously realized than elsewhere, and every effort was made by the emperor and the patriarch to impress their imaginations and convince them of the superiority of the Greek Church. They were dazzled by the magnificence of the court, and transported by the splendor and imposing ceremonies of the ritual. "When we stood in the temple," said they, on their return, "we hardly knew whether or not we were in heaven, for, in truth, upon earth it is impossible to behold such glory and magnificence; we could not tell all we have seen; there, verily, God has His dwelling among men, and the worship of other countries is as nothing. Never can we forget the grandeur which we saw. Whoever has enjoyed so sweet a sight can never elsewhere be satisfied, nor will we remain longer as we are."[1] They adduced Olga's example as an additional reason for adopting the Eastern faith: "If the Greek religion had not been good," they urged, "thy grandmother Olga, wisest of mortals, had not embraced it." Vladimir still hesitated; but when, in the following year, his armies were held in check before the walls of Kherson, he made a vow to be baptized if he captured the city. It fell, and then the crafty prince, eager for every advantage, demanded as a condition of peace and of his conversion the hand of Anna, sister of Basil II., in marriage, threatening otherwise to march on Constantinople. An old prophecy of unknown origin was current in the tenth century on the shores of the Bosphorus, and had been inscribed on the statue of Bellerophon within the city walls, that "the Russians would some day seize upon the capital of the Empire of the East." It has not yet been forgotten, and it may, in those ancient days, have influenced the emperor's decision. The danger was imminent, and in order to avert it and to bring so powerful an enemy under the banner of the cross, the haughty Greek consented, and, in spite of her reluctance, sent the Princess Anna, with a retinue of priests, to Kherson. On her ar-

---

[1] Nestor, vol. i., p. 122.

rival she found Vladimir suffering from a sudden attack of blindness; but when the bishop laid hands upon him in baptism he recovered his sight and exclaimed, "Now it is that I know the true God!"

On his return to Kiev he commenced, with characteristic energy, the propagation of the new faith; his twelve sons and all the people, by his command and under penalty of his anger, were baptized; idols were overthrown, the great statue of Peroun was cast into the Dnieper, and the entire nation, with a unanimity and suddenness that have no parallel in the religious history of Europe, turned from paganism to Christianity at the bidding of its prince.

Doubtless the labors of early missionaries, in neighboring countries, had prepared the way, while the translations of the Bible and of the Liturgy into Slavonic by Cyril and Methodius assisted in the dissemination of the truth. By popularizing the holy books, they tended to impart, from the first, a religious tone to the literature of Russia, and a national spirit to its religion.

The docile and submissive nature of the people had been exemplified centuries before, when they summoned Ruric to reign over them. "Our country is vast and fertile," said they to him; "all things abound therein, but order and justice are wanting; come, therefore, govern and rule over us."

It was again illustrated by their ready compliance in matters of belief with the commands of their ruler, and explains the character, at once popular, national, and loyal, of the Russian Church. At the same time, the extraordinary power of sacred pictures, and the devotional feeling which they excite in the Russian mind, the regard for ceremonial and external rites, the rigid adherence to ancient forms, the strong tincture of Orientalism which pervades the Church, mark the influences which surrounded its birth and its affiliation with Constantinople.

Vladimir, from his conversion to his death, remained steadfast and zealous in the faith. He exhibited by his acts, throughout his later career, the depth and earnestness of his convictions. Architects and builders, bishops, priests, and teachers, were summoned from the East. In all the cities of his realm he erected churches and established schools; at Kiev he built a cathedral and there founded the metropolitan see, over which St. Michael, and, after him, St. Leontius, prelates from Constantinople, were called to preside. By a formal decree he provided for the regular support of the Church establishment and the clergy, setting aside for the purpose a tenth part of the revenues of his kingdom and of his subjects. He based his legislation upon the Greek Nomocanon, which embodies the canons and decisions of the seven œcumenical councils, and, in accordance therewith, he gave to the Church exclusive jurisdiction over ecclesiastical affairs, pronouncing his curse upon any of his descendants, or any officers of state, who should, in the present or the future, disturb or infringe upon the regulations thus declared. The authenticity of this enactment, which is attributed to him, is doubtful; but his persistent devotion to the interests of the Church is abundantly proven. Few princes can show better title to the admiration of posterity than Vladimir, who, a rude pagan warrior, became a wise and Christian ruler. Known in history as the "Great," and canonized by the Church as "Equal to the Apostles," he lives also in popular song and tradition; his exploits are related in Byzantine annals, Arab chronicles, and Scandinavian sagas. He cleared forests, sent colonies into the wilderness, reclaimed deserts, founded cities, promulgated laws, administered justice, encouraged learning and the arts, overthrew paganism, established Christianity, and called into Russia all the civilizing influences that the world, in his time, could offer.

CHAPTER III.

The Russian Church from its Establishment to its Independence of Constantinople.—The Unia and the Orthodox Church in Poland; Separation of the Latter from the Church in Russia.

AFTER the death of Vladimir, in 1015, bloody and fratricidal strife between the appanaged princes desolated Russia until Yaroslav, his son, succeeded in uniting the whole kingdom under his sway.

Yaroslav, great among the greatest of Russian monarchs, followed his father's example. He sedulously fostered the growth of the Church as an element of his own power. With its growth its national character was developed. It evinced its jealousy of foreign influence by the election, in 1051, of Hilarion, a native Russian, as metropolitan, without reference to Constantinople. Churches were multiplied in all the cities, and the first monastic establishments were founded. The most celebrated of these, from the great influence which it exerted upon the civil and religious destinies of Russia, and from the profound veneration in which it is and always has been held by the people, merits more than a passing notice.

A pilgrim from Lubetsch became a monk in the Holy Land, under the name of Anthony, and was distinguished for exemplary humility and devotion. His superiors marked his vocation for cœnobitic life, and, giving him their blessing, ordered him back to Russia, prophesying the success which would attend his labors in his native land. On his return, about 1013, he was divinely guided, in his search for a retreat, to the mountain near Kiev, where the metropolitan Hilarion had, when a simple priest, been wont to resort for solitary prayer and meditation; there, in the cave, two fathoms deep, dug out for himself by Hilarion, Anthony took up his abode and lived a hermit's life of fasting and self-denial. The fame of his piety spread through the land, and the people far and near revered him as a saint. Yaroslav and his son Isiaslav, with the court, came frequently to implore his blessing; and soon other devotees joined him, and dug their caves by his. As their numbers increased, Anthony appointed Barlaam to rule over them as abbot, and retired farther into the forest to be alone. A church and a cloister were added to the subterranean dwellings which burrowed far into the mountain, and by degrees other churches and an immense monastery, dedicated to the Assumption of the Virgin, arose around and above the caves of the early brethren, in memory of which it was called the Petcherski.[1]

The prince and the great lords were prodigal of their riches in founding and endowing other religious establishments, but none, writes Nestor, one of its inmates, prospered as did the Petcherski, "created without silver or gold, of which Anthony had none, but by fasting and watching, by tears and prayers." Feodoceï, "humblest of the brethren," succeeded Barlaam. He completed the organization of the brotherhood according to the strict rules of the Studium monastery of Constantinople. As it was the first, so it became the most celebrated of the monasteries of Russia, and the source from which many sprang.

---

[1] From *petchera,* meaning cave or cavern.

What Jerusalem and the Temple were to the Jews, Kiev and the Petcherski are to the Russians. The vast and mysterious catacombs are peopled by the bodies of thousands of holy men, who still rest in the caverns where they lived; miracles are worked by their remains, and keep alive the ardent devotion of innumerable worshippers at their shrines.

When Christianity was introduced in Russia the schism dividing the East and the West, although threatening, was not declared, and the Russian establishment was a branch of the Church universal, still, in theory, one and indivisible. The final separation, consummated in 1054, aroused but little, if any, attention in Russia. The Church there, deriving its origin, its creed, and its ritual from Constantinople, followed as of course the fortunes of its parent stem. It ignored the doctrines of Rome, and, while it watched with jealousy any unnecessary interference on the part of the patriarch, whom it acknowledged, it resented from the first all pretensions of the popes to jurisdiction over it. Its flourishing condition had already attracted notice, and Rome was in haste to commence the long series of her attempts to bring it under her authority.

Yaroslav's reign was followed by long and bloody civil wars. Isiaslav, his son, driven from power, found refuge in Germany and obtained promises of support from Pope Gregory VII. upon condition of submitting his kingdom and the Church to the Roman see. In the bewildering maze of revolution and counter-revolution Isiaslav regained his throne without foreign aid, and Gregory's schemes came to naught.

The short reign of Vladimir II., Monomachus, a wise and pious prince, was the only respite in a century and a half of anarchy. During this dreary period of civil wars, culminating in national subjugation by the Tatars, the history of the Church alone affords some relief to the gloomy picture. It extended its peaceful conquests over the North and towards the West, and its annals are illustrated by the lives of holy men and devoted missionaries. As a body it gained in strength and vigor; its influence was courted and its assistance invoked by the rival claimants of the crown, but it suffered in its purity and dignity by stooping to favor the pretensions of the, for the moment, successful competitor, transferring its support from the weaker to the stronger, as they fell and rose. The fortunes of its primates depended upon those of the princes, and, as they passed in rapid succession on the throne, so bishop after bishop sat in the metropolitan chair, and, in the twelfth century, three rival prelates at one time claimed possession of ecclesiastical sovereignty.

Amid civil dissensions the Church again manifested its spirit of nationality and its impatience of foreign dictation. In 1147 a synod of native bishops elected Clement, a Russian prelate, as metropolitan, without reference to Constantinople.

Political anarchy had its parallel in doctrinal differences among the clergy, and then, as in the graver schisms to arise in later years, these differences related to matters of practice and not of dogma.

At the commencement of the twelfth century religious antagonism to the Church of the West was stimulated by national feeling in a struggle with a foreign enemy.

The orders of the Teutonic Knights and of the Brethren of the Sword, incited by Rome, had subdued Lithuania and Livonia. Under the banner of the Latin Church they attacked Russia on the west, aiming not merely at conquest, but at the establishment of papal supremacy.

Soon after, the Tatars appeared on the east, crossed the Volga in 1237, and, in successive invasions, spread over the country like an overwhelming deluge. Notwithstanding the patriotic efforts of the popular hero and saint, Alexander Yaroslavitch, known in Russian history as the "Nevsky," for his great victory over Swedes and Lithuanians on the banks of the Neva, the Tatar khan was everywhere triumphant, and Russian princes accepted his sway. Finally the Church recognized his authority, but it is her glory that she was the last to submit; that even then she maintained the faith, never lost hope for the future, and strove ever to keep alive the dying pulsations of national life.

Russia's extremity was Rome's opportunity. Pope Innocent IV. offered to arouse the Christian princes of Europe in a crusade against the Mongols, if the Russian Church would unite with that of Rome and acknowledge his supremacy. His proposals were disdainfully refused; Russian princes and the Church preferred submission to the khan rather than recognition of the pope.

The Tatar conqueror speedily realized the mighty influence of the Church and the clergy over the people, and endeavored to enlist their support to strengthen his authority. By his favor and protection, amid the general ruin, they increased greatly in power and wealth; but, during this period of anarchy and disorder, grievous abuses crept into the one, while ignorance and corruption degraded the other. The metropolitan Cyril, a Russian, keenly sensible of these evils, was indefatigable in his efforts to correct them. By his direction a synod was convened in 1247 for the reformation of the Church and to inflict discipline upon the clergy. His patriotism equalled his religious zeal, and he labored incessantly to create among the Russian princes a spirit of harmony and unity as the only hope for the future.

Maximus, a Greek from Constantinople, followed Cyril on the metropolitan throne. Although a foreigner, he proved a worthy successor, and, like Cyril, endeavored to check the never-ending feuds and wars between the native princes. His virtues and Christian character inspired the Tatar conquerors with respect, and, by personal intercession with the "Horde," he added greatly to the power and prosperity of the Church. The clergy, under his direction, always sympathizing profoundly with the people, availed themselves of their increased influence and wealth to protect the victims of Tatar tyranny, and to assuage their misery and sufferings.

As Kiev was in ruins, Maximus transferred the primacy to Vladimir, then chief among the Russian cities.

Moscow soon rose to importance under Ivan (John) I., surnamed "Kalita," from his habit of bestowing alms upon the poor from his purse.[1] This prince, established in authority and protected by the khan, maintained comparative peace and order within his principality; with its prosperity his power increased, and he became pre-eminent among the native magnates. He was wise and politic, ambitious yet patriotic. While keeping faith with his Tatar sovereign, he endeavored to unite the native princes under one head, which head he aspired to be, as the only means of securing present tranquillity for Russia and its eventual liberation. He also fully realized the vast power wielded by the Church, which, by affording protection to the people and maintaining them steadfast in the faith, had alone preserved any semblance

---

[1] *Kalita* means a pouch, or a purse.

of national life. This power it was his constant aim to increase and to enlist in support of his own authority. His purpose had the quick sympathy of the metropolitan Peter, who had succeeded Maximus. Ambition, patriotism, and religion were combined to one common end. Prince and primate were united in hearty, harmonious co-operation. By their joint action the primacy was transferred to Moscow, henceforth to be the capital of the empire and the seat of the head of the Church. Peter died before the transfer was effected, and his last words were a prophecy of the future greatness of the new imperial city, and of the glory therein awaiting the Church. His body was placed at the corner of the cathedral erected to commemorate the event, and he, with his illustrious successors, Alexis, Jonah, and the martyred Philip, are accounted the foundation stones of the Russian Church.

Ivan's efforts towards the creation of an independent and united Russia were recognized in the title bestowed upon him by his people of "the Restorer of the Country." They were, however, not destined to bear immediate fruition. The future of the empire was jeopardized, in successive reigns, by renewed dissensions among the princes and by dangers threatening from hostile neighbors.

The turbulent republics of Novgorod and of Pskov were ever at variance with the great prince of Moscow, but the powerful kingdom of Poland and Lithuania, extending beyond the Dnieper and including Kiev, was a more terrible enemy. Within its territory the influence of Rome was paramount.

In these critical times the Church in Russia, though torn by intestine dissensions and claims of rival pontiffs for pre-eminence, remained faithful to the national cause.

Its acknowledged heads labored with unswerving patriotism against the difficulties surrounding the new birth of the nation. The dynasty of Ivan Kalita had been set aside by the khan. Dimitri II., the Tatar nominee, planned the retransfer of the primacy to Vladimir; but Alexis, the metropolitan, successfully maintained the supremacy of Moscow as both the religious and political capital. By his influence Ivan's family was restored to the throne, and the accession of Dimitri III., his grandson, was welcomed by the princes, who began to appreciate the policy advocated by the Church, of hereditary succession and of union under the most powerful of their number.

The activity of the Church was further manifested in its own domain by the erection of innumerable churches in the different cities and by an extraordinary development of monastic life, which led to the creation of many great and powerful religious establishments. The most celebrated among them is the monastery of the Troïtsa, or the Trinity, near Moscow, founded by St. Sergius of Radonegl. Like St. Anthony of the Petcherski, St. Sergius retired to the wilderness to lead a hermit's life in a little wooden hut built by himself, and which he called the "Source of Life." From this humble origin sprang the "ever glorious Lavra" of the Troïtsa, destined, on many a memorable occasion, to be the bulwark and preserver of the national existence. Under the blessing of Providence, favored and fostered by the princes of Moscow, it increased with unexampled rapidity in riches and consideration, and became a city and fortress as well as a monastery.

Macarius, in the seventeenth century, after describing its wealth and splendor, its buildings and churches, dwells on the extent and strength of its walls and bastions, on its armory "furnished with cannon without number," "with arms and accoutrements for more than thirty thousand men," and "its guns in numberless quantities." [1] The military glory of this sacred fortress dates from the great victory of the Don. When Dimitri went forth to do battle with the Tatar, St. Sergius gave him his blessing, and sent his brother monks, Peresvet and Osliab, to fight by the prince's side.

Dimitri III., "the Donskoï," ascended the throne in 1362. Skilful and prudent in warfare, chivalrous, while politic, in dealing with his rivals, beloved by his people, he was also devoted to the Church, whose vast influence was constantly exerted in his behalf. Victorious in repelling Polish invasions, he finally succeeded in uniting the whole country under his sway.

The metropolitan Alexis, to whom, more than to any one, were due the establishment of the empire and the revival of Russian nationality, lived to see the fruition of his labors. He was very old, but, while yet alive, the patriarch of Constantinople, with indecorous haste, moved perhaps by anxiety at the progress of the Roman Church in Poland, appointed Cyprian as his successor. The great prince indignantly resented this unseemly premature act, and Cyprian retired to Kiev. At Alexis's death Dimitri hurried his favorite, Mitai, to Constantinople to obtain the investiture, although he was not a prelate of the Church. He died on the way, and his companion, Pimen, fraudulently secured his own nomination by forged letters of credence. On his return he was thrust into prison for this scandalous abuse of confidence, and Cyprian was summoned from Kiev.

During these ecclesiastical disputes the Tatar power

---

[1] Macarius, vol. ii., p. 144.

was broken by the great battle of the Don, and Dimitri, henceforth the Donskoï, was hailed as "The Deliverer of the Country." The victory over Mamai, the Tatar khan, was complete, but its fruits were lost; Dimitri returned to Moscow to enjoy his triumph, instead of pursuing and annihilating the enemy. His glory and increasing power aroused the jealousy of his neighbors, and his supineness revived the feuds of the native princes. The empire was attacked from the west, and its unity within was disturbed, when its independence was again threatened by its formidable and hereditary foe. Toktamuish, a descendant of Genghis Khan, destroyed the shattered forces of Mamai, seized upon the khanate, and, with fresh legions from the depths of Asia, swept over the empire and brought Russia once more under the Tatar yoke. Dimitri returned to his ruined capital to find the Church deserted by its head. Cyprian had fled to Tver for safety, and the prince, indignant at his pusillanimity, removed him from office and installed Pimen.

The terrible calamities of the barbaric invasion were accompanied by anarchy in the Church. The clergy had become corrupt and rapacious; its ranks were swelled by multitudes of greedy, selfish drones, who throve and fattened in sloth and idleness. The people despised them for their ignorance, vices, and gluttony, groaned under their oppression and rebelled against their exactions. Popular indignation found public expression in sects hostile to the Church. Amid disputes of rival pontiffs, the degradation of the clergy, foreign invasion, domestic treachery and revolt, the whole fabric of the empire, social, political, and religious, seemed tottering to its fall. Some degree of order was restored by the energetic and skilful policy of Dimitri, assisted by dissensions among his enemies.

The death of Pimen left Cyprian sole claimant of ecclesiastical sovereignty, and, in the succeeding reign, he returned to the capital and united the whole Orthodox Church of Russia and Poland under his jurisdiction. His subsequent career marks his place in the history of his country. While he may be reproached for his hasty flight from Moscow, the services which he rendered the Church and the nation cannot be overestimated. By his Christian virtues, his zeal, tempered by prudence, his discretion and ability, he preserved the existence of the Orthodox faith in Poland and Lithuania, whose rulers professed the Latin creed, favored the efforts of Rome, and viewed with jealousy the control of a foreign prelate over their Orthodox subjects. As metropolitan, Cyprian's administration was wise and energetic; he repressed disorder, corrected abuses, and strictly enforced purity of morals and discipline among the clergy. He encouraged the labors of St. Stephen and other missionaries of the Church, and established regular ecclesiastical government over the converted heathen tribes of the vast countries stretching to the Ural Mountains.

As patriot and statesman, he ably seconded the efforts of the great prince Vassili II., to recreate a free and independent Russia, conciliating the native princes, opposing the formidable pretensions of Vitoft, King of Poland, resisting, with all the power of the Church, the Tatars under Toktamuish and Tamerlane. When dying, in 1406, Cyprian wrote to the great prince and his boyars, to the clergy and the people, asking forgiveness of his offences, and giving them his benediction. Tears and lamentations followed the reading of his words at the altar of the great cathedral, and from this time metropolitans of Moscow, at the approach of death, have addressed similar farewell messages to the nation.

Cyprian's death was a public calamity. His successor, Photius, a Greek, had no sympathy with the national sentiment, and estranged both the people and the princes by too zealous care of the temporal interests of his see. Vitoft, no longer checked by Cyprian's influence, determined to free the Orthodox Church within his dominions from the control of a foreign prelate. The see of Kiev was declared independent of that of Moscow in 1415; rejoined to it a few years later, its independence was again and finally established in 1433.

Under Vassili III. the fortunes of Russia sank to their lowest ebb. Civil wars, foreign invasion, and Tatar tyranny brought the country to the verge of ruin. The metropolitan see remained vacant after the death of Photius, and anarchy reigned supreme in Church and State.

During a short respite from turmoil and trouble, Jonah of Riazan was elected metropolitan by a synod of bishops, but already the patriarch had appointed Isidore of Thessalonica, bishop of Illyria, as primate of Russia. With his advent upon the scene opens an interesting phase of ecclesiastical history, in which, not only Russia, but the other powers of the civilized world were concerned.

The Byzantine empire, a mere shadow of its former greatness, was tottering to its fall. The emperors, dependent alternately on Turkish forbearance and European favor, sued to or slighted both Moslem and Christian powers according to their fluctuating fortunes, cunningly, and with deliberation, playing one against the other.

John Palæologus, as long as Bajazet spared his throne, turned an indifferent ear to papal advances, but when he had been threatened he had humbled himself before the pope, kissed his slipper at St. Peter's, and led his mule by the bridle. The Greek people, on the contrary, were fanatically attached to their ancient religion, although among them it had degenerated to mere formalism.

The Roman Church was torn by faction and schism; rival pontiffs disputed St. Peter's chair, the pope's supremacy had been denied by its prelates and councils, as well as by princes, and his authority was no longer absolute over either the Western Church or the Western powers.

When John Palæologus, again menaced by the Turks under Amurat II., turned to Europe for succor, Pope Eugenius IV. eagerly seized upon the opportunity thus presented of reconciling and uniting the Churches of the East and of the West, in the hope that the glory of this achievement would, by re-establishing the supremacy of Rome over the whole Church, redound to his advantage and silence all opposition to his claim to be its legitimate head. He relied upon the support of Isidore, an adroit, ambitious schemer, distinguished for his eloquence and diplomatic tact, celebrated for theological erudition and learning. He was, moreover, a personal friend of the pope, whose influence is supposed to have assisted in his elevation to the exalted position of chief of the Russian Church.

In furtherance of his plans Eugenius convoked an œcumenical council in Italy, where his own influence was paramount. All the Western powers were present, and, by specious promises of material assistance, he induced the Greeks to join. The participation of so powerful a member of the Eastern Church as Russia was most important, and Isidore had scarcely taken possession of his see ere he was summoned, and craved of Vassili permission, to attend. Vassili yielded a reluctant assent, and charged Isidore to strenuously uphold the Orthodox faith, and to return with it intact. "Our fathers," said he, "and our ancestors would never listen to the reunion of the Greek and Latin religions, nor have I any such intention. Yet you may go, if such be your desire; I will not oppose your departure, but remember the purity of our faith and come back with it unsullied." [1]

The council met at Ferrara in 1438; adjourned to Florence, and separated in 1439. Its sessions were violent and stormy, its debates acrimonious and endless. Accord between the opposing parties which composed it was hopeless, but the emperor and the pope were determined not to lose the fruit of their labors, and to secure, by any possible means, at least the semblance of a union. Private negotiations supplemented public discussions, and with more profitable results. Isidore was promised a cardinal's hat, and, by similar influences, opposition was gradually reduced to the single voice of Mark of Ephesus, who denounced the compact in unmeasured terms, and was compelled to seek safety in flight.

The reunion of the Churches was proclaimed by the council, and the articles of reconciliation, subscribed to unanimously by the members present, bore on four important points. They declared,

That either leavened or unleavened bread might be used in the Eucharist.

That, as regards purgatory, the righteous enjoy eternal happiness in heaven; unrepentant sinners suffer eternally; while those who have relapsed into sin after baptism and repentance are purified in some intermediate state, by various torments, until penance be accomplished;

---

[1] Karamsin, vol. v., p. 335.

and, at the resurrection of the body on the last day, all men must render an account before the judgment-seat of God.

That the pope of Rome is the vicar of Jesus Christ, the head of the Church on earth, and the patriarch of Constantinople holds the second place after him.

That the Holy Ghost proceeds from the Father and from the Son.

The pope and the emperor reaped their rewards. Eugenius was hailed as the sole vicar of Christ on earth, the faithful shepherd who had brought the sheep of the East and the West into one fold after a separation of centuries, and John returned to Constantinople, loaded with presents and with abundant promises for the future, to be, however, but scantily fulfilled.

To Isidore, made cardinal and apostolic legate, the ultimate results proved less fortunate. His return to Russia was awaited with the keenest impatience and anxiety, intensified by the pastoral addresses, which, issued by him from time to time, had preceded his arrival.

Finally, in the great cathedral of the Assumption at Moscow, before the great prince and an august assembly of the highest dignitaries of the Church and the State, and, to the profound astonishment of them all, he celebrated mass after the custom of the Latin Church, and solemnly proclaimed the act of union. Wonder at the innovation in the service, respect for a decree of a council called œcumenical, and for the illustrious names of the emperor, the patriarch, and the Greek fathers appended to it, held the vast assemblage mute for a space; but soon indignation overcame amazement. Vassili, although a weak and vacillating prince, was firmly attached to the national belief, and, recovering from his stupefaction, he protested indignantly against the sacrifice of his own and his people's religious birthright. He passionately apostrophized the metropolitan as a recreant priest, treacherous to his holy trust, a false teacher, and heretic.

A synod of bishops immediately condemned and disavowed the action of the council. Isidore was deposed and sentenced to confinement; he escaped from his prison to Rome, where, by favor of the pope, he enjoyed the barren title of Bishop of Russia, and, at the fall of the Byzantine empire, was made patriarch of Constantinople under the jurisdiction of Rome.

Gregory, one of Isidore's disciples, and a partisan of the union, became metropolitan of Kiev in 1443, by the protection of Casimir, King of Poland; he endeavored, unsuccessfully, to extend his sway over the see of Moscow, and was, with his doctrines, excommunicated by the Russian bishops, who preserved the Muscovite Church steadfast in the ancient faith, while Kiev and Southern Russia fell under the domination of the pope.

At Constantinople, although the people and the great body of the Church rejected the acts of the council and persevered in asserting their independence of papal authority, the emperor and the patriarch acquiesced in the union. As henceforth any Orthodox patriarchal confirmation of a metropolitan in Russia was impossible, Jonah of Riazan, who had been elected prior to Isidore's appointment, remained, by common consent, in charge of the Church, and in 1448 was formally consecrated as its head by a synod of bishops. He endeavored in vain to bring the Churches of Poland and Lithuania under his control, and for his efforts was excommunicated by the pope; despairing of success against the will of the Polish king, at that time a more powerful potentate than the great prince of Russia, he abandoned the attempt and relinquished the empty title of Kiev, to assume that of metropolitan of Moscow, by which he and his successors were thenceforth designated.

From this period dates the complete independence of the Church of Russia. The necessity of its separation from the see of Constantinople was recognized by all the Orthodox members of the Greek communion, and with them all it continued in close bonds of spiritual union.

CHAPTER IV.

The Church in the Fifteenth Century.—Effect of Tatar Occupation.
—Liberation of Russia from the Tatars.—Attempted Reforms in
the Church.—The Orthodox Church in Poland.—Establishment of
the Patriarchate in Russia.

THE restless spirit of inquiry and enterprise, the prodigious mental activity which, at the end of the fifteenth century, had aroused Southern and Western Europe, spread into Russia and agitated the stagnant pools of Muscovite barbarism and prejudice. Civilization, elsewhere progressing with gigantic strides, was there creeping onward with slow and sluggish steps, hampered by the fatuity and apathy typical of its Oriental origin. Belief in the approaching end of the world turned men's minds towards the Church. Among the Russian people, pre-eminently ignorant and superstitious when ignorance and superstition were everywhere characteristics of the people, this expectation was generally prevalent, and the consequent devotional feeling correspondingly intensified. Public churches were multiplied, the rich erected private chapels and founded religious establishments; innumerable ecclesiastics were required for their services; restrictions for admission to the clergy were disregarded, and its ranks invaded by multitudes from the poorest and lowest of the population, seriously debasing its morals and lowering its character.

Among the great events of which this age was prolific, the greatest for Russia was its liberation from Tatar tyranny; national independence followed close upon independence of the Church.

The long period of foreign subjugation was productive of many grave and abiding results, and among the most noticeable are those affecting the clergy, as a body, and the Church.

The Tatar princes, recognizing the vast influence of the Church over the people, afforded it protection in order to enlist its support in favor of their authority. They were also not indifferent to the virtues and self-abnegation displayed by its members, and treated its bishops and dignitaries with respect, accepted their mediation, and yielded frequently to their solicitations on behalf of the suffering population. These marks of consideration, shown by infidel and lawless tyrants, inspired the people with increased veneration for their pastors, whom they found able to obtain for them protection and redress of wrongs. For this reason, apart from the influence of religious sentiment, they became more than ever accustomed to turn to the Church for relief, and to implicitly accept its guidance.

The monasteries and religious bodies, exempted from taxation and protected from spoliation, had grown rich and prosperous amid the general ruin, and afforded a haven, not only to the poor and needy, but also to such of the better class as, timid or weary of strife, were glad to sacrifice property and escape the responsibilities it entailed in order to secure safety or a peaceful refuge. Many of the rich and noble poured their wealth into the coffers of the Church from gratitude for protection, in expiation of crimes, or to purchase future happiness. Nearly all the great religious institutions of Russia arose during this period of the Tatar conquest.

The position and attitude of the clergy towards the

governing powers were not so much changed as confirmed, in accordance with the submissive spirit of the Greek Church, always content to be the coadjutor or servant of the civil authority. Recruited in great measure from the people, the clergy sympathized profoundly with their feelings and sufferings, shared their aspirations for deliverance from oppression, and was inspired by the same ardent affection for the soil, but it was also deeply imbued with popular superstitions and prejudices. Deprived, under Tatar rule, of all right of interference in State affairs, it became devoid of ambition beyond its immediate sphere. Seldom, even with its native princes, did any of its members attempt to control, although they may have endeavored to direct, the civil power and stimulate it to action. While largely contributing to the maintenance of national sentiment, and devoted to the welfare of the people, it suffered in its tone and character from the general disorganization of society. The destruction of the seats of learning at Kiev and throughout the captured and plundered cities of the empire, the suppression or interruption of schools and academies almost completely annihilated facilities for education. With a few exceptions among the higher dignitaries, the great body of the clergy were hopelessly ignorant and illiterate; possessing barely the knowledge requisite for celebration of the Church service, they conceived religion to exist only in the formal routine of ceremonial observances. The standard of morality among them was lowered, their character as a body was debased, while their numbers were prodigiously increased.

Ivan III. came to the throne in 1462. He was zealous for the protection of religion, ambitious, but prudent and politic. He reduced nearly all the principalities and cities of Russia to his authority, and laid the foundations of the future greatness of the empire. Sophia, heiress of the Byzantine emperors, was his second wife. This alliance was favored by Rome in the hope that, educated in the Catholic Church, this princess would induce her husband to acknowledge the act of union decreed by the Council of Florence. The hope was vain; Sophia abjured the Roman creed and maintained Ivan steadfast in the Orthodox faith, while the Russian clergy strenuously asserted the independence of their Church.

His authority firmly established within his dominions, Ivan aspired to free his country from Tatar vassalage, and the whole nation arose at his call. He refused tribute to the khan, and summoned the entire forces of the empire to repel the invasion of Ahkmet. The armies were in presence on the banks of the river Oka, called by the people "the girdle of the Mother of God." Ivan's throne trembled in the balance; he faltered and feared to risk all upon a single battle, but, as in every great crisis of Russian history, the Church was strong on the side of nationality and independence. The clergy, by the voice of its prelates, urged him to combat. Vassian, the aged archbishop of Rostov, rebuked his timidity. "Dost thou dread death? Death is the lot of all; of man, beast, and bird alike; none can avoid it. I am old, borne down by weight of years, but give these warriors into my hands and I will brave the Tatar sword and never turn my back."

Gerontius, the metropolitan, was no less urgent: "Be thine, oh, my son! the courage and strength of mind that belong to a soldier of Christ. A good shepherd will die, if needs be, for his flock. May God protect thine empire and give thee the victory!"[1]

---

[1] Karamsin, vol. vi., p. 183.

As Ivan still hesitated, and from his camp continued negotiations, Vassian again argued and earnestly besought him, in "the name of the metropolitan and of us all, representatives of Jesus Christ," to march against Akhmet, blessing "him and his son and his warriors, children of Christ."

A sudden and extraordinary panic spread through the hostile camps, and each fled from before the other, without striking a blow. The Russians were the first to rally, and Ivan reaped the fruits of the campaign.

The Tatar power, exhausted and broken by dissensions among its chiefs, was no longer formidable to the empire.

Victorious in war, Ivan was, in peace, a wise, enlightened, and magnificent prince. He assumed great state, embellished his capital, welcomed at his court scholars fleeing from the infidel conquerors of Byzantium, and endeavored, in Moscow, to revive the glories of Constantinople. He extended his favors to all members of the Greek communion; prelates came to the Russian metropolitan for consecration, and the patriarch of Jerusalem found refuge in Russia from the tyranny of the Sultan of Egypt. While solicitous for the national faith, he was tolerant of other religions. He protected Mahometans and Jews, and exhibited a leniency, extraordinary for the age, towards the dangerous and wide-spread heresy of the Judaizers, which, promulgated in secret, penetrated into high places of both State and Church.[1]

The metropolitan Zosimos, whom Ivan, in the plenitude of his power, had arbitrarily appointed, was convicted of participation, but was simply deposed and relegated to a monastery without further punishment.

---

[1] See p. 183.

Persecution was forbidden, and the votaries of this erratic religious movement were lightly dealt with, until their obstinate persistency, after years of forbearance, necessitated more rigorous measures of suppression.

With greater dignity assumed by the monarch came increased expenditure and a higher sense of imperial authority. Notwithstanding the great services rendered by the Church, Ivan, like his contemporary Louis XI. of France, became jealous of its power and envious of its enormous wealth. He attempted to sequestrate its landed property, and to render it more subservient to his will; but the determined opposition he encountered was too powerful, and a council confirmed its ancient grants and privileges. Simon, the successor of Zosimos, sturdily maintained its rights, and at the same time carefully watched over its discipline and the habits of the clergy. The monasteries for men were separated from those for women; priests and deacons who had lost their wives were prohibited from officiating at mass; simony, corruption, and irregularities of all kinds were severely punished, and every effort made to purify the morals and elevate the tone and character of the clerical profession.

During this period of consolidation in Russia the Church in Lithuania and Poland was exposed to trial and suffering. After the death of the Uniate metropolitan Gregory, its bishops repudiated the decrees of the Council of Florence, refused to acknowledge their dependence on the pope, and insisted upon the consecration of their metropolitans by the patriarch of Constantinople. The rulers of the country, on the contrary, professed the Roman creed, and subjected their Orthodox population to annoyance and persecution. When Ivan married his daughter Helena to Alexander of Lithuania, he carefully

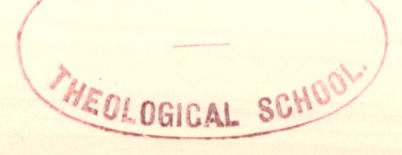

PERSECUTION IN POLAND.—GROWTH OF MOSCOW. 45

stipulated for freedom in the exercise of her religion, and earnestly exhorted her to be steadfast herself, and to be constant in her efforts for the protection of others of their faith. This family alliance was insufficient to prevent dissensions between neighboring princes, each grasping and ambitious, and with religious antagonism to whet suspicion and create irritation. Helena's influence was often, although ineffectually, exerted to alleviate the oppression to which the Orthodox were exposed, but her husband was under pressure from the papal element, which also had his sympathy, and Helena herself was made to feel it. Joseph Saltan, promoted to the see of Kiev, became, in gratitude for his elevation, a convert to the prince's views, and joined in his efforts to crush Orthodoxy and strengthen Romanism. Helena discreetly concealed her own vexations, but the cry of the people reached her father's ears and aroused his indignation. Political relations between Lithuania and Russia were always strained, war was constantly breaking out or imminent, and in such conditions the state of the Orthodox Polish Church was melancholy and distressing.

Under Ivan's son, Vassili IV., the Church in Russia enjoyed a long season of tranquillity; the missionary spirit was strong within it, and it sent forth priests to Christianize and colonize through Lapland to the shores of the Northern seas.

The glory of Moscow, as a centre of learning, the seat of the mightiest prince and most potent prelate of the Orthodox Church, attracted thither monks and emissaries from the convents and holy places of the East in quest of alms and succor. Vast collections of religious manuscripts and books had been accumulated in former reigns, and more recently by Sophia. Vassili sent to Constantinople for theologians of competent erudition for their examination and study. The patriarch selected for the purpose Maximus, a Greek monk of Mt. Athos, distinguished for learning, piety, and ability. He applied himself assiduously to the task, discovered and corrected many errors which had crept into the Church books by the negligence of transcribers, and, by his emendations, restored the ritual in its original purity. His virtues, the wisdom of his counsels, his unaffected piety and religious zeal, greatly endeared him to the prince. Notwithstanding his frequent requests, now that his labors were ended, for permission to return to his convent home, Vassili would not consent, but retained him near his person.

In 1519 Pope Leo X. urged the Russian monarch to unite with the Christian princes of Europe, for the glory of God, against the Turks. He suggested that Constantinople was his legitimate inheritance as son of a Greek princess. He further offered to raise the see of Moscow to a patriarchate, preserving all the "allowable" practices of the Eastern Church, thus speciously disguising, while asserting, his assumption of jurisdiction. Vassili, however, mindful of the Te Deums celebrated by Leo for the great victory of the Lithuanians over the "heretic" Russians at Orscha, declined his advances, and refused others of a similar nature from Clement VII.

Vassili's attachment to the national religion was sincere, but he was impatient of clerical dictation. He forced Barlaam, for his uncompromising austerity, to retire from the primacy, and raised Daniel to his place. The new metropolitan was a man of elastic principles, of narrow, selfish views, unscrupulous, complaisant, devoured by ambition and by jealousy of Maximus, a foreigner.

In common with most of the clergy, Daniel was fanatically attached to the ancient ceremonies of the Church ritual, and opposed to reforms. To strengthen his position and ingratiate himself with the prince, Daniel authorized Vassili's divorce from his wife Salomina, on the plea of her sterility, and celebrated his marriage with Helena. On this matter Vassili had set his heart, but for a long time in vain, as it was contrary to ecclesiastical canon. It is related that, by Daniel's advice, Vassili consulted the Eastern patriarchs, and Mark of Jerusalem replied by a prediction terribly fulfilled in the succeeding reign—

"Shouldst thou contract a second marriage thou shalt have a wicked son; thy states shall become a prey to terror and to tears; rivers of blood shall flow; the heads of thy mighty ones shall fall; thy cities shall be devoured by flames."

Maximus agreed with the other prelates in condemning the proceedings, and Daniel seized upon the occasion to accomplish his ruin. Vassili's affection was turned to hatred, and, deprived of this support, Maximus was summoned before a council, convicted of heresy and sacrilege for tampering with the Sacred Books, and sentenced to reclusion. Daniel's triumph was of short duration; during the infancy of Vassili's son Ivan this scheming prelate and his successor were actively engaged in court intrigues and conspiracies, and both suffered from the vicissitudes of the struggle between rival factions; one was forced to abdicate, and the other was banished. The primacy was in the gift of the party in power, and the selection of the incumbent was of grave importance from the influence he might exercise over the young prince, to whom, by virtue of his functions, he had free access, and from his authority as head of the Church. Macarius, archbishop of Novgorod, an ambitious man, but of recognized piety and ability, was chosen in 1542.

Ivan IV. was an infant when his father died; his youth was turbulent and riotous; gifted by nature with great talents and force of character, with lofty aspirations, but strong and ungovernable passions, with untiring energy and unbounded confidence, his education was purposely neglected by his guardians, who, while intriguing and disputing among themselves for power, each in turn, in order to strengthen and prolong their authority, gratified his caprices, encouraged his excesses, pandered to his vicious propensities, sedulously fostered his harsh and tyrannical disposition, and, by adulation and flattery, imbued his mind with the conviction that as Tsar he could do no wrong. In early life he gave evidence of his impatience of control and of his cruel nature. When but thirteen years of age he joined in the overthrow of the ruling faction, viewed with complacency the torture and death of its chief, whose body he ordered to be thrown to his dogs to be devoured. At seventeen years of age, in 1547, he assumed sovereign authority, and was crowned as Tsar. This title, derived from the Hebrew, borne by Chaldean kings of Biblical history and by Greek emperors, sometimes adopted by his father and grandfather, was henceforth to be the designation of the monarchs of Russia. He married Anastasia Romanoff, a native princess of great beauty, rare intelligence, and piety.

By a singular contradiction, Ivan, in his wildest excesses, always exhibited extraordinary regard for devotional observances, scrupulous adherence to religious ceremonial, and superstitious reverence for the Church.

In the year following his marriage Moscow was destroyed by a furious conflagration; popular insurrections broke out, and general anarchy threatened the stability of the government. At this juncture, when Ivan was terrified and dismayed by these calamities, Sylvester, a monk of Novgorod, revered for his sanctity and holy life, appeared before him, and, like a prophet of old, boldly rebuked his shameful excesses and cruelty, declared the ruin of Moscow to be the sign of divine wrath, invoked upon him the vengeance of the Almighty if he did not turn from his wickedness, and exhorted him to give heed to the Gospel injunctions if he would escape from the hand of God and live. Ivan was moved to tears, and promised amendment. Among his companions was Alexis Adaschef, a youth of great personal attractions, of pure and elevated character, and signal ability, who valued royal favor only as a means for noble ends, and who joined Sylvester in his efforts to reclaim the prince. Henceforth the influence of these virtuous, patriotic men was paramount, and, guided by them, Ivan, with characteristic energy, summoned the bishops of the Church, made public confession of his faults, and besought the metropolitan to aid his youth and inexperience.

Success to his arms abroad and prosperity within his realm followed the wise and prudent administration of his new counsellors. The civil laws were reduced to a code in 1550, and the year following an assembly, known as that of "the Hundred Chapters," from the number of its decisions, was convened to confirm the legal code and to take into consideration all matters pertaining to clerical discipline and reform. It was opened by Ivan in person, who appealed to the fathers present to "enlighten and instruct him in all godliness," not to spare his weakness, but to "rebuke his errors without fear;" "so shall my soul live and the souls of all my people."

From the scanty records of this council it would seem to have undertaken a thorough reform of the Church and of the ritual, but its action was incomplete and most unfortunate. Many superstitious practices were preserved, and the alterations of the Church books were superficial and incorrect. Errors, allowed to stand, received thereby additional confirmation, and were more widely disseminated by the introduction of printing.

Meanwhile Russian arms were everywhere victorious. Kasan and Astracan were subdued, the Golden Horde crushed, and the dominion of the Church was extended over the conquests of the State. Ivan, yet faithful to his virtuous resolves, loved by his people, feared by his enemies, realized a crowning happiness in the birth of a son.

A change was imminent, terrible as it was unexpected. During a serious illness of the tsar intrigues and disputes regarding the succession filled his soul with doubts of the loyalty of his most faithful friends. His mind, unhinged by sickness, was painfully affected by the sudden death of his child and of his beloved wife, and perfidious counsels fostered suspicions, to which his dark and sombre disposition was prone. He sought advice from a former favorite of his father, Vassian, ex-bishop of Kolomna, who had been deprived of his diocese for crime. This old man, whose heart was filled with gall and envy, whispered suggestions which found ready response in Ivan's diseased fancies.

"If," said he, "you wish to be absolute monarch, have no confidant wiser than yourself; give orders, but receive advice from no one; always command and never follow the lead of others; thus you will be indeed a king, terrible to your lords. Remember, above all, that a counsellor, even of the wisest prince, inevitably becomes his master."[1]

---

[1] Karamsin, vol. viii., p. 234.

The poisonous seed bore fatal fruit. Ivan, then but thirty years of age, seemed to lose all faith in mankind. He surrounded himself with sycophants and parasites, and plunged anew into the wild excesses of his youth; he pursued his former friends with relentless cruelty, arraigned and condemned Adaschef and Sylvester for treason. His tyranny grew with its indulgence; every one became an object of suspicion; prisons were filled with victims; blood ran like water: no head was too high, no character too pure, for attack. The natural ferocity of his disposition broke through all restraints, and he seemed to be possessed by a wild, insane fury to torture, slay, and destroy; yet, with strange inconsistency, making profession of earnest devotion all the while, constantly humbling himself before the altar, and, cleansed of past enormities, going forth with fresh thirst for blood.

Anastasius succeeded Macarius, but, terrified at the atrocities committed by the tsar, and at his impatience of all remonstrance, he soon retired to a monastery.

Ivan, apprehensive of the possible consequences of his cruelty and oppression, removed with his court to Alexandrov; his people, in consternation at his departure from Moscow, implored him to return, and he yielded to their solicitations only upon condition of absolute submission to his will. This they promised, and their obedience never faltered through a long reign distinguished in all history for its unspeakable horrors.

"He who blasphemes his Maker will meet with forgiveness among men, but he who reviles the Tsar will surely lose his head," is a Russian saying, and loyalty was a principle of religion ingrained in the Russian soul. A nobleman impaled by Ivan, for some trivial offence, while languishing in agony, constantly repeated, "Great God, protect the Tsar!" "Neither tortures nor dishon-

or," writes a chronicler of the times, "could shake their devotion to the sovereign."

On returning to the capital, Ivan, in a wild caprice, established the "Opritchnina,"[1] and divided the empire into the so-called "personality" and "communality;" the one to be his individual property, under his personal rule, and the other to be governed by the boyars and ordinary officers of the State. He formed a body-guard called the "Opritchniki," or Legion of the Elect, chosen for their debauched and lawless habits, and sworn to obey him only, and in all things, ignoring all other authority. With them he gave free vent to his fiendish passions and diabolic cruelty. City and country, noble and peasant, were alike subjected to pillage, extortion, and torture. At Alexandrov he established a chapel and monastery, where he and his familiars, in the garb of monks, officiated and assiduously followed the strictest rule of monastic life. He spent hours in prayer and self-flagellation, as if to quiet remorse, and then, unable to control his thirst for blood, he passed from the fatiguing and exhausting service of the altar to rest and refresh himself by superintending the rack. Vain of his theological acquirements and devotional practices, he was wont to vary his occupation as torturer and executioner by admonishing the clergy to be faithful, and to take pattern from him in the discharge of their duties.

Before the Church fell into ignominious subserviency a martyr was added to its list of saints. When Athanasius retired, Germanus refused the primacy and rebuked the tsar for his crimes. Philip, a monk of noble birth, distinguished for piety and learning, was sum-

---

[1] *Opritchnina,* or *opritchina,* is an old Russian word, now obsolete, meaning privilege; *opritchniki,* the persons who are "privileged."

moned from the distant monastery of Solovetsk. Mindful of the grave responsibilities and duties of the high office offered him, he declined its acceptance unless the tsar would abolish the Opritchnina and restore the unity of the empire. Finally, hoping to mitigate the evils of this institution, if he could not obtain its suppression, he yielded to the solicitations of the people.

Ivan's diseased imagination saw conspiracy and rebellion threatening his throne, and, to strike his enemies with terror, he redoubled his persecutions. Philip, by his constant exhortations to mercy and amendment, became odious to the tyrant, who at times seemed possessed by an insane fancy to mock the Church which generally he so much feared. He presented himself, on one occasion, dressed in strange attire, accompanied by a band of his Opritchniki, before the primate at the altar, to receive his blessing. Philip took no notice of his presence, but when the boyars announced to him that the tsar was before him, he replied, "I do not recognize the tsar in any such dress; I do not recognize the tsar in his acts. What is this that thou hast done, O tsar! to put off from thee the form of thine honor? Fear the judgment of God. Here we are offering up the bloodless sacrifice to the Lord, while behind the altar there is flowing the innocent blood of Christian men." Ivan, furious, tried to stop his lips with menaces. "I am a stranger and a pilgrim upon earth," was the reply, "as all my fathers were, and I am ready to suffer for the truth. Where would my faith be if I kept silence."

Ivan was awed, but greedily listened to accusations of seditious intrigues brought against Philip, and a packed tribunal of venal prelates condemned him. He calmly submitted and resigned the insignia of his office, but was ordered to officiate again at a solemn festival. When on the steps of the altar, arrayed in his pontifical robes, a troop of armed men invaded the sanctuary; their leader proclaimed the primate's deposition, and the soldiers, with blows and insult, tore the sacred vestments from his back and dragged him to prison. Philip exulted in being permitted to suffer for the truth, and, turning on the steps of the Church, he gave his blessing to the horror-struck worshippers, with the single admonition, "Pray."[1] Transferred to the Otroch monastery, he was strangled in his cell by the tsar's command, and died a martyr; to the honor of Russian monarchs, be it said, the only one the annals of the Church record.

After the death of Philip, weak and pusillanimous prelates, humbly submissive to the tyrant's will, occupied the metropolitan throne, and all attempts to check the tsar's excesses ceased. The Church sanctioned his frequent marriages, in scandalous violation of ecclesiastical canons, and, unable to protect even its own members, was a silent witness to scenes of atrocious cruelty and unbridled license. An imaginary conspiracy was Ivan's pretext for the destruction of Novgorod, still boasting the name of "Great," but sadly fallen from its ancient high estate. The unhappy city was given over to sack and pillage; churches and monasteries were sacrilegiously plundered; the miserable inhabitants led forth by thousands to be broken on the wheel, boiled in oil, sawn between planks, or flayed alive, while Ivan looked gleefully on, racking his hellish ingenuity to devise new tortures. Pskov was saved from a similar fate by the bold interposition of a religious fanatic named Nicholas, who, feigning insanity, dared upbraid the savage tyrant, and so aroused his superstitious fears that he left the

---

[1] Mouravief, pp. 116, 117.

city in peace. It is related that he offered Ivan raw meat, and, it being Lent, the tsar replied, "I am a Christian, and eat no meat in Lent." "Thou doest worse," was the hermit's rejoinder; thou feedest upon human flesh and blood, forgetting, not Lent indeed, but Christ Himself."

Notwithstanding the subserviency of the clergy, its patriotic spirit was not extinct. In 1580, when Russia was sore beset on every side, a council assembled at Moscow eagerly responded to the monarch's call for aid, and relinquished to the crown all the landed estates which the Church had acquired by gift or purchase from the princes of Moscow. At this critical juncture Ivan's wonted energy deserted him. Hidden from his people in the gloomy retreat of Alexandrov, he revelled and caroused with his favorites, giving his son in marriage and espousing his seventh wife, while defeat and disaster overwhelmed the empire. He was compelled to humble himself before the Polish king and sue for peace.

The pope Gregory XIII. deemed the opportunity propitious for renewing the oft-repeated attempt at union of the Churches, and, in 1581, despatched to Moscow Anthony Poissevin, a Jesuit of wily and insinuating manners, of great diplomatic skill, to act in his name as mediator between the combatants. Although the vast resources of Russia were far from being exhausted, Poissevin, adroitly playing upon the pusillanimous fears of the tsar, induced him to conclude an armistice upon disadvantageous terms, and Livonia was lost to Russia, after nearly six centuries of possession. During the negotiations with Stephen Batory, King of Poland, the tsarevitch Ivan, who, though educated in vice, inherited the manliness of his father's youth, indignant at the national humiliation, begged permission to lead an army against the enemy; but the jealous tyrant, in a fit of frenzy, suspicious of treachery even in his own son, felled him by a fatal blow from his iron staff.

Poissevin, relying on his success in securing the peace which Ivan desired, proceeded to Moscow to develop the future plans of Rome. In return for the services he had rendered he urged the tsar to recognize the fusion of the Churches promulgated by the Council of Florence, to enter into an alliance with the other European powers, and thus array the whole Christian world in a crusade against the Turks. He eloquently discoursed on the glorious opportunity of restoring unity to the universal Church, not, he claimed, by abjuring the Greek religion, but by preserving it in its ancient purity, as established by the early Councils, as decreed at Florence, recognized by the Greek emperor, the patriarch, the clergy of Constantinople, and by Isidore, the former illustrious head of the Russian Church. He adroitly insinuated the prospect of recovering Kiev, the ancient patrimony of the race of Ruric, and of grasping the sceptre of the Byzantine Empire. His arguments fell on a listless and unwilling ear. Ivan, consumed by remorse at the murder of his son, his anxiety about foreign invasion allayed, his youthful energy dulled by excesses and indulgence, felt no kindling ambition for a shadowy empire in the East. He ridiculed the Orthodoxy of Western Christians, who shaved their beards, and the pretensions of the pope to sit on a throne above kings, and give them his toe to kiss. "We earthly sovereigns," said he, "alone wear crowns. The heir of the apostles should be meek and lowly in spirit. We reverence our metropolitan, and crave his blessing, but he walks humbly on earth, and seeks not, in pride, to raise himself above princes. There is but one Holy Father, and He is in heaven; whoso calleth himself the companion of Jesus Christ, but is carried on men's shoulders, as if borne up on a cloud by angels, is no true shepherd, but a wolf in sheep's clothing."[1]

Poissevin's persistence and eloquence were exerted to no purpose; the utmost concession he could obtain was that Catholics, like other heretics, might dwell in Russia without molestation on the score of religion, but the erection of Latin churches and the propagation of their faith were prohibited.

The erudite Dionysius, surnamed "Grammaticus" for his learning, had, during the last years of this reign, by his prudence, virtues, and energy, somewhat restored the dignity of the metropolitan see.

Worn out before his time by the warring of his fierce passions, alternating with fits of remorse and repentance, Ivan, in his latter days, turned again to the Church for relief; he showered rich alms on the holy convents of Sinai and Athos, exhorted his youthful son and heir to rule with mercy and charity for his subjects, and, receiving tonsure from the priest's hands, the "Terrible" Tsar yielded up his soul as the simple monk Jonah.

"He had passed over the land of Russia," says a great poet, "like a blast of divine wrath," and now, on the throne of this "scourge of God," sat a gentle and pious youth, who seemed lost in the gloomy precincts of the Kremlin, a wandering monk who had strayed from his monastery.

Feodor (Theodore) I. was small in stature, weak in health and intellect; he joined to extreme mildness of disposition a timid spirit, excessive piety, and a profound indifference for this world's affairs; he passed his days in listening to pious legends, singing hymns with monks,

---

[1] Karamsin, vol. ix., p. 460.

and his greatest pleasure was to ring the convent bells and share in the services of the Church; "He is a sacristan," said his father, "and no tsarevitch."

Yielding in character, and fondly attached to his wife, Irene, he reposed implicit confidence and trust in her brother, Boris Godounov, who, during the entire reign, wielded the supreme authority in the young tsar's name.

Godounov, by his energy and ability, restored strength to the crown and prosperity to the State. Looking forward with far-sighted and patient ambition, he saw the sceptre within his grasp. So important an element, in his calculations, as the clergy, was not neglected; Dionysius, the metropolitan, penetrated the secret of his treacherous designs, and, anxious regarding the succession, as Irene was childless, he instigated a petition, notwithstanding its uncanonical object, to the tsar for his divorce. His machinations resulted in his ruin; he was deposed, and confined in the convent of Khoutinsk. Godounov was all-powerful, and by his influence Job, archbishop of Rostov, was installed as primate.

The Russian Church was still nominally under the ecclesiastical jurisdiction of the patriarchal see of Constantinople, but the Eastern Church had fallen to a state of lamentable decrepitude and degradation. The patriarch, although elected by a synod, was dependent on the Turkish emperor for confirmation, which was to be obtained only by intrigue and bribery; the ambition of Eastern prelates to wield the pastoral staff was a never-failing source of revenue to the sultan and his favorites. Each incumbent was in turn the victim of the jealousy of his competitors, and scarcely had he mounted the slippery steps of the throne ere he was removed to make place for a rival more fortunate from influence at court or with a heavier purse to support his pretensions.

DEGRADATION OF THE EASTERN CHURCH. 59

During the century subsequent to the fall of Constantinople suffering and martyrdom were the general lot of the successors of St. Chrysostom, but it was suffering without good for the Church, and martyrdom without dignity. Their procession is a melancholy one; Joasaph Cocas, persecuted by his clergy, attempted, in despair, to drown himself in a well; rescued, and reseated on the throne, he was driven into exile by the sultan; Mark Xylocaraboeus was exiled; Simeon paid a thousand gold florins for his seat, and was thrown into a monastery; Dionysius had the same fate; Raphael, to secure his nomination, doubled the tribute hitherto exacted; unable to pay the sum promised, he was thrust forth, loaded with chains, to beg by the roadside, and died in misery; Nyphon had his nose cut off, and was forced into exile; Joachim raised the tribute to three thousand ducats, was exiled, recalled, and again exiled; Pacome was poisoned; Jeremiah I. started on a pastoral tour, his vicar deserted him on the way, hurried back, bribed the vizier, and usurped the see; he was driven away by a popular outbreak, and Jeremiah's friends purchased for him permission to resume his seat; Joasaph II. again raised the tribute, was deposed and excommunicated by his clergy for simony; Gregory was cast into the sea; Cyril Lucar was exiled and strangled; Methrophanes, accused of simony, was induced to resign by the offer of two dioceses; he sold the one and administered the other; Jeremiah II., bishop of Larissa, was elected and confirmed in 1572; his funds were exhausted by the tribute, then fixed at ten thousand florins, and he piteously complained, in his correspondence, that he dared not undertake a pastoral tour to replenish his treasury from the alms of the faithful for fear that, in his absence, some ambitious brother might seize upon the throne. The danger was real; Methrophanes reappeared, and reasserted his claims to the patriarchate; as his purse was the longer, he was reinstated on appeal to the sultan. At his death Jeremiah again enjoyed a brief spell of power, but, accused of conspiracy against the government, he was imprisoned, then exiled to Rhodes. Theoptus, his accuser, seized the vacant seat, disputed, also, by Pacome, a monk of Lesbos, and, by the opportune payment of a double tribute, secured the imperial confirmation; imprudently he ventured on a pastoral visit to Walachia, and in his absence Jeremiah's friends purchased *his* pardon, and reseated him on the throne.[1]

The dilapidation of the finances of the patriarchate, the ruin threatening the whole fabric, and the exhaustion of all parties, brought about perforce a general reconciliation, and Jeremiah was left in undisputed possession. A common effort was made to heal the wounds of the unhappy and suffering Church; missions were despatched to various countries in search of succor and alms, and Jeremiah himself, for the same purpose, undertook a journey to Russia, the wealthiest and most powerful member of the Orthodox communion. His arrival was happily timed for the designs of the ambitious Boris.

Under his influence the pious Feodor had eagerly seized upon the idea of freeing the national Church from all dependence, however slight, upon foreign jurisdiction. Probably to prepare the way for this step, early in his reign he sent an embassy to the sultan, and charged his envoy with rich gifts for the patriarch and kindly assurances of good-will towards the Church. In 1586 Joachim of Antioch appeared in Russia in quest of

---

[1] De Vogüé, *Revue des Deux Mondes*, Mars, 1879.

ESTABLISHMENT OF RUSSIAN PATRIARCHATE.

alms, and, during his visit, Feodor announced to his council and clergy his intention to elevate the see of Moscow to the rank of patriarchate. They approved of his project, but urged that the assent of the whole Eastern Church be first obtained, in order to forestall any reproach from schismatics or heretics, that the change was due to a merely arbitrary act of the tsar. Joachim, while favoring Feodor's plan, concurred in the wisdom of delay, and, abundantly rewarded for his compliance, took his departure for the East, promising to press the matter upon his brother patriarchs. A year or more passed; the œcumenical fathers delayed their answer; doubtless the proposition met with little favor in their eyes; they feared to affront a powerful friend, yet, unwilling to assent, sought refuge in procrastination.

At this juncture Jeremiah arrived at Moscow, and was welcomed with all the honors that a pious monarch could render to one of his exalted rank. Touched with gratitude at his reception, he expressed his approval of the tsar's desire to institute a Russian patriarchate. To his surprise, Godounov, by the tsar's orders, proposed to him that he should abandon his poverty-stricken capital on the shores of the Bosphorus, escape from humiliating subjection to the infidel Turk, and assume charge of the newly-established primacy over rich, powerful, Orthodox Russia. Jeremiah, dazzled by the brilliant prospect, willingly assented, but it formed no part of the plans of the astute Godounov that a stranger should occupy in Russia so exalted a station. While laboring for the aggrandizement of the national Church, he intended that it should also serve his ambitious ends, and reserved the primacy for a friend and partisan upon whose support he could rely. At his suggestion the tsar intimated his intention to fix the residence of the new primate at Vladimir, which city was, after Kiev, the ancient ecclesiastical capital of the empire. Jeremiah demurred, and insisted that Moscow was the only proper abode of the head of the Church. He appealed to former precedents in the East, and claimed it to be his province to be near the sovereign. This was inadmissible; the presence of a foreigner at court in such intimate relations with the tsar would shock national prejudices; the necessity of an interpreter between the sovereign and the prelate would bring a third—possibly an indiscreet—person into secrets of state or religious polity. Moreover, it would entail the forced retirement of Job, who was still the actual head of the Church, a sorry reward for years of zealous and faithful service.

During the negotiations which ensued the wily Greek soon perceived that he was but a tool in the hands of the unscrupulous Godounov. He began, also, to weary of the strange, and, to him, savage habits and customs of the country; waxing old and feeble, he became apprehensive, and sighed to return to milder climes and scenes to which he had been accustomed. When, therefore, the alternative was placed before him of a residence at Vladimir or the appointment of a native prelate to fill the patriarchal throne, he chose the latter.

A synod of all the Russian bishops was solemnly convoked at Moscow for the election, the result of which was a foregone conclusion; three names were submitted to the tsar, and he selected the first on the list, that of Job, the metropolitan, the friend and faithful adherent of Godounov. Jeremiah, whose expectations had been raised only to be disappointed, now earnestly craved permission to depart, although with his desire to escape from Russia were mingled grave apprehensions of the reception that might await him at Constantinople for his complicity with these serious changes in the constitution of the Church. His presence at Moscow was, however, yet necessary to add to the dignity and sacredness of the event, and he was detained, sorely against his will, to officiate at the ceremony of installation. As the elder and first of the pastors of the Eastern Church, he solemnly imposed hands and blessed Job as "Chief of Bishops, Father of Fathers, and Patriarch of all the Countries to the North, by the grace of God and the will of the Tsar."

A formal record of the proceedings was subscribed to by the tsar, with the great seal of the State, by all the Russian bishops and dignitaries present, by Jeremiah and the Greek prelates who accompanied him. It was therein set forth that ancient Rome had fallen into heresy, and the Western Church was polluted by false doctrines; that new Rome was in the hands of the infidel Turk, and henceforth a third Rome had arisen at Moscow; that the first œcumenical prelate of the Church was the patriarch of Constantinople, the second the patriarch of Alexandria, the third the patriarch of Moscow, the fourth the patriarch of Antioch, the fifth the patriarch of Jerusalem. It was further declared that the patriarch of Moscow should be elected and consecrated by the clergy of Russia, without any necessity of reference to other authorities of the Greek Church.

In order to complete the hierarchy of the Russian establishment four metropolitan sees were instituted—at Novgorod, Kasan, Rostov, and Kroutitsk—and six archbishops, with eight bishops, were added to the ranks of the clergy.

The reorganization of the Church thus completed, Jeremiah, loaded with presents, was dismissed, with all possible honors, in the spring of 1589.

His apprehensions of an unfriendly reception at the hands of the vain and intolerant clergy of the East, hostile to any intrenchment upon the shadowy dignity of their position, were fully realized, and he found it by no means an easy task to reconcile his brother patriarchs of Asia and Africa to the proceedings authorized by him. His own companions disavowed his acts, regardless of their signature to the record at Moscow, but, after much mutual recrimination, the Oriental fathers acquiesced in the inevitable, and signified their assent to what they could not have prevented and could not now undo, stipulating, however, with clerical jealousy of rank, that the Russian patriarchate should, as the youngest, be fifth in order of precedence instead of third, and that its incumbent should seek investiture at Constantinople.

These conditions were never enforced, and within a century were formally abolished.

CHAPTER V.

Boris Godounov.—The Church in Poland.—Peter Mogila.—Liberation of Russia from the Poles.—Philaret.—Alexis.—Nikon and his Reforms.—Dissent.

BORIS GODOUNOV was now at the height of his power, screened by the arm of the Church and strong in his sovereign's affection. Dimitri, last heir to the throne, was secretly assassinated by his orders, and Feodor's daughter died in infancy. All obstacles thus removed, he waited patiently for the feeble tsar's death to seize upon the crown.

A successful campaign against the Crimean Tatars added the glory of a warrior to his fame as administrator. He drove the invaders from the walls of Moscow, while the monkish prince prostrated himself before the altar with sublime confidence in the efficacy of prayer. "Have no fears," he prophesied to the aged men and weeping women who remained within the beleaguered city, "to-morrow not a Tatar shall be in sight."[1]

The singular piety of the monarch greatly endeared him to his devout and superstitious people. He lost all chance of election to the throne of Poland by his unswerving Orthodoxy, and declined the pope's proposals for union of the Churches in a general crusade against the Turks.

Under his fostering care the Church increased enormously in wealth and influence. Moscow became a

---

[1] Karamsin, vol. x., p. 206.

"holy city;" there were four hundred religious edifices within its walls, and thirty-four within the precincts of the Kremlin.

At his death, in 1598, Irene, in furtherance of her brother's ambition, retired to a convent. Feodor left no direct heir; Boris was the choice of the nation, and a general assembly summoned him to the throne. After repeated refusals, with great apparent reluctance, and pretending to yield only to threats of excommunication by the Church, he assented to the popular wish and was crowned tsar.

During these events in Russia the Polish Church had passed through trying vicissitudes. About 1520 Jonah II., an Orthodox prelate, had succeeded Joseph Saltan as metropolitan of Kiev. He and his successors were zealous defenders of the Orthodox faith against the encroachments of the kings of Poland. Liberty of religious worship was allowed, and the independence of the Church was recognized in principle, but severe pressure was exerted upon the nobles who professed the Greek faith. Their social and political privileges were seriously curtailed; they could not occupy any of the higher offices of state, nor sit as senators in the national diet.

When Sigismund, of Sweden, was elected king, in 1587, his zeal for the Catholic Church led to more systematic and persistent persecution of members of the Orthodox communion. Their fidelity to their creed was undermined by appeals to their interests and ambition, and many of the clergy, as well as of the nobles, became lukewarm and indifferent to the fortunes of their Church.

The Jesuit Poissevin had not forgotten his ill success at the Muscovite court, and, during the reign of Stephen Batory, he had urged upon Pope Gregory XIII.

the policy of weakening the stronghold of Orthodoxy by attacking its outposts in Lithuania.

He suggested the establishment of a Jesuit college at Wilna, and translated into Russian many works of Latin theology. He continued his labors with unremitting zeal, and earnestly advocated unity of belief as essential to the welfare of the kingdom; he insidiously urged upon the nobles of Lithuania the advantages they would gain by adherence to the faith of their sovereign, and the new fields of honor and distinction thereby to be opened, and from which they remained debarred. His reasoning was persuasive and his arguments cogent, substantiated, as they were, by royal and papal promises. The incipient and growing discontent, thus artfully fomented, was further stimulated by the severity exercised by the patriarch Jeremiah, who visited Kiev on his return from Moscow to Constantinople. He endeavored to purify the Orthodox Church of Lithuania by the removal of unworthy members of its hierarchy, and hoped to impart fresh life and vigor by wholesome correction. He deposed the metropolitan Onicephorus, and consecrated Michael Ragosa in his stead. The new primate, yielding to the blandishments of the court, induced the bishops of his see to consent to union with Rome, and the synod sent ambassadors to Pope Clement VIII. to signify their submission.

In vain did Jeremiah threaten the apostates with excommunication. Sigismund assured them of his protection, and defied the patriarch's anathema. Te Deums were sung in St. Peter's, and medals were struck commemorative of the event, but the results were not as satisfactory as had been anticipated. The seceding prelates did not meet from their Latin brethren the hearty recognition they had expected, and were not admitted to the senate as equals in rank, while a strong opposition denounced the union as fraudulently and treacherously proclaimed. Each party deliberately anathematized the other, and the Church of Little Russia was from this period, 1596, divided into the Orthodox and the Uniates, both sects preserving the same forms and ceremonies of worship, and, at first, professing the same creed, differing only as regards acknowledging or rejecting the supremacy of the pope. Rome, with considerate moderation, was content, for the time being, to waive questions of doctrine. The Uniates, exulting in their success, and relying on the hearty support of the secular power, were eager to enjoy the fruits of their victory; Dominican convents were established; the Orthodox were excluded from the schools, while ordination was refused to all save graduates; the Orthodox churches, monasteries, and religious establishments were seized, and their revenues confiscated; Orthodox prelates were replaced by Uniates, until but a single bishop of the Greek religion remained in the realm.

The Cossacks of the Don were steadfast in their adherence to the ancient creed, and frequently rose in arms for its defence. The strong leaven of faith among them and the people, kept in active ferment by persecution, greatly facilitated the conquest of Little Russia by Alexis Romanoff fifty years later.

In Russia the brilliant prospects attending Boris Godounov's usurpation were undergoing a gradual but radical change. His presence on the throne grated on the loyalty of the Russian people to the blood of Ruric; he was not of the royal race, but of comparatively mean, even of foreign, origin, a descendant of a Tatar mourza.

The nobles yielded unwilling obedience to one of inferior birth. Serfdom, which he rigorously enforced, revolted the peasantry, and was irksome to the landlords. The protection which he accorded to foreigners and his encouragement of foreign arts and sciences were a terrible grievance to the clergy and the people. To Russians a foreigner was not only a stranger, he was an alien in blood, language, and religion. They divided mankind into three categories, and, leaving aside the "Busurmani," or Mussulmans of the East, the remainder of the human family was composed of the "Slovenie," or those having the gift of speech—their own and kindred races who could comprehend, or "speak" with, each other, and of the "Nyemtsi," or the "Dumb," who could not "speak" with them, comprising all Western nations.[1] They did not esteem them Christians, and used the same term indifferently to designate the heathen. The Russian people was the Orthodox people; their country was "Holy" Russia; the presence of a foreigner therein was pollution, and to visit foreign lands was a sin. The youths who were sent abroad by Boris for study were mourned by their families as lost beyond hope.

Boris was devout in his religious duties, and his devotion was called hypocrisy, or was attributed to remorse. He withdrew from the eyes of his subjects, and claimed veneration as the vicar of God on earth; he ordered prayers to be recited in every household, at each repast, "for the salvation of the body and soul of the servant of God, the Tsar, chosen by the Eternal, Lord of all lands of the North and of the East, the only Christian monarch of the universe, whom all other sovereigns obey as slaves, whose mind is a well of wisdom, whose heart is full of love and mercy,"[2] and his self-exaltation was deemed sacrilegious.

---

[1] Haxthausen, vol. i., p. 272. [2] Karamsin, vol. xi., p. 122.

Old stories of Dimitri's assassination were revived, and suspicions became convictions; Boris was accused of having summoned the Tatars, that, in the danger to the empire, his crime might be forgotten; a terrible pestilence and famine was a token of divine wrath, and his beneficent measures to relieve the suffering were made a reproach. Discontent fed on calumny, and the country was ripe for revolt.

Godounov met the hostile feeling by harsh and tyrannical treatment of all who, from birth, rank, or influence, were objects of suspicion. The Romanoffs, who, from relationship with Anastasia, the virtuous wife of Ivan IV., shared the popular affection in which her memory was held, fell into disgrace. Their head, Feodor Niketitch, afterwards the celebrated patriarch Philaret, was forced into a monastery as a tonsured monk.

The apparition of Dimitri, claiming to be the son of Ivan IV., was the breeze which fanned into open flame the kindling embers of disaffection.

The Church remained loyal to the tsar, and hurled its anathema against the pretender as an unfrocked monk and arrant impostor, but the nobles and the people, weary of Boris's tyranny, hailed him as their deliverer and true-born lord.

In 1603, by the influence of Claudio Rangoni, papal nuncio at the Polish court, Dimitri was acknowledged by King Sigismund as the rightful tsar. His apparition, at the moment when the struggle in Poland between Orthodoxy and the Unia was at its height, was most opportune for the Catholic party; money and men were promised him upon condition of his embracing the Latin faith; and he, nothing loath, agreed, but secretly, in order to avoid arousing the prejudices of his Russian subjects. Clement VII., rejoicing at the prospect of extending the sway of Rome over the North, joyfully received him into the Church, and gave him his benediction. Supported by the Poles and Cossacks of the Don, aided by treachery, his march on Moscow met with no effectual opposition. Boris, enfeebled by disease, betrayed by his generals, and abandoned by all, was spared by death, in 1605, the final ignominy of submission.

In the last terrible moments that decided the fate of the empire the courage and constancy of Job, the patriarch, may have faltered; he is said to have proffered, with other bishops, his submission to the pretender, but he nobly redeemed this momentary weakness. When Moscow, in flames, proclaimed the downfall of Boris, Job proceeded to the cathedral, and, while he was officiating at mass, the infuriated mob broke into the sanctuary, seized and dragged him from the altar. Job, in a loud voice, denounced the sacrilegious intrusion, and the rebellion against the Lord's anointed. "Here," said he, "before this sacred image of the Virgin, for nineteen years, I have fought the good fight and preserved the unity of the faith. Now I foresee the troubles of the Church and the triumph of falsehood and impiety. Mother of God, save Orthodox Russia!" Degraded from his office, insulted and beaten, he was hurried to confinement in the monastery of Staritza.

Dimitri signalized his accession to power by acts of clemency, especially directed towards such as had suffered from the tyranny of his predecessor; Philaret Romanoff became a recipient of his favor, and was made metropolitan of Rostov.

Once firmly established in the capital, the pretender gradually yielded to his predilection for foreign manners and customs. He no longer hesitated to display his contempt for the antiquated, barbarous usages of his

Muscovite subjects, or feared to shock their national and religious prejudices. He surrounded himself with Poles, and took for his wife the beauteous Marina, a Polish princess. To the horror of all pious Russians, and notwithstanding the remonstrance of the Church, this heretic and foreign woman was crowned tsarina before her marriage, before she had abjured the Roman faith or made profession of Orthodoxy. She encouraged Dimitri in the blind infatuation which led to his ruin. He threw off the dreary state and ceremony which hedged in the dignity of a tsar; mocked at pious superstitions, refusing to cross himself before the sacred images or to have his table blessed and sprinkled with holy water; partook of impure meats, and carelessly evinced his indifference towards the Church and his ignorance of ecclesiastical history. He tolerated Lutherans, and welcomed Jesuits at his court; allowed the erection of a Catholic church and the celebration of the Latin mass within the sacred precincts of the Kremlin. He graciously received apostolic benediction from the pope, and renewed his promise of abjuration.

A more serious act was the nomination of Ignatius, a foreigner, as patriarch. This prelate had been archbishop of Cyprus; exiled from his see, he had, on pretence of suffering for the faith, imposed upon the pious credulity of Feodor, and obtained the bishopric of Riazan. He was a Greek of wily, insinuating address, but of dubious orthodoxy, willing to be a pliant tool in his master's hands.

Popular discontent, artfully fomented by the nobles, who had favored the pretender only to compass the downfall of Godounov, stimulated by Dimitri's supposed intention to recognize the authority of the pope over the Church of Russia and to sacrifice national interests to those of Poland, broke out into open rebellion.

The usurper was slain, his foreign favorites and priests were massacred, and a council of boyars proclaimed Vassili Shouesky as tsar. The Church ratified and blessed the choice. It deposed the foreign intruder, Ignatius, and placed Hermogenes, a prelate of unblemished character and exemplary piety, on the patriarchal throne.

The new tsar professed ardent devotion to the Church, and, to conciliate its powerful influence, as well as gratify the religious sentiments of his subjects, he craved for himself and the whole people absolution for the crimes of treason to the son of Godounov and of submission to an impostor. The venerable Job was summoned for the last time from his convent cell for this solemn ceremony. Blind and infirm, tottering on the brink of the grave, he stood by the side of Hermogenes, clad in the simple black gown of a monk, and received the confession of national repentance. As former patriarch and head of the Church, he pronounced the pardon and remission of the nation's sin, and invoked the blessing of God on the tsar and on Holy Orthodox Russia.

Vassili Shouesky's reign, thus auspiciously commenced, was doomed to end in disaster and ruin.

A second and a third Dimitri, and an impostor pretending to be Peter, son of Feodor, appeared to claim the throne. Intestine strife and foreign invasions by Poles, Cossacks, and Swedes brought the empire to the verge of destruction. "Mounds of graves," says an ancient chronicle, "dotted the land of Russia." The Church throughout remained loyal to Shouesky, the legitimate tsar, and faithful to the cause of national independence.

At Tver the archbishop roused the people against the insurgent bands, and was slain; at Pskov the bishop,

Gennadius, died heartbroken at the treason of his city; Gelaktion, Bishop of Souzdal, perished in exile rather than acknowledge a pretender; Joseph, Bishop of Kolomna, was dragged in chains from town to town by another usurper for exhorting the marauders to obedience; at Novgorod the metropolitan Isidore kept the citizens true to their allegiance, and led them in a vigorous, though hopeless, resistance against a Swedish army; when the convent of Solovetsk was summoned, by the victorious Swedes, to surrender, with promise of a garrison for its protection, its hegumen Anthony stoutly replied, "The Lavra needs no protection from foreign soldiers, and no stranger shall ever be tsar of Russia;" when Rostov was captured Philaret Romanoff, the bishop, refused to abandon his flock, and endeavored to protect it by the power of the Church; seized by the victorious rebels while he was administering communion at the altar, dragged to the presence of their chief, the third Dimitri, the "Robber of Touschina," whom Marina had joined and married, he defied his authority; the great monastery of the Troïtsa successfully maintained for months a siege against an army of thirty thousand Poles, poured out its treasures without stint, and the blood of its brethren like water for the defence and relief of the capital. When Vassili Shouesky, driven from the throne, was a captive in a Polish jail; when Moscow fell, and Hermogenes, deposed by the invader, was thrust into prison to die of starvation; when the empire was thus without a tsar and the Church without a head, the Holy Lavra of St. Sergius refused to submit or to acknowledge a foreign prince, and, under the leadership of its archimandrite Dionysius and of its bursar Abram Palitsin, bravely continued the almost hopeless struggle for the national existence and the national faith. "Its light," says a chronicle, "shone like a sun over all Russia."

The record of the Church during these fearful years of anarchy and disaster is indeed glorious. Not one of its officers gave adherence to a pretender or acknowledged the authority of a foreign usurper. When, in 1610, Vassili was deposed by the Poles, forced to submit to tonsure, and immured in a monastery, Hermogenes, the patriarch, raised his voice in protest; when, subsequently, in a council of rebellious boyars and Polish nobles, some proposed the false Dimitri as tsar, and others successfully urged the election of Vladislas, son of the King of Poland, again the venerable prelate remonstrated, and implored the council neither to recognize a rebel nor to sanction the choice of a heretic and foreigner.

From the Troïtsa monastery the courageous Dionysius, by emissaries and letters, made earnest and constant appeal to the patriotism of the people. The Polish governor of Moscow and the rebellious Russian nobles ordered Hermogenes, as head of the Church, to forbid any national uprising. "I will forbid it," was the reply, "when I see Vladislas baptized and the country freed from Poles; if this is not to be, then I enjoin upon all to rise, and I absolve them from their oath to the king's son. I will give my blessing to all who are ready to die for the Orthodox faith."

Moscow was sacked and destroyed by the Polish soldiery. Hermogenes was deposed, and suffered martyrdom in prison. Ignatius, formerly a creature of the first pretender, Dimitri, now willing to be the minion of a foreign invader, was again seated on the patriarchal throne, amid the smoking ruins of the capital. Universal anarchy reigned supreme, and yet there was hope for Russia in the undying attachment of the people for their native soil and their national religion, and from among the people was to arise their deliverer.

An obscure citizen of Nijni-Novgorod, a butcher, Kozma Minime, raised the standard of revolt in behalf of Holy Russia and the persecuted faith. In rough and ready eloquence he appealed to the nation; "Let us rise," said he, "one and all, young and old; the time has come for us to risk our lives for the truth, but this even is not enough, we must sell our houses and lands, pledge our wives and children, to raise up armies for the deliverance of our country." As he spoke so he acted; he gave all he possessed to the common cause, and the people, electrified by his appeal, shamed by his example, rallied at his call, and chose him for their chief, with the title of "The Chosen One of all the Russian Empire." Minime was gifted with sound sense, ready tact, utter disinterestedness, and self-abnegation. He gave as leader to the army Prince Dimitri Pojarsky, an able soldier, a true and honest patriot. A solemn fast was enjoined upon the whole land, and this furious outburst of national feeling, stimulated by religious enthusiasm, was universal and irresistible. Traitors and pretenders vanished before it; foreign invaders were driven from city to city. Moscow was recovered, and, in 1613, a great council of the clergy and people, in harmonious accord, renounced allegiance to Vladislas, and acclaimed Michael Romanoff, son of Philaret, as tsar. When Moscow was retaken Ignatius had fled to Poland for safety, and, in the absence of a patriarch, Michael was crowned by three metropolitans, one of whom, Jonah of the Steeps, was placed in charge of the patriarchate until more tranquil times might permit a regular election of a head of the Church.

The struggle against the Poles and the Swedes still continued, with varying success. The Trinity monastery was again besieged by a foreign army, but patriotism and religion were triumphant, and, under the walls of the sacred fortress, a truce was finally concluded, though at costly sacrifice of territory, and the empire gained breathing-time in which to recruit its shattered strength.

The young tsar Michael, educated in a convent, under a pious mother's eye, was by natural inclination, as well as from early training, of a devout and religious character, and the interests and welfare of the Church were the earliest objects of his solicitude. The first step towards its reorganization was the election of a head to replace the fugitive Ignatius. Philaret Romanoff was the common choice of the tsar, the clergy, and the people. It was approved, also, by Theophanes of Jerusalem, who, sent by his brother-patriarchs of the East to the assistance of the Orthodox in Lithuania, visited Moscow, and gladly lent his aid to restore order and discipline in the Church of Russia.

Worn out by the hardships and misfortunes of his checkered life; in youth a victim of Godounov's tyranny, made a monk against his will, confined, banished, driven from his diocese by violence, long separated from friends and family, for nine years a captive in a Polish prison, now, in old age, restored to his native land, Philaret's only desire was to end his days in peace, and he yielded a reluctant consent to assume the high office and grave responsibilities pressed upon him. By his elevation to the ecclesiastical throne "the extraordinary spectacle, never before or since seen in the annals of the world, was presented of a father as patriarch and a son as sovereign governing the empire,"[1] an event most characteristic of the nation and typical of the indissoluble connection in Russia of the Church and State.

---

[1] Mouravief, p. 177.

Animated by the same high motives, united in mutual affection and confidence, the tsar and the primate labored in harmony for the restoration of civil prosperity and of religious order and discipline.

The long period of anarchy and confusion had seriously aggravated the evils arising from errors in the Church books, ritual, and ceremonies. All previous attempts to correct them had been incomplete or unsatisfactory. A thorough reform was indispensable to check abuses, eradicate erroneous or superstitious practices, and preserve the integrity and spirituality of Church worship. Michael urged upon the clergy the necessity of undertaking anew the work of expurgation and correction, and was supported by the patriarchs Philaret and Theophanes. Any change was, however, repugnant to the people and to the more bigoted of the clerical body; they were strongly attached to what they conceived to be the ancient forms, and angrily opposed any innovations. The controversy on the subject was violent and bitter, and this reformation made comparatively little progress. Much, however, was done to extend the power and influence of the Church. Loftier titles and greater dignity were conferred upon the patriarch, and the privileges of the clergy, dating back to Vladimir the Great, were renewed and increased.

The property and ministers of the Church were exempt from civil dues. The officers, servants, and serfs of the patriarch were made amenable to him or to his court alone, save for crimes involving life, and upon these the patriarchal court first pronounced. The great monasteries of the Troïtsa, of the Ascension, and of the Novodyevitchi,[1] were subjected to his direction. These, and

---

[1] Convent of the "Maidens."

all ecclesiastical establishments appertaining to the patriarchate, with their lands, clergy, and following, were placed under his special charge, and, in the event of civil suits, were to be judged by the court of the Great Palace, that is, before the sovereign in person. The extension of the privileges of the clergy was accompanied by a renewal of the restriction established by Ivan III., rendered advisable by the enormous increase of their wealth; the monasteries were prohibited from further acquisition of landed property without special authorization.

Philaret was as solicitous for the internal discipline of the Church as for its material prosperity, and shared the desire of its more enlightened prelates to free it from superstition and error. Efforts in this direction, led by Dionysius, the celebrated and patriotic superior of the Troïtsa monastery, had, immediately prior to Philaret's elevation to the primacy, been checked by clerical intolerance; Dionysius, with his adherents, had been subjected to severe punishment for alleged tampering with sacred mysteries. This persecution was stopped, the reformers were released, and encouraged to persevere in their labors.

The pious zeal of the patriarch, stimulated by the fierce religious struggle in Lithuania and Poland, led him to draw a stronger line of demarkation between the Churches by re-establishing a custom, which had fallen into disuse and was afterwards abrogated, of rebaptizing converts from the Latin faith upon their admission to the Greek communion.

The Church, in remote provinces of the empire, felt his paternal care. The archbishoprics of Kasan and Astracan were reorganized; in them, and in Siberia, regular ecclesiastical administration replaced chaos and anarchy. The savage and predatory population of these countries, which had relapsed into barbarism, were brought under the civilizing influences of religion.

Philaret's anxiety for the interests of the Church was not restricted by the limits of the empire. The close spiritual connection he maintained with Novgorod hastened its final reunion to Russia, and his sympathy was constantly directed towards the suffering Orthodox population of the neighboring realm.

After the reorganization of the Church in Russia the Eastern patriarch proceeded on his mission to Poland. There active and cruel persecution by the Uniate and Catholic prelates, aided by the weakness and vacillation of King Sigismund, had reduced the Orthodox Church to the direst extremity. For upwards of twenty years it had been deprived of a head and of all means of united action. Its dioceses were without bishops; its clergy, pursued with systematic severity, were forbidden to officiate, were imprisoned, tortured, and slain, but the great body of its adherents among the people, together with most of the Cossack population, were ardently attached to their religion. They evinced their devotion, not merely by patient endurance, but also by frequent rebellion against the intolerance of their masters. Theophanes was at first received with scant courtesy by the king, but, after reference to Constantinople, his dignity as patriarch was recognized, and he was allowed to remain at Kiev. Proceeding with exemplary moderation and caution, he succeeded gradually in obtaining permission to open schools for his clergy and to establish charitable and religious institutions for members of his Church. Encouraged by the immunity attending his early efforts and by the renewed life and vigor aroused with return of confidence and hope for the future, he steadily pursued the work of reorganization. In 1620 he installed

THE ORTHODOX CHURCH IN POLAND.—PERSECUTION.

Job Boretsky as metropolitan of Kiev, and appointed bishops to the various dioceses. Having thus re-established the Church, with its hierarchy complete, Theophanes returned to Jerusalem.

This period of tranquillity was but the precursor of a more violent storm. Sigismund, always weak and easily swayed, yielded to the influence of his Romish advisers, and permitted a revival of the contest between the hostile factions, one struggling for existence, the other striving for domination. The Catholics and Uniates, strong in the support of royal authority, pursued the Orthodox with all the rancor and ferocity of clerical fanaticism. Their schools were suppressed; their churches closed or turned into inns, barracks, and mosques; their clergy were deprived of protection from the mob, and prevented from officiating; congregations were dispersed by force; the dead were left without burial rites; sanctuaries and cemeteries were rifled and desecrated. The people, goaded beyond endurance, rose against their oppressors, and exercised fearful reprisals. The Cossacks massacred the Catholics at Kiev; Jehosaphat, the Uniate archbishop of Polotsk, infamous among the Orthodox for his bloodthirsty cruelty, and canonized at Rome for his righteous zeal, was killed by a mob, and the vicar of the Uniate metropolitan was drowned.

The two primates, Job the Orthodox and Joseph the Uniate, convoked rival synods, and were engaged in mutual excommunications when the death of Sigismund checked the fever of persecution. His son and successor, Vladislas IV., signalized his accession to the throne by an edict of toleration. Freedom of worship, with the right of electing their metropolitan, was granted to the Orthodox, and the ancient cathedral of St. Sophia, at Kiev, was restored to them.

Job died in 1632. Peter Mogila, who succeeded him, was a man eminently qualified, by his firmness and decision of character, as well as by erudition and piety, to be head of the Church in difficult times.

This distinguished prelate, son of Simon Ivanovitch, hospodar of Moldavia, was educated in Paris, and in his youth had served with distinction in the wars of the Poles against the Turks; renouncing the career of arms, he entered the monastery of the Petcherski, at Kiev, and soon rose to be its superior. Appointed exarch by Cyril Lucar, patriarch of Constantinople, he boldly and courageously upheld the rights of the Greek Church at the Diet of Warsaw. To his able advocacy was mainly due the liberty of conscience proclaimed by King Vladislas and the restoration to the Orthodox of the churches, convents, and estates wrested from them by the Uniates. He established libraries and printing-presses, reopened seminaries and schools for the clergy, and sent chosen pupils to study in foreign universities. The celebrated academy of Kiev, founded by him in 1634, was a lasting memorial of his name.

During the reign of Vladislas the Orthodox Church enjoyed a short respite from persecution, during which Peter engaged in active theological controversy with its enemies. He issued from his presses the writings of the Greek fathers and books of the Church; he restored the purity of the ritual, and, with the assistance of the archimandrite, Isaiah Trophimovitch, he drew up a confession of the Orthodox faith, in order to authoritatively establish the cardinal points of its doctrine, and clear away the subtile errors and conflicting distinctions thrown around it by the writings of Jesuit and Roman theologians. This confession was revised by a council of bishops, and sent to Constantinople for approval and confirmation. Peter's former patron, Cyril Lucar, was no longer alive to encourage his efforts; this energetic and learned Cretan had, in his extensive travels throughout Europe, become imbued with the reformatory tendency of the age, and, in accordance with it, had attempted the regeneration of the Eastern Church; he was five times deposed from and reinstated upon the patriarchal throne, and was finally murdered by the Turks, in 1628. Parthenius was patriarch when the confession of Peter Mogila was referred to the Eastern fathers. At a synod convened at Jassy, in 1643, it was amended by Meletius Striga, of Constantinople, and in its revised form was approved, and again confirmed, by the council of 1672, under the direction of the patriarch Dositheus of Jerusalem.

This confession was generally received by the Russian Church, and was formally adopted by Adrian, Patriarch of Moscow from 1690 to 1700. With the exception of the doctrines regarding the supremacy of the pope and the Double Procession, it was in general accord with the teachings of the Roman Church, towards which the theologians of Kiev were, from the influence of their surroundings, more strongly inclined than their Muscovite brethren. No other authoritative expression of belief was put forth until 1766; but while Peter's confession has been considered correct in its fundamental principles, it has, since that date, been modified by Russian prelates, and the doctrines of the Russian Church, as now set forth by its catechisms, issued under authority of Philaret, Metropolitan of Moscow from 1820 to 1867, and used in its schools since 1839, may be summarized as follows:[1]

---

[1] This summary has been taken from an article on the Greek Church in the *Encyclopedia Brittanica*, vol. xi., p. 158, by Rev. T. M. Lindsay, D.D. Small capitals denote differences from Roman Catholic, italics differences from Protestant, doctrine.

Christianity is a divine revelation, communicated to mankind through Christ; its saving truths are to be learned from the Bible *and tradition*, the former having been written *and the latter maintained uncorrupted* through the influence of the Holy Spirit; *the interpretation of the Bible belongs to the Church*, which is taught by the Holy Spirit, but every believer may read the Scriptures.

According to the Christian revelation, God is a Trinity; that is, the Divine Essence exists in Three Persons, perfectly equal in nature and dignity, the Father, the Son, and the Holy Ghost; THE HOLY GHOST PROCEEDS FROM THE FATHER ONLY. Besides the Triune God there is no other object of divine worship, *but homage* (ὑπερδουλία) *may be paid to the Virgin Mary and reverence* (δουλία) *to the saints and to their pictures and relics.*

Man is born with a corrupt bias which was not his at creation; the first man, when created, possessed IMMORTALITY, PERFECT WISDOM, AND A WILL REGULATED BY REASON. Through the first sin Adam and his posterity LOST IMMORTALITY, AND HIS WILL RECEIVED A BIAS TOWARDS EVIL. In this natural state man, who, even before he actually sins, is a sinner before God by original or inherited sin, commits manifold actual transgressions; *but he is not absolutely without power of will towards good, and is not always doing evil.*

Christ, the Son of God, became man in two natures, which, internally and inseparably united, make one Person, and, according to the eternal purpose of God, has obtained for man reconciliation with God and eternal life, inasmuch as He, by His vicarious death, has made satisfaction to God for the world's sins, and this satisfaction WAS PERFECTLY COMMENSURATE WITH THE SINS OF THE WORLD.

Man is made partaker of reconciliation in spiritual regeneration, which he attains to, being led and kept by the Holy Ghost. This divine help is offered *to all men without distinction, and may be rejected.* In order to attain salvation, man is justified, and, when so justified, CAN DO NO MORE THAN THE COMMANDS OF GOD. He may fall from a state of grace through mortal sin.

Regeneration is offered by the word of God and in the sacraments, *which, under visible signs, communicate God's invisible grace to Christians when administered "cum intentione."*

There are *seven* mysteries or sacraments. Baptism *entirely destroys* original sin. In the Eucharist the true body and blood of Christ are *substantially present, and the elements are changed into the substance of Christ, whose body and blood are corporeally partaken of by communicants.* ALL Christians should receive the bread and the WINE.

The Eucharist is also an expiatory sacrifice. The new birth, when lost, may be restored through repentance, which is not merely (1) sincere sorrow, but also (2) *confession of each individual sin to the priest,* and (3) *the discharge of penances imposed by the priest for the removal of the temporal punishment which may have been imposed by God and the Church. Penance, accompanied by the judicial absolution of the priest, makes a true sacrament.*

The Church of Christ is the fellowship of ALL THOSE WHO ACCEPT AND PROFESS ALL THE ARTICLES OF FAITH TRANSMITTED BY THE APOSTLES AND APPROVED BY GENERAL SYNODS. *Without this visible Church there is no salvation.* It is under the abiding influence of the Holy Ghost, and *therefore cannot err in matters of faith.*

Specially appointed persons are necessary in the service of the Church, *and they form a threefold order, distinct, jure divino, from other Christians, of bishops, priests, and deacons.* THE FOUR PATRIARCHS, OF EQUAL DIGNITY, HAVE THE HIGHEST RANK AMONG THE BISHOPS, *and the bishops, united in a General Council, represent the Church, and infallibly decide,* under the guidance of the Holy Ghost, all matters of faith and ecclesiastical life. All ministers of Christ must be regularly called and appointed to their office, and are consecrated by *the sacrament of orders. Bishops must be unmarried*, and PRIESTS AND DEACONS MUST NOT CONTRACT A SECOND MARRIAGE. To all priests in common belongs, besides the preaching of the word, the administration of the SIX SACRAMENTS—BAPTISM, CONFIRMATION, PENANCE, EUCHARIST, MATRIMONY, UNCTION OF THE SICK. The *bishops* alone can administer the *sacrament* of orders.

Ecclesiastical ceremonies are part of the divine service; most of them have apostolic origin; and those connected with the sacrament must not be omitted by priests under pain of mortal sin.

The Cossacks of the Ukraine and "of the Horde beyond the Falls" were ardently attached to the Orthodox faith, and had frequently risen in its defence. Although pacified by the promises of Vladislas, they were again aroused to revolt by renewed persecution on the part of the Romish and Uniate clergy, and religious antagonism led to a long and bloody struggle, during which these disaffected subjects of the Polish king made repeated appeals to Russia for assistance. Early in the century Job, Metropolitan of Kiev, had urged the tsar to extend his protection over the Ukraine, but Russia was too weak to cope with Poland. Michael dismissed the Cossacks with ample, but empty, assurances of sympathy.

Alexis, son of Michael, vigorously pursued his father's

task of pacifying and reorganizing the empire, still torn by intestine contentions and groaning under onerous, but necessary, taxation. He convened a national assembly for the formation of a code which should embody all the regulations requisite for the efficient government of both the State and the Church. While inheriting his father's pious and devout disposition, he felt the necessity of curbing the excessive power of the Church, which threatened to overshadow that of the crown. To this end he established the "Monastery Tribunal," consisting of lay members, which was empowered to deal with matters concerning the clergy and their estates, over which hitherto the patriarchal court had held jurisdiction. He further ordered that the domains and acquisitions of the Church and clergy, which had enormously increased, in violation of the ordinance of Ivan III., should be made the subject of investigation.

Then commenced in Russia the mighty struggle between the civil and ecclesiastical powers, in which the final victory was to remain with the State, and then appeared the great reformer and champion of the Church, a man destined to exercise a deep and lasting influence upon the Russian nation and the national Church.

Nikita, who subsequently bore the name of Nikon, was born of obscure parentage, in the district of Nijni-Novgorod, in 1613. In early life he felt an imperative call to enter the Church, and secretly left his home to become a monk. At his father's earnest entreaty he returned, married, and was ordained a parish priest; his children died in infancy, and this affliction seemed to him a summons from on high to renounce the world. He persuaded his wife to enter a convent, and took upon himself vows of strictest reclusion in the Solovetsk monastery, on the shores of the White Sea. In this forlorn and desolate retreat of almost perpetual winter he passed many years, living apart from the brotherhood, on a desert island, mortifying the flesh by rigid discipline and fasting. Disagreeing with his fellow-monks as to the employment of the convent funds, and unable to submit to dictation, he sought refuge at the Kojeozersk monastery, where, by his austere life and exemplary devotion, he gained wide-spread reputation for sanctity. Made superior of the monastery, he was called to the capital by the duties of his charge, and while there he officiated and preached before the tsar. His striking personal appearance, his gigantic stature, his earnestness and fiery eloquence, made a deep impression upon the young and pious monarch. Alexis, hearing of his holy life, wished to retain him near his person, and made him archimandrite of the Novospassky[1] monastery at Moscow.

The strength and originality of Nikon's character, the bold frankness of his disposition, his eager, self-sacrifising zeal, his lofty and far-sighted genius, both in political and ecclesiastical matters, his indomitable courage and independence, his generous spirit and high sense of justice, made him a fit counsellor for the sovereign. He has been variously judged by his countrymen and posterity; he has been compared to Thomas à Becket and Wolsey, his ambition condemned as dangerous to the State, his pride and arrogance as insufferable, but the savage, barbarous condition of the people whom he was called to govern, the disordered state of the country, the ignorance and superstition of the clergy and the degradation of the Church, must not be forgotten. His faults were

---

[1] Of the Saviour, from *Spass*, Saviour.

those of a great and noble nature; his object was not personal or selfish; his energies were exerted for the aggrandizement of the Church of which he was the faithful pastor, for its elevation and purification from error; his patriotism was sincere, and his devotion to the tsar never faltered, even during the years of persecution and suffering which closed his life.

Alexis took pleasure in his conversation and companionship, and leaned upon him, in utter confidence, as a trusty servant, a true and honest friend. He made him Metropolitan of Novgorod, and then, wearying at the separation, called him constantly to his side for consultation and advice; he delighted to do him honor, and gave him the lands about the beautiful Lake of Valdai, where Nikon built, upon a wooded island, the Iversky Convent, as a resting-place on his long and frequent journeys to and from the capital. In his capacity of metropolitan he was, by special favor, invested with extraordinary powers; his court was authorized to adjudicate all ecclesiastical matters within his see, and its jurisdiction was extended over all cases in which the Church or the clergy were concerned. While at Novgorod his administration was distinguished by characteristic energy; he visited the prisons and dispensed justice in person; he watched with paternal care over the material, as well as over the spiritual, welfare of his people. During a terrible famine he spent his revenues in building hospitals and houses of refuge, and in relieving the poor and suffering. When a rebellious outbreak threatened the imperial authority, and the governors of Pskov were massacred by the populace, he was the uncompromising defender of the law; at the risk of his life, he faced the insurgents, and gave shelter to the fugitive magistrates; maltreated by the mob, and left for dead in the street, he no sooner recovered consciousness, than he appeared again in their midst, exhorting them to submission. He prevented the betrayal of Novgorod to the Swedes, and hurled the anathemas of the Church against the traitors to the tsar; his firmness and courage gave time for succor to arrive and preserved the city to the empire, while his subsequent mild and judicious measures effectually quelled the rebellion.

His energy in civil matters was equalled only by his zeal in affairs of the Church. He insisted, among the clergy, upon cleanliness of person and apparel, decency of life, and purity of morals; he encouraged the decoration of churches, chapels, and altars, and surrounded the ritual with extraordinary ceremony and pomp; he regulated anew the order of divine service, and introduced harmonious chants from Greece and the East, with well-drilled choirs of soft Cossack voices; he condemned the idolatrous worship of the sacred pictures and their meretricious adornment by foreign art; gifted, himself, with fluent eloquence, he supplemented, by preaching, the monotonous reading of the lessons.

His imperious, domineering disposition had created many enemies, and the changes he introduced into the service, although they were a return to the original practices of the Greek Church, had aroused a feeling of strong antagonism on the part of the people and of many of the clergy, who were fanatically attached to their own, and, in their opinion, the ancient, forms, but this hostility dared not manifest itself by open opposition, and found vent only in secret murmurings. Nikon, strong in the affection and support of the tsar, distinguished for the purity and austerity of his life and for untiring zeal, was, notwithstanding latent discontent, called by unanimous desire to the patriarchal throne. Aware of the enmity he had excited, yet conscious of high purpose and determined to persevere, he consented to accept the post only upon condition that his control over the Church should be absolute and unfettered, and should be so declared by imperial decree.

His elevation to the primacy was signalized by more energetic action, and his measures of reform aimed higher than at mere restoration of accurate ceremonial observance. He punished with relentless severity all transgressions of the clergy, all indifference and sloth in the discharge of their duties, and, especially, he set his face against their besetting sin, intemperance. Heads of monasteries and high dignitaries, as well as simple monks, were made to feel the weight of his displeasure; the distant convents of Siberia were filled with dissolute, wretched priests, condemned without appeal and banished without mercy. He endeavored to give life to the Church, and to create a sense of the moral obligation imposed by religion. As supreme pontiff, he continued his former habit of expounding and preaching. In the account of Macarius's travels there is frequent allusion to the surprise of the Eastern prelates at this innovation, of which they were witnesses, and to the long and "copious" patriarchal sermons, "until our spirits were broken within us the tedious while." Their chronicler, Paul of Aleppo, also expatiates, with pious joy, upon the extraordinary devotion manifested by the emperor and the people. When Alexis took the field against the Poles "the patriarch stood before him, and raised his voice in prayer for the emperor, making a beautiful exordium with parables and proverbs from the ancients . . . and with much prolixity of discourse, running on at his leisure, like a copious stream of running water. . . . No one seemed to find fault with him, or to be tired of his discourse; but all were silent and attentive as if each were a pauper or a slave before his master. But what most excited our admiration was to see the emperor standing with his head uncovered while the patriarch wore his crown before him; the one with his hands crossed in humility, the other displaying them with the action and boldness of an orator addressing his auditors; the one bowing his bare head in silence to the ground, the other bending his towards him with the crown upon it, speaking to him; the one guarding his senses and breathing low, the other making his voice to ring like a loud bell; the one as if he were a slave, the other as his lord! What a sight for us! God knows our hearts ached for the emperor; was not this singular humility?" And upon another occasion Paul relates: "We returned to our monastery astonished and wonder-struck at the constancy and firmness of this nation, from the emperor to their very infants. We entered the church as the clock struck three, and did not leave it till ten; having stood there with them about seven hours, on our legs, on the cold iron pavement, enduring the most severe cold and piercing frost. But we were consoled for all this by witnessing the admirable devotion of this people. Nor was the patriarch satisfied with the ritual and the long service, but he must crown all with an admonition and a copious sermon. God grant him moderation! His heart did not ache for the emperor nor for the tender infants! What should we say to this in our country? Would to God we were thus patient! Without doubt the great Creator has granted to this nation to be His peculiar people, and it becomes them to be so because all their actions are according to the spirit, and not to the flesh, and they are all of this disposition."

Of Nikon's influence, and of the trust reposed in him by the tsar, and of the dignity and state he assumed, this eye-witness goes on to say: "Before the emperor's departure (against the Poles) he appointed a vice-regent and many ministers; the patriarch he placed as inspector over all, so that no affair, whether superior or inferior, should be decided without his advice, nor without their declaring it before him every morning of every day as it occurred. Thus, even in the frosty season, we observed the greatest among the ministers, the emperor's Vakeel or Deputy, repairing to the public office. Whenever it happened that the ministers were not all assembled in the divan when the patriarch's bell rang for them to repair to his palace—as the door is always closed during prayers—those archons who were too late were obliged to wait at his door in the excessive cold until he should order them to be admitted; . . . on their being permitted to enter, the patriarch would turn to the images, and, in secret, repeat a prayer, whilst they bowed to him all together to the ground, with their heads uncovered, as they remained until they went out. Thus he conversed with them standing, while they presented to him their accounts of everything that was passing. To each he gave answer concerning every affair, commanding them what they should do. By what we observed of the grandees of the empire they do not much fear the emperor, nor entertain much dread of him; they rather fear this patriarch, and by many degrees more. His predecessors in the patriarchal dignity did not interfere at all in affairs of the State, but this man, from his ingenuity, comprehension, and knowledge, is accomplished in every art and skill as regards the affairs of the Church and the State, and all temporal affairs whatsoever." [1]

In the plenitude of his power Nikon steadily pursued

---

[1] Macarius, vol. ii., pp. 51-74.

the reformation of the Church, and, as the chief means to this end, he determined upon the purification of its service and ritual, and the correction of the sacred books. This undertaking, in which the tsar evinced the strongest interest, commenced under Vassili IV. and continued at different periods, had never been satisfactorily accomplished. Former errors remained, and fresh ones had been ingrafted upon the old, which, by time and sufferance, had taken deeper root. The churches and monasteries throughout the empire were ransacked for ancient manuscripts; missions were sent to the Holy Places of Palestine, and to Constantinople for information and authoritative records. Paisius, the Byzantine patriarch, and his œcumenical brethren offered their co-operation, and supplied the writings of the Greek fathers, the early canons and creeds of the Church, and decisions of Councils. They proposed the adoption of the Confession of Peter Mogila as the accurate embodiment of Orthodox doctrine, and urged adherence to the rules of the primitive Church, as well in rites and ceremonies, as in dogma. The presence of Macarius, patriarch of Antioch, and of other Eastern prelates, gave additional solemnity to the proceedings of the synod, convened in 1654, over which Nikon and the tsar presided.

The points of divergence which had gradually arisen between the Russian and the other Greek churches related more to matters of ceremonial observance than to those of doctrine. Trivial as they may appear in the light of modern criticism, they were then held to be of vital importance, involving the very essence of the faith, and only by the practice of the primitive Eastern Church could the truth regarding them be authoritatively established. "I am a Russian, son of a Russian," declared Nikon, "but my faith and my religion are Grecian."

The principal differences to be settled were: whether a *triple* halleluia should be pronounced, in honor of the Trinity, or a *double* halleluia, in reference to the double nature of Christ; whether processions around the churches should march *against* or *with* the sun; whether it be *right* or *wrong* to shave the beard; whether at mass there should be upon the altar *one* or *many* loaves—the Russian used seven; whether the name Jesus should be spelled *Iissous* or *Issous;* whether, in prayer, the Saviour should be addressed as *our God* or as *the Son of God;* whether it be right to say of God, whose reign *is eternal*, or whose reign *shall be eternal;* whether the cross should have *four* or *eight* points; and whether the sign of the cross should be made with *three fingers extended*, as denoting the Trinity, and *two closed*, in reference to Christ's double nature, or with *two fingers extended*, in allusion to the double nature, and *three closed*, in token of the Trinity.

The hidden and typical significance of these ceremonies and symbols constituted their special importance. The Greeks, in each case, followed the former, and the Russians the latter, of the above alternatives, and in these respects a change, so as to conform to the Greek practice, was ordained by the synod, and was confirmed by subsequent councils in 1666 and 1667.

The Russian form of the cross, however, prevailed in the empire: the lower branch is not at right angles with the stem, but is slanting, in consequence of a tradition that Christ was deformed, with one leg longer than the other, and the lower branch of the cross, upon which his feet rested, was made to meet this personal defect. In popular belief, the Saviour was made to share to the utmost the degradation of humanity, and, in the words of Isaiah, "he hath no form nor comeliness; . . . he is despised and rejected of men; . . . he was despised and we esteemed him not; . . . we did esteem him stricken, smitten of God, and afflicted."[1]

During the Tatar subjugation the cross on the churches was replaced by the crescent, and, after their expulsion, the crescent was not removed, but was surmounted by a cross, in significance of the triumph of Christianity.

In addition to the changes enumerated above, another decree of the council, secured by Nikon's influence, evinced the larger spirit of Christian charity which characterized his efforts at reform; the validity of baptism by the Latin Church was recognized, which, although contrary to the decision of his great predecessor Philaret, and to the practice at Constantinople, was in accordance with the rules of the churches in Palestine. The alterations in the service, decided upon after much and stormy discussion, were at once promulgated and enforced throughout the empire. The people, filled with superstitious veneration for familiar forms, received these innovations with strong dislike, as an impious profanation of what they deemed most sacred, and a very large body of the clergy shared this feeling.

Nikon's enemies fomented the spirit of discontent, but his power was yet too firmly established for any successful resistance. The members of the clergy who ventured to oppose his plans were made to feel the impotency of their endeavors by banishment and prison. Paul, Bishop of Kolomna, was arbitrarily deprived of his diocese and exiled to Siberia, without trial by his peers, and in violation of ecclesiastical law.

Nikon's intolerant exercise of authority, his severity towards the clergy, his overbearing arrogance towards all, increased the growing hostility to his power; but,

---

[1] Hare, "Studies in Russia," p. 221.

conscious of the rectitude of his intentions, and confident in his influence over the tsar, he disregarded and set at naught the machinations of his enemies.

While thus zealously engaged in ecclesiastical reform, his restless energy found other spheres of action in civil matters. He was a patriot as well as churchman, and eagerly favored all measures conducing to the aggrandizement of Russia, especially where the interests of the Church were likewise involved. The supplication of the Cossacks of the Ukraine for protection, formerly presented under Michael, and now renewed to Alexis, appealed to his sympathies on both civil and religious grounds, and received his earnest support. The consequent war with Poland, advocated by him, resulting in the conquest of Little Russia and its reunion to the empire, added to his influence and increased his arrogance.

His arbitrary government, while left as regent during the absence of the tsar in the field, his haughtiness and impatience of advice in civil, as well as in ecclesiastical, affairs, excited the bitter animosity of the great lords and boyars, who submitted with ill-concealed repugnance to the supremacy of a low-born peasant. A double danger threatened the all-powerful favorite—jealousy and hatred on the part of the great nobles and the high dignitaries of the Church; superstitious fears and a holy horror of sacrilegious innovations on the part of an ignorant and fanatical people and clergy. Reverses and disaster in foreign wars followed the season of success, and the national humiliation was laid at his door; pestilence and famine visited the land, and his impious tampering with divine institutions was cursed for bringing God's wrath upon the country. The affection and confidence of the tsar was Nikon's only support, and this was soon to fail. Time, separation, and misfortune had weakened the monarch's trust and dependence upon his counsel; his opposition to the Monastery Court, established by Alexis, and his sturdy assertion of the prerogatives of the Church, excited the tsar's displeasure, who began to chafe under the arrogance of his favorite, and to resent his assumption of authority; palace intrigues undermined his position, the tsaritsa joined his adversaries, and, jealous of his influence over her husband, artfully fomented the growing coolness between them. By carefully-contrived and skilfully-veiled slights Nikon's impetuous disposition was incited to bursts of furious indignation, rendered the more violent by the tsar's apparent indifference and tardy response to his complaints, and Alexis, himself by no means patient, grew weary of his intolerant and inconvenient friend. An open rupture was inevitable; at a state reception a follower of the patriarch was abused and struck by a noble of the court; Nikon's demand for reparation was ignored, admittance to the monarch denied, and the supercilious demeanor of the boyars, encouraged by Alexis's indifference, soon roused the hot anger of the impatient prelate to explosion. While yet smarting at this indignity, he was soon after reproached, at the altar, by a powerful lord, for his pride and presumption, whereupon, perhaps hoping by extreme measures to revive the sympathy of his former friend and protector, he doffed his pontifical robes for the simple garb of a monk, laid down his pastoral staff, and renounced his office. Humbling himself before the people, he proclaimed his sins and unworthiness, sent his abdication to the tsar, craved permission to retire, and, covering his head with his mantle, sat down upon the altar steps to await a reply. Alexis was troubled, but sent no responsive message. Nikon's enemies triumphed, and, broken in spirit, he departed on foot to the Iversky Convent, from whence he renewed his resignation of the patriarchate, begged forgiveness for his unauthorized absence, and asked permission to retain charge of the monasteries which had been under his control.

The sacrifice thus made in anger he sorely repented, and would fain have recalled, but it was too late; the see was declared vacant, his enemy, Pitirim of Novgorod, appointed its guardian, and Nikon was left in solitude to brood over his disgrace.

Boyars and bishops, rejoicing in their liberation from his intolerable domineering, leagued together to complete his downfall. Fearing the influence of his personal intercession with the tsar, in whose heart there yet lurked some tenderness for his former friend, they prevented any interview, save in their presence; they baited and worried the hasty, impetuous priest to fresh bursts of violence and temper; his private papers were seized for proof of undue assumption of authority and dignity; he was accused of repeating the one hundred and ninth psalm in his daily convent service, and of directing its curses against the tsar; his indignant denials, his fierce invective, his vehement vindication of his acts and the recital of his wrongs, were made fresh pretexts for denunciation. For eight years Nikon maintained the contest, with unabated energy and independence; his spirit was not dismayed, nor his courage daunted; he anathematized his adversaries for his personal insults and injuries, but, more than all, for the scandal brought upon the Church; he loudly asserted his loyalty, and declared, "I have not cursed the tsar, but I have cursed you, ye noble prelates of the Church; and, if you care to hear it, I will have the same words sung over again in your ears." He could not forget that he had been, and, save for his own rash act, was still patriarch of Russia, and he refused, by deed or word, to recognize any successor; meanwhile the government of the Church was intrusted to a board of bishops, presided over by Paisius Ligarides, a Greek prelate, whom Nikon had befriended in former years, but who was now his bitter enemy.

Alexis, weary of the protracted struggle, called upon the Eastern patriarchs to form a tribunal before which to arraign Nikon for trial.

At this juncture the interposition of a friend at court aroused hopes of reconciliation. The boyar, Nikita Zuizin, of his own authority, and trusting to the great love Alexis had borne the patriarch, urged him to return, without warning, on the festival of St. Peter, the first metropolitan of Moscow, and, ignoring the past, to invite the tsar to join, according to ancient custom, in the prayers at the cathedral. Nikon, meditating upon this suggestion, retired to rest upon the stone couch of his hermit cell; as he slept he saw, in a vision, the long line of his predecessors rise, one by one, from their graves, at the call of the "wonder-worker," Jonah. Passing before him, they stretched out their hands, raised him up, and seated him on the patriarchal throne. Comforted by his dream, he departed secretly, by night, to Moscow, entered the cathedral of the Assumption, saluted the holy relics, and took his stand in the patriarch's place, clothed in his robes and holding the pastoral staff. The metropolitan, Jonah of Rostov, who had succeeded Pitirim as guardian of the see, was amazed to find him there at early dawn, but welcomed him with respect, and was sent by Nikon to the palace to announce his arrival, as if from a journey, and to invite the tsar to receive his blessing and to assist at the prayers. Alexis, taken by surprise, hesitated, and summoned his ministers for consultation. The moment was critical, as a meeting of the friends under such circumstances might jeopardize all that had been accomplished; to prevent it was, for Nikon's adversaries, a matter of life or death, and their influence prevailed. The tsar refused to go to him, and sent orders that he should retire to the Voskresensk[1] Monastery, and there await the assembling of the ecclesiastical council.

Nikon obeyed the harsh commands. His disgrace was complete, and, despairing of reconciliation with his former patron, he endeavored, but in vain, to make terms with his enemies. He was shorn of all authority, and placed under strict supervision until the council should decide upon his fate.

This assembly, the most august in the annals of the Church of Russia, met in the halls of the Kremlin in 1667. The patriarchs of Alexandria and Antioch, eight metropolitans of Greek churches without the empire, the archbishops of Sinai and Walachia, were joined to all the great dignitaries of the Russian hierarchy, and the tsar presided in person.

Cited to appear before them, Nikon, prior to his departure from the Voskresensk monastery, received extreme unction, as if in presentiment of approaching death. Mindful of his dignity and conscious of his innocence, he entered the council-chamber, arrayed in the insignia of his rank, with the cross borne before him; as no seat had been reserved for him with the other patriarchs, he refused to occupy a lower place, and, proudly facing his enemies with unmoved countenance, his gigantic stature towering above all around him, he remained standing to listen to the accusations read out by the tsar.

---

[1] Convent of the Resurrection.

He was charged with tyranny and oppression, with arbitrary and illegal exercise of power, with interference in matters beyond his province, with malversation of ecclesiastical revenues, with capricious abandonment of his office, with frivolously preventing the election of a patriarch after his own abdication, with offending the majesty of the sovereign and calumniating the clergy, thus bringing disorder upon the State and scandal upon the Church.

For the first time in eight years the two friends stood again face to face, and Alexis's heart was moved with pity and compassion. As he read the long list of accusations, tears flowed from his eyes, at the recollection of their former friendship and loving intercourse; yielding to his emotion, he descended from the throne, and, to the consternation of the hostile assemblage, took Nikon by the hand, and earnestly abjured him: "Oh, most holy father, why hast thou put upon me such a reproach, preparing thyself for the council as if for death? Thinkest thou that I have forgotten all thy services to me, and to my family, during the plague, and our former friendship?" The danger of reconciliation at the last hour seemed imminent, and the affecting scene was interrupted by violent denunciations on the part of the patriarch's enemies, anxious to destroy the effect of tender memories of the past. Nikon was speedily aroused to anger, and, in the bitterness of his heart, gave full course to his indignation, loudly denying the charges brought against him, and vehemently asserting the duties and prerogatives of his office; he fiercely inveighed against his accusers, and defied them to prove aught against him. "Why not bid them take up stones? so they might soon put an end to me, but not with words, though they should spend nine years more in collecting them." The critical moment had passed, and the threatening danger was averted by the tumult; although the deliberations of the assembly continued for many days, Alexis and Nikon parted then never to meet again.

The primate's condemnation was a foregone conclusion; he was sentenced to be degraded from his rank to the condition of a simple monk, and to do penance in a distant monastery for the remainder of his life. Alexis refused to witness his humiliation, and the council assembled, for the last time, in a small church, beyond the precincts of the palace. When summoned to hear its decision, Nikon still maintained his proud and lofty bearing; "Why," said he, "do you degrade me in this little chapel, without the presence of the tsar, and not in the cathedral, where he and you implored me to ascend the throne?" He reproached the Eastern patriarchs for their mean subserviency to power, in expectation of reward; "Take these," said he, stripping pearls from his vestments, which they removed in pursuance of the sentence; "they will help support you under Turkish oppression; get you home; better stay there than go wandering like beggars about the world."

It was midwinter, and the place of his banishment was far distant; the tsar sent him money and furs for the journey, and asked his forgiveness and blessing; but the indomitable prelate sternly refused all gifts, and withheld his benediction. "He loveth not blessing, and therefore it shall be far from him," was his reply. To a noble, who mockingly swept up the dust he shook from his feet, he said, pointing to a comet then flaming in the sky—the broom-star, as it is called in Russian—"God's besom shall sweep you all away."

To the people, who, in spite of prejudices against his reforms, reverenced him for the holiness and austerity of his life, and, pressing round, urgently besought his blessing, he, like the martyred Philip, spoke but a single word, "Pray." Still retaining his pontifical staff and mantle, which the patriarchs, "for fear of the people," had not ventured to take from him, sheltered from the cold by a cloak thrown over him by a pitying bystander, he was hurried away to close confinement in the Therapontoff Monastery, on the bleak shores of the White Lake.

Nikon's career marks a great epoch in the history of the Russian Church.

His purpose and aim have been variously estimated; loudly extolled as a reformer and saint, he has been as severely condemned as an ambitious and narrow-minded bigot. An impartial study of his life would seem to show that he was animated by a double motive, and addressed the wonderful energies of his powerful genius to a double end. On the one hand, to the reformation of the Church by purifying it from error, by endeavoring to impart spiritual life to the whole fabric, while restoring its ceremonies and ritual, and by elevating the character of the clergy in morals and intelligence; on the other, to the liberation of the Church from civil control by freeing it from debasing subjection and submission, in spiritual matters, to the temporal power, and by asserting its independence within its special domain.

The whole course and practice of Nikon's life bear evidence to his solicitude for reform in, and of, the Church; in this cause his zeal knew no languor, and only the untiring perseverance and savage energy he displayed, only the granite-like obduracy and firmness of purpose he evinced, could hope to triumph over the besotted ignorance, prejudice, and superstition he encountered. His personal example as priest, prelate, and pontiff, the severity of the discipline he shared and enforced, the reforms he inaugurated, his encouragement of learning, are recognized, and his lofty conception of the mission and prerogatives of the Church is stated boldly, and with rugged eloquence, in his voluminous replies to the council.

While recognizing the duty of submission, in all temporal matters, to constituted authority, he earnestly maintained the independence of the Church in spiritual affairs. He appealed to the ancient ordinances of the "apostle-like" Vladimir, re-enacted by successive tsars, and confirmed even by Tatar khans. Taking higher ground, he averred that "the pontificate is more honorable and a greater principality than the empire itself; . . . the priest is seated very much higher than the king. For, though the throne of the tsar may appear honorable from the precious stones set in it and the gold with which it is overlaid, nevertheless they are only the things of the earth, which he has received power to administer, and beyond this he has no power whatever. But the throne of the priesthood is set in heaven; . . . and the priest stands between God and human nature, as drawing down from heaven graces unto us, carrying up from us utterances of prayer to heaven, reconciling Him, when He is angry, to our common nature, and delivering us, when we have offended, out of His hand. For these causes kings themselves, also, are anointed by the hands of the priests, but not priests by the hands of kings, and the head itself of the king is put by God under the hands of His priests, showing us that the priest is a greater authority than the king, for the lesser is blessed by the greater. . . . Is the tsar the head of the Church? No! The head of the Church is Christ. . . . The tsar neither is, nor can be, the head of the Church, but is as one of the members, and on this account he can do nothing whatever in the Church. . . . Where is there any word of Christ that the tsar is to have power over the Church? ... The tsar has committed to him the things of this earth, but I have committed to me the things of heaven."[1] He vehemently assailed the Monastery Court, instituted by Alexis, establishing lay jurisdiction over the clergy and Church property, as illegal by the ancient ordinances of the empire, and unrighteous by the canons of the Church. Discussing the possible conflict of authority, he declares: "In spiritual things, which belong to the glory of God, the bishop is higher than the tsar, for so only can he maintain the spiritual jurisdiction. But in those things which belong to the province of this world the tsar is higher, and so they will be in no opposition, the one against the other."

The man fell a victim to bigotry, ignorance, malevolence, and jealousy, but of his work much, though the least valuable portion, remained. The council which sent him into banishment acknowledged, by its acts, the purity and orthodoxy of his faith, and, after electing Joasaph II. archimandrite of the Trinity Monastery, to fill the vacant patriarchate, it established authoritatively the changes introduced by Nikon, and annulled the decisions of the Council of the Hundred Chapters, which for many years had been a fruitful source and support of error. A few years later, during the succeeding reign, the Monastery Court was abolished, and the patriarchal tribunal re-established. But the power of inveterate habit and the force of prejudice are great, and the attachment of the people and of many of the clergy to their ancient forms was stronger than the enactments of the assembly, though backed by all the authority of the civil power. Teachers of false doctrine, pretending to be de-

---

[1] "The Patriarch and the Tsar," pp. 127, 251, 292.

fenders of the old national religion, disseminated their heresies throughout the empire, at first in secret, then openly, as they met with widespread sympathy.

Internal disorders, revolt in Little Russia, unsuccessful wars, and the consequent heavy burdens laid upon the people, aggravated the ferment of religious discontent. Numerous sects, asserting a purer Orthodoxy, arrayed themselves in opposition to the national Church; the most dangerous of these sectarian movements was that among the population about the White Sea; its adherents, called "Pomorians," or "Dwellers by the seashore," gathered around the great fortress convent of Solovetsk as their stronghold. This brotherhood of ignorant monks, isolated in their wintry home, had ever been noted for their fanatical devotion to ancient forms; they had, in previous reigns, remonstrated against, and refused to accept, changes ordered by Church authority, and now, with overweening confidence in the strength of their walls and the number of their partisans, they ventured upon open rebellion, and for ten years defied the power of the tsar; though finally, and by force, reduced to submission, their heretical doctrines spread through the North and into Siberia.

Three patriarchs—Joasaph II., Pitirim, and Joachim—followed in rapid succession on the throne, each hostile to Nikon; but time had softened the resentment of the sovereign. Rebellious chieftains had falsely claimed the influence of Nikon's name under which to shelter their pretensions, but Alexis disbelieved all accusations against his loyalty, and, in compassion, greatly mitigated the severity of his punishment. When dying, the tsar sent to crave his full forgiveness, and, at Alexis's death, Nikon wept bitterly, and mourned the loss of his friend. "The will of God be done," he exclaimed; "what though he never saw me, to make our farewell peace here, we shall meet and be judged together at the terrible coming of Christ."[1]

Under Alexis's son, Feodor III., the malignity of Nikon's enemies revived, and the full rigor of his sentence was enforced. The young tsar was Nikon's godson; but, weak and sickly, he was easily swayed by his spiritual advisers, and left the unhappy prelate, broken by suffering and disappointment, to languish in solitary confinement. A revulsion of feeling was, however, aroused in the prince's breast by the contemplation of the great Church establishments projected and commenced by Nikon, but now abandoned and falling to decay. A few friends who still remembered him ventured to raise their voices in his behalf. Among them was Simon Polotsky, in Feodor's youth his preceptor, in after-life his friend and counsellor. Polotsky was a wise and erudite monk, of liberal and advanced ideas, without sympathy with the harsh and bigoted patriarch Joachim. He was filled with admiration for the genius of the great reformer, and shared his aspirations for the glory of the Church. He appreciated the power which unity and centralization gave the Roman Church, and conceived the plan of a similar consolidation in the Russian establishment by raising the four metropolitan sees to patriarchates, and placing Nikon over all as supreme pontiff.

The scheme was too visionary, and too much at variance with the spirit of the Greek Church, for realization, but Polotsky's efforts for Nikon's restoration to favor were happily timed, and found quick response in the tsar's reawakened affection for his godfather.

Nikon, conscious of failing strength, had long and

---

[1] Mouravief, p. 243.

earnestly sought permission to return to his favorite monastery of Voskresensk, the "New Jerusalem," and there end his days.

Feodor granted this request, and the primate Joachim yielded a reluctant assent.

The dying patriarch's journey was a triumphal procession. As his barge dropped slowly down the Volga, the people pressed into the stream to crave his blessing. From the monasteries, which crown the high banks of the river, the brethren came forth to greet him with prayers and chants. Sergius, once his bitter enemy, and now, in disgrace, sentenced to reclusion, heard, in a dream, Nikon's voice calling him, "Brother Sergius, arise, let us forgive and take leave of each other;" and, hastening to the water-side, asked forgiveness on his knees. "The citizens of Yaroslav, hearing of his arrival, crowded to the river, and, seeing the old man lying on his couch all but dead, threw themselves down before him with tears, kissing his hands and his garments, and begging his blessing. Some towed the barge along the shore, others threw themselves into the water to assist them, and thus they drew it in and moored it against the monastery of the 'All-merciful Saviour.' Just then the bells were struck for evening prayer. Nikon was at the point of death. Suddenly he turned and looked about, as if some one had come to call him, and then arranged his hair, beard, and dress for himself, as if in preparation for his last and longest journey. The brethren, standing round, recited the prayers for the dying, and the patriarch, stretching himself out to his full length on the couch, and laying his hands crosswise upon his breast, gave one sigh, and departed from this world in peace."[1]

---

[1] Mouravief, p. 246.

Joachim's enmity did not cease at the grave, and, under plea of Nikon's degradation, he refused to render episcopal honors to his remains. It required the tsar's interference to check these manifestations of clerical malignity, and, at his command, Cornelius, Metropolitan of Novgorod, officiated at the burial. The monarch himself helped bear the body to its last resting-place, on the spot which Nikon had chosen, and, subsequently, he obtained from the four œcumenical patriarchs letters of absolution for Nikon's soul.

Over the tomb are hanging still the iron cross and heavy chains he wore upon his body, and Russian pilgrims venerate his shrine as a holy place, although solemn condemnation was passed upon him by a council of almost œcumenical dignity.

CHAPTER VI.

Reunion of the Polish to the Russian Church.—Dissent.—Peter the Great and his Successors.—Substitution of the Holy Synod for the Patriarchate.—Absorption of the Unia by the Russian Church.—Reforms.

During Feodor's short reign energetic measures were devised to arrest the progress of heretical and dissenting opinions, which had taken deep root among the peasants and lower classes. Strong efforts were made for the dissemination of education, as the most efficient mode of combating false doctrines, but they ceased at Feodor's death, when the country was again plunged into confusion by the disputed succession.

The patriarch Joachim favored Peter, to the exclusion of his imbecile elder brother Ivan, and the bloody struggles of rival factions resulted in the joint government of the two, with their sister Sophia as regent.

The period of Sophia's regency was signalized by the reunion of the Orthodox Churches of Little Russia and Poland to that of the empire.

When Little Russia was brought under the sway of Alexis, its Orthodox clergy, and that of Poland, asserted their affiliation with Constantinople, preferring a nominal dependency upon a distant see to real subjection under a powerful neighbor. Anarchy and intestine strife in succeeding years, aggravated in Little Russia by Polish invasion, were accompanied by dissensions in the Church. Rival prelates, supported by different factions, and each claiming ecclesiastical sovereignty, maintained their independence of Moscow.

The Russian patriarchs appointed guardians of the see of Kiev, but their authority was ignored.

To heal these divisions, and to settle the question of supremacy by an authoritative decision, reference was made to the Byzantine patriarch. The ecclesiastical dispute was decided simultaneously with the pacification of the Ukraine under the Hetman Samuelovitch, and its cession, with Kiev, to Russia by John Sobiesky, in 1685, as the price of her neutrality in his wars with the Turks. A formal decree from Constantinople united the Orthodox Churches of Russia and Poland under the see of Moscow, and terminated their separation of two centuries and a half.

This auspicious event was, however, followed by unfortunate and unforeseen consequences to the Polish establishment. Shorn of the comparative independence it had so long enjoyed, and insufficiently protected by Russia, it gradually lost energy and vitality, and yielded to the surrounding pressure. The government, jealous of any control by a foreign pontiff over its dioceses, endeavored to supplant Orthodox prelates by others of the Catholic or Uniate creeds. Its efforts were crowned with success, and eventually but a single Orthodox bishop remained in the realm. From the people, deprived of their spiritual advisers and exposed to unremitting and persistent persecution, nearly every trace of Orthodoxy disappeared, save among the peasantry of the more remote districts.

In Russia, meanwhile, the absence of a firm and settled government, and the disorder consequent upon the strife of rival factions greatly facilitated the growth and development of religious dissensions among the people.

GROWTH OF DISSENT.—ITS POLITICAL ASPECT.

Although they were subjected to strict supervision, and all overt manifestations were suppressed by force, the feeling, among them, of hostility to the innovations inaugurated by Nikon had spread throughout the empire. The superior clergy, who generally accepted the reforms and were in sympathy with the nobles, treated the village priests, who were recruited chiefly among the people and shared their feelings, with arrogance and contempt. This aggravated the popular discontent, which, in turn, reacted upon the minor clergy. The prevalent and increasing dissatisfaction of the lower classes was fostered by unscrupulous and designing men in furtherance of their ambitious ends. The inveterate hatred of Russians for everything foreign was, notwithstanding the Greek origin of their Church, artfully fomented against innovations brought from Constantinople and against their advocates. In all the schemes and intrigues, in all the insurrectionary and political movements of those troublous times, the element of religious discord played an important part. Discontent and Dissent, acting and reacting, grew into a formidable political power, dangerous and threatening, even to the stability of the government.

The only military organization existing in Russia was that of the "Streltsi,"[1] an irregular kind of national guard, first created under Ivan IV. It was officered exclusively by Russians, and was largely recruited from among the people, with whom, as a body, it was in general accord, especially in dislike for everything of a foreign origin or nature. This turbulent militia, ever clamoring for whatever they deemed national or Russian, sympathized with the popular attachment to the

---

[1] From *Strelets,* meaning archer or bowman.

old forms and ceremonies of religious worship; they joined the outcry raised against the changes introduced into the Church service as being heresies, subversive of the true faith, and demanded a return to ancient custom.

In order to check the prevalent dissatisfaction, which ever and anon found seditious expression, the authorities consented to a public disputation upon the points in controversy. Nikita, formerly a priest, then a dissenter, and who, under threat of punishment, had recanted and again relapsed, led the popular side; but the meeting, convened with due solemnity in presence of the tsars and the regent, with the patriarch and clergy, ended in a noisy riot, put down with a strong hand. The Streltsi, overawed by display of force, and cajoled by promises, abandoned Nikita, with his adherents, to their fate. He, and many of his disciples, were executed and order restored. Notwithstanding vigorous measures of repression, the great mass of the people were infested with the poison of Dissent; sect after sect arose, each with its local following and peculiarities, but all professing, as their single common bond of union, opposition to reform and to the established Church, as having fallen away from the ancient and true faith.

As Peter grew to man's estate, a giant in mind and body, his haughty, imperious nature could ill brook a divided authority. Sophia was equally ambitious, and incited the Streltsi to rise in her behalf. Peter, warned in season, fled to the Troïtsa monastery, where already, when a boy of ten years of age, he had, with his mother Natalia, found protection against rebellious subjects. There the patriarch and his clergy, together with the loyal nobles, rallied to his support. The insurrectionary movement was checked and Sophia was deposed.

Ten years after, in 1698, this wild and undisciplined

soldiery again raised the standard of revolt. Peter was absent from Russia, but, hurrying back, he abolished the institution, and wreaked such fearful and bloody vengeance upon the rebels as to call forth remonstrance, "in the name of the Mother of God," from Adrian, who was then patriarch. "Get thee home," was the fierce reply; "know that I reverence God and his most Holy Mother more earnestly perhaps than thou dost. It is the duty of my sovereign office, and a duty that I owe to God, to save my people from harm, and to prosecute, with direst severity, crimes that tend to the common ruin." His impatience of control and his growing determination to break down all opposition, even that of the Church, to his will, were thus early made manifest.

The patriarch Joachim died in 1690; although a lifelong enemy of Nikon, he, with the higher clergy, had accepted the changes in the Church service which Nikon introduced, but he shared the general dislike felt by all Russians of high and low degree for foreigners, and mourned the tsar's deplorable predilection for their society. His opposition to them, otherwise unavailing, was successfully exercised against teachers of foreign religions; the toleration hitherto extended to Calvinists and Lutherans was greatly restricted; Catholics were prohibited from celebrating mass in public; the Jesuits were banished; and Germans, accused of disseminating false and blasphemous doctrines, were burned at the stake. He left testamentary admonitions to the tsar, urging him to drive from Russia all heretics and unbelievers, enemies of the Orthodox faith, and to destroy their places of worship. His administration of the Church was characterized by decision and energy, and, notwithstanding the growth of Dissent and the influx of foreign ideas, its power and the extent of its sway was largely increased. Its conquests followed those of the State, and spread Christianity to the farthest regions of Eastern Siberia; a bishopric was established at Irkutsk, and the incumbent, Innocentius Koulchinsky, was head of a church mission to Pekin. In 1684 a garrison of four hundred Cossacks defended a frontier fortress at Albasin, on the river Amoor, with such distinguished bravery that their survivors, when compelled by starvation to capitulate, were granted their lives and were settled in Pekin, with permission from the Emperor of China to retain their religion and to receive priests of their Church from Russia. Descendants of this captive colony of Christians exist in Pekin at the present day.

Peter was but eighteen years of age, and the gigantic schemes which were to immortalize his name, and transform the empire, were still ideas or aspirations vaguely conceived, without having as yet assumed in his mind definite shape and proportion. He did not then probably realize the importance for his plans which attached to the choice of a head for the Church, and while preferring Marcellus, Metropolitan of Pskov, a "learned and civilized" person, he acquiesced in the selection of Adrian, Metropolitan of Kasan, an aged prelate, narrow-minded, strongly imbued with antiquated and national prejudices, the favorite of the lower clergy, and of what may even then be considered as the old Russian party. He was a rigid Churchman, and during his pontificate the confession of Peter Mogila, which had been generally received in Russia, was formally adopted as embodying the doctrines and belief of the Church. His influence was in constant opposition to the wishes of the tsar; Western habits, which Peter was eager to follow, were an abomination in his sight; the use of tobacco, the wearing of foreign apparel, he condemned as sinful; by a decree in due form he anathematized all who shaved their beards, an "ornament given by God to man, whom He created in His own image, which had been worn by all the holy prophets and apostles, by the saints of the Church, and by our Saviour Himself."

Peter's growing determination to bring his people within the pale of Western civilization was strengthened by his travels. He was the first tsar who had left Russia since Isiaslav took refuge in Germany with the emperor Henry, in 1073. On his return from foreign countries Peter applied himself vigorously to his task, with haughty disregard of edicts of his predecessors, of decrees of patriarchs, and of ancient customs.

The social and civil changes he first introduced struck a fatal blow at the most cherished prejudices, and at the religious belief of his people. They were followed by others more radical and fundamental, as well in the Church as in the body politic.

During his travels he had examined for himself the different religious systems of Western Europe. He had listened to Protestant preaching in Holland, to exhortations of Quakers and of Anglican divines in England, and, in Austria and Poland, had lent an apparently willing ear to arguments of Catholic priests in favor of a union of the Greek and Latin Churches, but always without conviction as to his religious belief. Gilbert Burnet, Bishop of Salisbury, judged him accurately in his shrewd remark, "that he was anxious to understand our doctrines, but he did not seem disposed to mend matters in Muscovy."

The Catholic prelates felt more encouragement, and the papal nuncio at Vienna reported to Rome that Peter had evinced a desire to be received into the bosom of the true Church. With them, however, the wish was father to the thought. While he evidently inclined to toleration, he violently resented any reflection, in his hearing, upon the Orthodox Church. At Mitau he attended mass, and a Polish senator ventured to urge upon him the union of the Greek and Roman Churches, but Peter replied: "Sovereigns have rights only over the bodies of their people; Christ is the sovereign of their souls. For such a thing a general consent is necessary, and that is in the power of God alone." Whatever may have been Peter's intentions towards the Church, in its relations to the State, he had no wish to disturb the religious belief of the people.

The patriarch, Adrian, died in 1700, at the moment when Peter was engaged in remodelling the national code, and in establishing clear distinctions between civil and ecclesiastical jurisdiction. The election of a successor was postponed by the tsar's orders, upon pretext of his absence with the army, and probably also on account of his solicitude that the choice should not, while he was away, fall upon a prelate hostile to his views. As a temporary measure, Stephen Yavorsky, Metropolitan of Riazan, a man of great learning, ability, and prudence, was named guardian of the see, with the title of Exarch.

The reorganization of the ecclesiastical administration was speedily commenced. Questions of theology, and of Church discipline, were reserved to the patriarchal tribunal, but the charge of the property and of the material interests of the Church, together with general supervision over clerical affairs, was confided to the "Department of the Monasteries," created for the purpose.

The religious establishments in Russia were very numerous and very wealthy; many were very ancient, with exclusive and peculiar privileges, dating back anterior to any codified laws. There were in all 557 monasteries and convents, whose vast possessions comprised 130,000 peasant houses and many hundreds of thousands of serfs; the richest was the great Troïtsa monastery, near Moscow, which owned 20,400 houses and upwards of 100,000 serfs, representing, at the present time, a value of nearly four millions sterling;[1] then came the official property of the patriarchate, which was reckoned at 8900 houses, and that of the see of Rostov, comprising 4400 houses, with proportionate numbers of serfs.

The Department of the Monasteries was empowered to take charge of, and manage, this enormous property for the general good of the Church, paying an annual sum to each establishment for the support of its inmates.

The thriftless and lazy thronged in and about religious communities in order to enjoy an easy and comfortable existence, and to secure exemption from military service. To remedy this evil, really serious from the sparseness of the population, the number of residents in each institution was prescribed by law, and stringent regulations were enacted for entrance to religious life. It was prohibited to minors—to such as could not read nor write— to those of noble birth, and to all in the employment of the State. The limit of age for admission was fixed at thirty years for monks and at forty for nuns, and the previous consent of the tsar was necessary. The inmates of each establishment were compelled to remain within its walls, and were subjected to rigid observance of strict monastic discipline. Allowances and salaries were assigned to the higher spiritual authorities in lieu of their estates, and of the dues hitherto exacted from the parishes. The surplus income of the fund was to be devoted to charitable objects and military hospitals, and finally to the current necessities of the State.

---

[1] Haxthausen, vol. i., p. 72.

The measure was calculated to elevate the character of the whole religious body, and, by depriving it of its worldly superfluity, to purify its ranks of the army of parasites and mendicants fattening upon it in sloth and ignorance. It was, however, practically, one of confiscation, and, together with strict enforcement of discipline, it caused very great discontent among the clergy, whose persistent and bitter opposition delayed its thorough execution until the reign of Catherine II. Clerical jealousy was also aroused by the reorganization of the Academy of Moscow, where the introduction of foreign teachers, and of professors from Kiev, was rendered necessary by the incapacity and ignorance of the native clergy.

Yavorsky was indefatigable in his efforts to regenerate and reform the Church, and was at first assured of the friendship and support of the tsar, but he was dismayed at the storm of opposition he encountered, by the clashing of conflicting authorities, by quarrelling between the monastic department and the patriarchal court; he was, moreover, subsequently discouraged by frequent differences with the sovereign, for whom the Church was rather a powerful political lever than an institution of peculiar sanctity. To share and lighten his labors there were, fortunately for Peter's plans, a few noble and disinterested men who could appreciate the wisdom of the changes inaugurated; who could rise above the narrow-minded bigotry of their clerical brethren and the prejudices of the day, to become able and zealous coadjutors in the great reformatory work. The archimandrite Dimitri brought to its support his earnest piety, profound learning, and historical research; he is famous in the annals of the Church for his "Lives of the Saints," which is still a religious classic, and has himself been canonized; his writings, aimed especially against the fallacies of Dissent, and intended to expose and dispel its errors, were widely disseminated. Job, Metropolitan of Novgorod, lavished the revenues of his see on establishments of benevolence and charity, and on institutions of learning; he created a school for the higher education of the clergy, and by his influence obtained the release from confinement of many victims of clerical intolerance and jealousy. Metrophanes, Bishop of Voronege, the last saint added to the Russian calendar, was animated by a spirit of unselfish patriotism. By exhortation and example he allayed the discontent of the peasantry of his diocese, who were impatient of the burdens imposed upon them, and induced them to labor willingly on the construction of the fleet which Peter destined for an attack upon Azov. His bold and fearless character was singularly attractive to the rough-and-ready tsar, whose irregularities and extravagances he did not hesitate to chide, while he proved his loyalty and devotion by the sacrifice of his private fortune to help relieve the pressing necessities of the government.

In 1702 Peter issued his famous manifesto inviting foreigners to Russia, and establishing the principle of religious toleration. He declared therein that, " as in our residence of Moscow the free exercise of religion of all other sects, although not agreeing with our Church, is already allowed, so shall this be hereby confirmed anew in such wise that we, by the power granted to us by the Almighty, shall exercise no compulsion over the consciences of men, and shall gladly allow every Christian to care for his own salvation at his own risk." [1]

The toleration shown by the tsar to foreign religions was not extended to Jews or to native Dissenters.

---

[1] Schuyler, vol. ii., p. 141.

The latter had increased in numbers as a result of the changes and innovations introduced in the State and Church; they enjoyed, at times, a precarious immunity as a consequence of the constant wars in which Peter was involved. When not engaged in weightier matters, he pursued them with relentless severity; less, however, from any religious motive, than from a stern determination to crush all opposition to his reforms.

Fanaticism grew with persecution; discontent among the people became hatred of the oppressor, and the traditional veneration for the tsar turned to pious horror. Serious outbreaks, which required a strong force for their repression, occurred in different parts of the empire, and even in Moscow. The frontiers of Poland and Livonia, the neighborhood of the great lakes, the marshes of Olonetz, the wilds of Perm and Siberia, the shores of the White Sea, the forests of Nijni-Novgorod, the banks of the Volga and of the Don, were thronged with colonies of schismatics, all at variance one with another, and proclaiming doctrines as extravagant as their enthusiasm was fervid, but all animated by a fanaticism stronger than death. Thousands left their homes to perish in the wilderness; whole families deliberately sought voluntary martyrdom in the flames of their burning houses, kindled by their own hands.

Against the fervor of this popular spiritual uprising the efforts of the Church and the power of the State were exerted in vain. Dissent was rooted in the hearts of the people, never again to be extirpated.

The relations between the tsar and the exarch were no longer harmonious. Peter was exacting and arbitrary, impatient of clerical control, and inclined to use ecclesiastical patronage in furtherance of his political plans. Yavorsky, while faithful and loyal, was independent, and rigid in his devotion to the Church. A new favorite supplanted him at court. Feofan Procopovitch attracted Peter's attention by his eloquence, and ingratiated himself by his wily and insinuating address. He preached absolute submission to the monarch's will, advocated his reformatory measures, and defended his private character. In the grievous dissensions between Peter and the tsarevitch Alexis, he energetically supported the father, while Yavorsky sympathized with the son. Procopovitch had studied under the Jesuits at Rome, and his religious convictions had varied with his prospects of advancement; alternately Orthodox, Uniate, and again Orthodox, his latitudinarian opinions were suspicious to Yavorsky, who accused him of heresy, and arraigned him before a council of the Church. By the tsar's favor he issued triumphantly from this trial, and Yavorsky, in comparative disgrace, was ordered to remove to the new capital, St. Petersburg.

When Peter was at Paris, in 1717, the theologians of the Sorbonne made him proposals for a union of the Greek and Latin Churches. They dwelt at length upon the general accord of their doctrines and sacraments, and on the similarity of their ecclesiastical discipline; they made light of the dogma of the Double Procession, instancing the creed of the Uniates, which, with the pope's assent, ignored it; and they laid still less stress upon recognition of the pope's supremacy, adducing the independence and liberties of the Gallican Church.

Procopovitch prepared the reply to these proposals. It declared that the Russian bishops could not venture to decide alone so momentous a question, which concerned the whole Church universal; it should be submitted to a general conclave, in which the Eastern patriarchs should take part, and, meanwhile, any close connection of their own with a foreign Church might seriously endanger the ancient unity of the Orthodox communion.

A similar movement towards union with the Russian Church was made by the English clergy, but it also proved abortive, and was again revived some years later.

In spite of all opposition, Peter had accomplished the cherished aim of his ambition, and given Russia her fitting place among the powers of the civilized world. Satisfied with the result of his changes in the constitution and government of the State, he turned his attention to the Church. For many years it had been deprived of its official head, and was administered by an authority, originally instituted as a temporary expedient, but which was no longer equal to the emergency. He was also pressed to a definite settlement of the ecclesiastical question by the urgent solicitations of the metropolitan Yavorsky, still guardian of the patriarchate, who, waxing old and no longer possessing the full confidence of the emperor, was anxious to be relieved from the increasing cares and responsibilities of the office.

To intrust the full power and influence of the Church to a single individual seemed a measure fraught with danger, and Peter was reluctant to feel again, by the side of the throne, a personal authority almost equal to his own, in a degree beyond control, and possibly antagonistic. The creation of a senate, the establishment of colleges, or boards of commissioners, for the administration of civil affairs, had proved successful; he had seen, in Protestant countries, the possibility of applying a similar form of government to the Church, and he determined to adopt it in Russia.

To Feofan Procopovitch, under his personal supervision, was confided the preparation of "The Spiritual Regulation," as the basis of the new reform.

It was put in force in 1721, and the motives which guided the emperor in his decision are thus plainly expressed in the document itself: "From the collegiate government in the Church there is not so much danger to the country of disturbances and troubles as may be produced by one spiritual ruler, for the common people do not understand the difference between the spiritual power and that of the autocrat; but, dazzled by the splendor and glory of the highest pastor, they think that he is a second sovereign of like powers with the autocrat, or even with more, and that the spiritual power is that of another and a better realm. If, then, there should be any difference of opinion between the patriarch and the tsar, it might easily happen that the people, perhaps led by designing persons, should take the part of the patriarch, in the belief that they were fighting for God's cause, and that it was necessary to stand by Him."

The supreme power of the Church was vested in a body, at first termed "the Spiritual College," and which was afterwards, and still is, designated as "The Most Holy Governing Synod." It was originally composed of ten members chosen from the different ranks of the clerical hierarchy, and, subsequently, the number was reduced to eight. To its charge were committed the administration of all the estates of the Church; the election of bishops; supreme jurisdiction over all the clergy, save in capital cases, and over all matters of heresy, schism, marriage, divorce, and Church discipline.

The "Spiritual Regulation" was submitted to a council convened at Moscow, comprising the highest dignitaries of the Church and the State. Notwithstanding the hostility of the old Russian party, and the objections urged by many prelates, who preferred the maintenance of the patriarchate, the authority of the tsar bore down all opposition, and the measure was approved. Yavorsky was made president of the Synod, with Feodoceï Yanovsky and Feofan Procopovitch as vice-presidents.

The new institution was announced to the patriarch of Constantinople in an autograph letter from the tsar, setting forth the necessities of the Russian Church and the reasons which had dictated a change in its form of government. He expressed the hope that the Synod might receive the recognition of the Eastern patriarchs, and ever maintain, in close communion with them, the ancient unity of the Orthodox faith.

Favorable replies were returned by them all, and the constitution of the Russian Church, thus confirmed and sanctioned by the œcumenical fathers, still continues in full force, as established by Peter.

A union between the Anglican and Oriental Churches, which had been already suggested to Peter, had meanwhile been pressed in the East by certain members of the English clergy, but without any prospect of success. This visionary scheme received at the same time a definitive settlement. The Eastern fathers and the Russian divines joined in emphatically repudiating the heretical and Calvinistic doctrines with which they declared the English Church to be tainted, and, mutually exhorting each other to be steadfast in the faith, they reasserted the truth of the Orthodox confession, as set forth by Peter Mogila and proclaimed by Dositheus, Patriarch of Jerusalem, at the Council of Bethlehem, in 1672.

Other questions, which at different periods of the Church's history had been decided and redecided, now, in one way and again in another, were discussed, and to Peter's influence was due the more Catholic and Christian spirit in which they were finally settled.

The rebaptism of converts from Romanism had been already abolished in Russia, and it was now declared to be equally unnecessary in the case of Protestant Christian sects. Marriage between members of the Orthodox Church and those of a foreign creed were permitted, upon condition that no attempt should be made to subvert the belief of the Orthodox husband or wife, and that the children should be educated in the Orthodox faith.

The changes and reforms which Peter imposed upon the nation, once definitively settled and accepted, his treatment of dissenting sects, whose hostility was no longer dangerous to his institutions, became milder. Peaceful subjects, who held aloof from political affairs, were assured of protection. In passing through the deserts along the river Vyg, he visited a flourishing colony of these schismatics, and encouraged them in their efforts to reclaim the wilderness. He bade them pray for him. "God," said he, "has given power over the nation to the tsar, but Christ alone has power over the consciences of men." Yet, as a true believer, he considered Dissent an error, the propagation of which he wished to prevent; hence its adherents were doubly taxed, and compelled to adopt a peculiar dress; attendance upon the church service on Sundays, and communion at Easter, were made obligatory upon all, and any attack upon the Orthodox faith met with severe punishment. He pursued a similar policy of toleration towards Western religions, and their establishments were numerous; the Jesuits alone fell under his displeasure, from their inveterate habit of meddling in politics, and were banished from the empire in 1710.

Peter's intention, not only to prevent clashing of authority between Church and State, but also to make the former a dependency upon, and an auxiliary of, the latter, proved successful, and the result was, to his own mind, eminently satisfactory. On hearing read a comparison between himself and Louis XIV., greatly in his own favor, he remarked: "I do not think I merit the preference given to me, but I have been so happy as to be superior to the French monarch in one essential point; I have forced my clergy to obedience and peace, and Louis allowed himself to be subjugated by his." Peter's sense of the great importance of the Church, as an essential element of government, was evinced by his solicitude for its prosperity and dignity, not only within his dominions, but wherever the Greek faith existed. His alms and donations to the churches of the East were large and frequent, and the influence of his government was constantly exercised for the protection of his co-religionists, wherever found.

At the union of the Orthodox churches of Lithuania and Poland to the see of Moscow, and as one of the conditions of the treaty with John Sobiesky, in 1685, liberty of conscience and freedom of worship were guaranteed to the adherents of the Greek faith. Diplomatic stipulations, however, proved no bar to the spirit of intolerance, and the Orthodox population of those countries were subjected to fierce and constant persecution on the part of the Catholics and Uniates. Within a few years every Orthodox bishop, except Silvester of Mogilev, was deposed and replaced by others appointed by Cyprian, the Uniate metropolitan of Polotsk, an apostate from Orthodoxy, and its bitter enemy.

Peter, although engaged in constant and terrible wars, earnestly remonstrated and threatened, but received in reply only empty promises, never fulfilled. The highhanded measures of Cyprian were continued by his successor, Leo Zishka, with the approval of the national diet. The few monasteries and churches, which, in spite of oppression, had maintained a struggling existence, were suppressed and their property confiscated, while all who professed the Orthodox faith were declared incapable of holding public office. From 1718 to 1720 fresh remonstrances of the tsar, then at the zenith of his power, led to an apparent amelioration in the condition of the Orthodox sufferers. Strict orders for their protection were issued by Augustus of Poland, and the papal nuncio at Warsaw threatened with his apostolic curse all who should disturb the peace of the Orthodox Church, but the change was more apparent than real. The government in Poland was never sufficiently strong to repress the intemperate zeal of the clergy and the Jesuits, or to afford efficient protection to the Orthodox peasant from the rapacious exactions of his Catholic lord. Continued persecutions led to renewed appeals of the unhappy sufferers to the Polish king, and to the national diet. Russia, under the successors of Peter the Great, constantly interfered in their behalf, but without effectual result.

In 1762, during the reign of Elizabeth, George Kominski, the Orthodox bishop of White Russia, laid before King Stanislas, and the diet, a statement of the sad condition to which the adherents of the Greek faith had been reduced, with an earnest appeal for the redress of their wrongs. Two hundred of their churches had been forcibly seized and given over to the Uniates; they were prevented from repairing their ancient edifices, falling into ruins, and forbidden to erect new ones; their priests were hindered in their ministrations, imprisoned, tortured, and put to death without any form of trial; congregations were dispersed by force; Orthodox believers were deprived of all civil rights; freedom of worship and liberty of conscience, so often promised, had become words without meaning.

The patience of Russia was exhausted, and when the Orthodox Poles appealed to Catherine II., as head or defender of their Church, their demands for religious toleration, and for the restoration of their political rights were supported by Russian armies assembled on the frontier. Stanislas was ready with promises, but his authority was impotent before the fanatical intolerance of the Catholic diet, which, in 1766, refused to accede to any change, or to sanction any reform. Catherine's ambassador, Repnine, proved equal to the emergency, and, calling Russian troops into Poland, he seized the Catholic prelates Soltyk, Bishop of Cracow, and Zalusski, Bishop of Kiev, who were most bitter in their opposition, and sent them prisoners to Russia. This energetic, but high-handed measure, although a violation of the law of nations, received general approval throughout Europe, as having been taken in defence of liberty of conscience. It produced the desired effect; the diet yielded, recognized the principle of religious toleration and the equal rights of Orthodox with Catholic subjects; but these concessions, exacted by force, and grudgingly assented to, only embittered the strife. This great religious controversy was eventually one of the chief causes of the first partition of Poland, and of its final division in 1795, when, by the absorption of Polish territory, the sway of Russia again reached the extreme limits of the ancient dominions of Ruric.

In strong contrast with the fierce intolerance of the Polish government, the rule of Catherine II., in matters of conscience, was mild and liberal. Catholics were protected, and assured of immunity from persecution; even Jesuits, then under the ban of Europe and of the pope, were allowed the right of residence in White Russia. Her wise and judicious policy was followed, in the Polish provinces, by a strong reaction in favor of the Orthodox faith, and, before the end of her reign, nearly two millions of the inhabitants returned to their former belief. The reactionary religious movement led, as a natural consequence, to the healing of the schism in the Church, and to the reunion of the Unia with Orthodoxy. This result became the ardent desire of the Uniate clergy. It was earnestly advocated by the metropolitan Heraclius Lisovsky, early in the nineteenth century, and met with warm encouragement from the Emperor Nicholas, upon his accession to the thrones of Russia and Poland. In 1828, he established in Poland a spiritual college for the Uniates, under the direction of the metropolitan Josaphat Bulgak, and raised the Uniate Church to a footing of perfect equality with the Roman Catholic, in all its rights and privileges. The Uniate services were purified of all changes and alterations introduced under the rule of former kings, and were restored according to the ancient rites and ceremonies of the Greek Church. In 1839, the Uniate bishops and clergy, assembled in council at Polotsk, under Joseph Siemaszko, then metropolitan, signed an act declaring it to be their wish, and that of their entire community, to be received back into full and complete communion with the "Holy Orthodox Catholic Eastern Church," and into inseparable union with the "Church of all the Russias." Their petition was presented to the Emperor Nicholas, and, by him, laid before the Most Holy Synod, accompanied by declarations to the same effect from the entire body of the Uniate clergy. The petition was at once granted, and the Holy Synod decreed, in March, 1839, with the ratification of the emperor, "To receive the bishops, clergy, and spiritual flocks of the hitherto-called Greek Uniate Church into full and complete communion with the Holy Orthodox Catholic Church, and so as to be integrally and inseparably incorporated with the Church of all the Russias."[1] By this measure about two millions of Uniates were joined to the National Church. The only act of profession required was the acknowledgment "that Our Lord Jesus Christ is the One True Head of the One True Church," and the Holy Synod, with wise and Christian forbearance, recommended "that an apostolic indulgence should be exhibited to local peculiarities not affecting the Sacraments or Faith."[2]

The position and constitution of the Church in Russia remained without material change under the immediate successors of Peter the Great. With the accession of Elizabeth, in 1741, the old Russian party obtained the ascendency, and their animosity against the German and foreign element, which had been so long predominant, was evinced by increase of Orthodox zeal, directed against heretics and schismatics. They were again subjected to violent persecution; their fanaticism had suffered no diminution, and, rather than yield, they sought voluntary immolation by hundreds in expectation of eternal happiness. Elizabeth was under the influence of priests, and acquiesced in their bitter opposition to native Dissent, and to the presence in Russia of strange religions.

The Synod ordered the suppression of Armenian and Protestant churches; Tatar mosques were closed, and Jews were expelled from the empire as enemies of "Christ our Lord." This revival of clerical intolerance was accompanied by efforts to improve the internal condition of the Church. Theological studies in Russian

---

[1] Mouravief, p. 445.   [2] Neale, p. 57.

schools were as puerile as at the universities of the Middle Ages, where it was discussed whether Jesus, at his ascension, had his clothes on or not; if not, did he appear naked to his apostles? if he had, what became of them? At the Academy of Moscow, divines seriously debated whether angels reason by analysis or by synthesis, and what may be the nature of the light of glory in the future life. The ignorance of the priests was severely reprobated; learned and intelligent professors were appointed in the ecclesiastical colleges, and attendance was strictly enforced.

The morals of the clergy were corrected by the rough discipline of the secular arm; drunkenness and disorder were punished by the lash; scandalous fairs, where dissolute priests and mendicant friars let out their services to the highest bidder, were suppressed, and the priests, who thus degraded their holy office, were sent to the whipping-post. The filthy condition of the sacred images, and of the churches, was stigmatized as a shame, and inspectors were appointed to keep them clean, to maintain decency of appearance among the officiating clergy, and to preserve order and decorum during the services. The necessity of issuing and enforcing regulations against abuses and evils of so gross a nature is sufficient comment upon the deplorable state of things existing in the lower ranks of the clergy, and among the devout, though superstitious, worshippers.

The short reign of Peter III., in 1762, inaugurated an era of toleration and religious freedom, as he felt no especial sympathy for the national faith, which he had embraced, under compulsion, at his accession to the throne. He checked the persecution of Dissenters, and, by promises of protection, and offers of grants of land in Siberia, he encouraged their return from exile. "Mahometans," he proclaimed by ukase, "and even idolaters, are tolerated in the empire; now the Raskolniks (Dissenters) are Christians."

The great Catherine continued, in matters of conscience, the liberal policy of her husband Peter III., and exercised severity only against those who disturbed public order, and, like Pougatchev, revolted against her authority as sovereign. Her measures of repression were not dictated by motives of religious intolerance, and she assured all Dissenters, who were willing to be law-abiding and faithful subjects, of immunity from persecution and of her protection, in earnest of which she relieved them of the double tax imposed by Peter the Great.

She permitted the establishment of foreign religions, and, in order to people the fertile, but uninhabited, regions of the Volga and the Ukraine, she encouraged immigration, and offered in her realm an asylum to all persecuted religious sects, with unrestrained liberty of conscience. Many thousands answered her appeal, and nearly two hundred towns sprang into existence as a consequence of this wise and enlightened policy.

Animated by views similar to those of her great predecessor, Peter, and determined to make the Church subservient to the State, she resumed, and carried into effect, the secularization of ecclesiastical property. An "Economical Commission" was charged with its administration; the monasteries, converted from land-owning proprietors to crown pensioners, received allowances, each in proportion to its wants, and the surplus revenues were applied to schools, invalid homes, and hospitals. In her correspondence with Voltaire she dwells with complacency upon this important measure, and upon the liberal spirit in which it was carried into effect. "I think," she writes, "you would be pleased with this assembly, where an Orthodox believer sits between a heretic and a Mussulman, the three listening to an idolater, and all four consulting together how to render their conclusions satisfactory to all."

Beyond her own dominions Catherine was the recognized, and oft-appealed to, protector of the Orthodox Church. She assumed the prerogative of "Defender of the Faith," not only in the countries along her borders, but also in the far East, where a quasi right of protectorate over the Christian subjects of the sultan was conceded by the treaty of Koutchouk-Kaïrnadji in 1774. This right, much cherished by Russian sovereigns, was frequently asserted and maintained by arms, until wrested from Nicholas by the disastrous war of the Crimea, in 1852.

The radical changes in the ecclesiastical organization made by Peter the Great, and maintained intact by his successors, aided by the extraordinary growth of the power of Russia and of its monarchs, the absolutely autocratic nature of its government, and the singularly submissive disposition of the Russian people, produced in time their anticipated result. The Church lost its individuality and independence, as a necessary consequence of the impersonal character of the Holy Synod, its governing body and head. Composed of many men holding, with few exceptions, their positions by the will and at the pleasure of the sovereign, severally liable to the influences of different, and possibly conflicting, motives, with a representative of the emperor, source of all power, in their midst, the Synod no longer possessed the singleness of purpose and the unity of action inherent to the authority of one supreme pontiff. By the suppression of the patriarchate all danger of rivalry, or conflict, between Church and State was averted, but with it disappeared, as well, the independence of the former, and much of its energy and vitality. It became practically, what it now remains, the vassal of the crown, an important, even the most important, of the departments of government, but still, only one of the many powers which make up the State, whereof the tsar is absolute head.

CHAPTER VII.

Influence of the Religious Element; its Development. — National Character of the Church; its Isolation.—Differences from Catholic and Protestant Churches.—Popes.—Development of Church and State in Russia.—Church Government.

The influence of the religious element in the history of Russia, and of its people, can hardly be exaggerated. In no country in Europe has it been greater, and yet, as one of those singular contrasts which the study of Russian civilization presents, while over the mass of the nation its power is and has been constant, nearly absolute, the upper classes have to a great degree become emancipated from its control, and indifferent to it. Since the days of Peter the Great the spirit of doubt and scepticism, characteristic of the eighteenth century, has pervaded the nobility and governing classes; among them Atheism is as general a doctrine as Christianity, and infidelity has supplanted faith; but the great body of the people have never risen above that degree of civilization in which all new ideas generally, and naturally, are imbued with a tincture of religion or superstition. Russian peasants are very devout, especially those who belong to the dissenting sects; among others, of the Orthodox creed, religion is rather a mechanical ritualism, but it holds them under bonds as severe as those of the most intense fanaticism. Evidence of the wonderful vitality of the religious principle among them is seen in its fecundity; it has given rise to innumerable sects, and others are constantly appearing; but this principle, so deeply rooted in the heart of the Russian peasant, is not entirely, and necessarily, always Christian in its nature. The conversion of the Russian people in the Middle Ages was sudden, and easily accomplished at the command of its princes, and was, in the same degree, superficial; the spirit of Christianity never permeated the masses so thoroughly, nor triumphed so completely over the ancient religions as elsewhere in the West. Many pagan ceremonies were partially engrafted on the services of the Church, while much of the old pagan superstition remained in the hearts of the people, covered up and concealed by a Christian exterior, but still exercising, even to the present day, unconscious influence over their religious conceptions.

The ceremonies of the Church recall to them the magical incantations of their heathen ancestors. The peasant imagines that the priest possesses the secret of propitiating the heavenly powers by the rites of the altar; that St. Vlas, the cattle-preserver, St. Elia, the rain-giver, St. George, the patron of wolves, all yield to priestly intercession. By it he can secure good harvests and increase of his flocks.

Attributes of pagan deities have been transferred to popular saints of the Russian calendar, and the whole universe teems with imaginary beings of superhuman nature, who, to the peasant, have a real existence; he believes that when Satan fell from heaven his hosts found refuge, some under the earth, as gnomes, others in the elements of earth, air, and water, or about the domestic hearth, as sprites; when hunting, he offers to the Lyeshi, or wood-demons, the first game he kills; if he be sick, he leaves in the forest a bit of bread or salt, with an invocation to the sylvan deity. The leaven of this pagan mythology still ferments in the peasant mind.

RELIGIOUS CONDITION OF THE RUSSIAN PEOPLE. 139

The old belief could not be readily set aside, and was engrafted on the new; hence the epithet "two-faithed," often applied to the Russian people by their old writers.

The three spiritual conditions—paganism, Christianity, and scepticism—which, in other countries, generally correspond to consecutive phases of their development, are, in Russia, still recognizable in singular admixture. Notwithstanding this apparent confusion of ideas upon religion, which seems to pervade whole classes of society, the Church, as such, has always carefully preserved the ancient purity of its faith, without change or corruption, as it came originally from the shores of the Bosphorus.

Christianity in Russia is not merely a creed or a religion; it is, above all, a national institution; the first, the most venerable, and the most popular. Scepticism, in modern days, may be rampant, self-asserting, and widespread, but the Church is never assailed; its children may have lost faith in its teachings, it still retains its hold upon their affection and their sympathies.

As in England, the Church in Russia is a national Church; it is also a member of a great Christian communion, which rises above kingdoms and nationalities, and claims universal homage as the Holy, Catholic, Apostolic, Orthodox Church. When it separated from Rome its adherents numbered barely twenty millions; now they exceed eighty millions; of these sixty are under Russian rule, and, of the remainder, about half are of the Slavonic race, subjects of Turkey or Austria. Although designated as the Greek Church, it embraces many branches of the human family, and, of these, the Slavonic is the one predominant; it rules over many nations, of which the most civilized, and by far the most powerful, is Russia. As Catholicism may be termed the Latin form of

Christianity, and Protestantism the Germanic, so Orthodoxy is the Slavonic.

There is a singular coincidence in the slight influence exercised by the Orthodox Church and the Slav race upon European civilization. Had they never existed their absence would have been hardly perceptible, whereas modern culture and development would be scarcely conceivable without Catholicism and Protestantism, or without the Latin and Germanic races.

The reasons for this striking inferiority, often and unjustly attributed solely to the Eastern Church, are manifold. Among them are, chiefly, the troubled, anxious political destinies of the nations acknowledging its sway; their isolated geographical situation, far from the centres of intellectual life; their position as forlorn hopes of European civilization and Christianity against barbaric and infidel invasion from Asia, and their religious, as well as their geographical separation from the rest of the civilized world, which was a consequence of the bitter hostility of Rome. Other reasons, of a secondary nature, may be traced to the different conceptions, in the East and in the West, of the mission and duty of the Church. The progressive element, and the gradual development of Christian truth, recognized by one communion, were ignored by the other. Rome admitted the principle of continual growth in religious knowledge, of constantly clearer manifestations of the faith, of further revelations of the sacred mysteries to be attained by study of the Word. To the Eastern theologian this idea was impious and damnable; for him the hour of discussion was closed by the decisions of the œcumenical councils anterior to the rupture between the Churches. The whole truth had been proclaimed, to which nothing could be added and nothing taken away. The limitations of the faith, thus forever established, without possibility of change, the Greek believer could, it is true, within those limits, exercise perfect freedom of personal interpretation, without fear of encountering more precise, authoritative definitions in the future, and the field open for discussion appeared the more vast, as the space circumscribed by unalterable dogmas was the more restricted. The result is apparent in the numerous sects and schisms within the fold of the Eastern, and, at a later day, of the Russian, Church, but the very immutability of the dogma tended to limit investigation to matters of minor importance, just at the period when human thought and study were concentrated chiefly on religious topics. At Rome, on the contrary, while individual opinion was always subject to decisions of the Church made obligatory on its adherents, the possibility of influencing those decisions was a constant stimulus to the development of intellectual activity upon questions of highest moment, and gradually extended its sphere of action to all branches of philosophy and modern science.

With this notable difference in the conception of the true development of Christian dogma, there is another, still more important, in the views held upon ecclesiastical authority. On this point the Greeks and the Latins are completely antagonistic. Bishops and priests are recognized among them both, but the Greeks do not accept any centralization of the power of the Church; they do not acknowledge any living chief before whom all must bow. Jesus Christ is, for them, the only Head of the Church, and He has no vicar on earth. The infallibility of the pope, and his supreme control, was the rock upon which the Churches split. The Greeks refuse allegiance to any other general authority than that of the whole Church in council assembled, and deny the existence of any permanent, living, personal head; no individual pontiff can speak in the name of the Church, or wield its power; that supreme prerogative belongs only to an Œcumenical Council. The Synod of Russia, the Patriarch of Constantinople, may censure or direct; their decisions are not infallible, nor are they binding beyond the limits of their own jurisdiction; even within them, personal opinions, individual consciences, are free, save in so far as the civil authority may lend its power to enforce the Church's decree. Recognizing no visible head, there has been no need of any local centre, of any Holy City, or of any spiritual monarch, vested, for his safeguard, with temporal power, and raised, as representative of divine right, by common consent of the faithful, above potentates and peoples.

As a consequence, nations following the Eastern creed have been spared the fierce and bloody struggles between Church and State which have devastated the West, but, as a further consequence, it has often happened that the State has encroached upon the Church, and made it subservient to its policy.

Decentralization has been characteristic of the Orthodox Church; it possesses unity of faith and of dogma without unity of government; it is modelled on the principle of nationalities, and is constituted of many national and independent establishments, auto-cephalous, each one having its own administration and language, and its peculiar rites, united only by the spiritual bond of a common belief; each one limited by the frontiers of its own country, and the extent of its jurisdiction measured by the territory of the State on which it depends. It is otherwise in the Catholic Church, where the constant tendency is to one centre, effacing more and more geographical separation and political boundaries, to claim universal dominion.

The inevitable result of this national character of Orthodox Churches has been increase of the influence of the civil power over the ecclesiastic, and, in proportion as the government has been the stronger, this result has been the more perceptible; it has been especially so in Russia, under absolute and autocratic rule. Throughout the history of this empire, harmony and concord have ever marked the relations of the two powers; religious zeal has stimulated patriotic devotion; the Church has earnestly co-operated in the creation and establishment of the State, and participated in its triumph over domestic, as well as over foreign foes; but it has fallen under the control of the State; the priest has become a functionary, and the Church, a department of the government. Intellectual stagnation followed the loss of its independence, and helped to aggravate the evil, peculiar to Russia, of isolation from the rest of the civilized world. The clergy submissively acquiesced in barring the influx of foreign ideas, and fostered the growth of national prejudices, as well as of patriotic sentiment. This isolation was also, in some measure, due to the national character which distinguished the Russian, as it did all Orthodox, Churches. Having no common religious centre, there was seldom need, or desire, for intercommunication; the various national establishments were interested, each only in its own domestic affairs, and their intercourse, one with another, was infrequent and exceptional. The use of the Slavonic tongue was an important element in the early success of the Church, and contributed largely to the rapid dissemination of its doctrines among the people, but it followed that Latin, the common medium of communication between the learned of all countries, was never an essential feature of clerical education, and, consequently, not only was the intellectual isolation of

Russia greatly increased, but the clergy, shut out from the study of classic literature, were, as a body, afflicted with gross ignorance, degenerating into superstition, and the standard of morals among them was lowered to the level of their intellectual condition.

As regards rites and ceremonies the Russian differs widely from the Catholic and the Protestant Churches. It is essentially ritualistic, and rigidly adheres to the practices of the fourth and fifth centuries. It is often reproached with stifling the essence of religious belief under outward forms. This accusation is, however, true only in part, and the fact, such as it exists, is attributable more to the character and disposition of the Slavonic and Eastern races, than to any fault of the Church; on the contrary, it has, from the earliest ages, endeavored to guard against superstition and the surreptitiously degrading influences of the senses. It has shown constant hostility to the most corrupting of all external observances, that of image worship; statues have never been admitted to its temples, and all pictorial illustrations have been restricted to unchanging traditional types, covered with metal, save the face and hands, ancient, expressionless, and austere; the bishop, at his consecration, promises "to provide that honor shall be paid to God only, not to the holy pictures, and that no false miracle shall be ascribed to them." The Virgin Mary, the apostles, and the saints receive, not adoration as gods, but a secondary devotion, as due to those cleansed from original sin, and admitted to behold the Deity.[1]

Musical instruments have always been prohibited, and the human voice only has been heard in its chants, as in its prayers. Its efforts in this direction have been in

---

[1] Hare, "Studies in Russia," p. 57.

DIFFERENCES IN RITES AND CEREMONIES. 145

vain, and even worse, as they have tended to deprive Russian civilization of the humanizing influences of the arts; but the spirit of formalism, of feticism, with which the Church has been so often, so bitterly, and so unjustly reproached, arises rather from the realistic, material character of the races subject to its sway, from their ignorance and proneness to superstition, and from their low intellectual development. For the Russian peasant, whose mind is still imbued with vague traditional reminiscences of his ancestral pagan worship, form and ceremony alone constitute religion; and his attachment to outward observances, his fidelity to rites consecrated by ancient usage, have given rise to obstinate schisms and dissensions, which still disturb the Church.

In the process of time, and notwithstanding their common origin, material differences have arisen in the form of the rites and ceremonies practised by the Eastern and Western Churches; these differences have been accompanied by a gradual, and finally a radical, divergence of opinion as to the essential meaning and importance of the ceremonial observances. The two Churches have the same sacraments, inherited from the same source, but they are conceived in a widely different spirit, and have a very different application and influence in the one, and in the other.

Among the Orthodox, baptism is administered by immersion only, and the validity of the Western ceremony, of merely sprinkling, is, by many of them, gravely questioned; it was for a long time absolutely denied, and converts to their faith were rebaptized, as a necessary introduction to the true Christian communion. In the Greek Church of Constantinople this custom is still maintained, and constitutes the only essential point of difference from the Russian Church, where, in this respect, more liberal ideas now prevail.

The Lord's Supper is administered by the Greek Church as it is among Protestants; the communicant partakes, with the clergy, of the consecrated bread and wine, and attaches vast importance to this privilege, as establishing his equality with the priesthood in the eye of God. Contrary to the custom of the Latin Church, it uses leavened, instead of unleavened, bread, as the true symbol of the Pascal feast; while it recognizes, like the Latin, the real presence of the body and blood of Christ, it does not pretend so precisely to designate the moment and manner of the transubstantiation, and claims, in consequence, a more spiritual interpretation of the mystery. A yearly confession and attendance at the holy table is made compulsory by law, and the great mass of the Russian people, although scrupulous to the extreme in the discharge of their religious duties, have come to consider an annual celebration of the festival as sufficient; the more piously inclined may, in the excess of their devotion, repeat it three or four times; but, even among the most devout, a monthly communion is more unusual than is its weekly observance among Catholics. So rare a participation in this most sacred of the sacraments, and the season of prayer and fasting enjoined as preparation for it, should, it would seem, invest it with peculiar solemnity; but the general habit of all flocking to the altar at the same period, together with its perfunctory nature, diminishes its effect upon the individual imagination, and has reduced it to the level of mere ceremonial routine. Being obligatory, and a pecuniary charge as well, the peasant, notwithstanding his devout and superstitious character, is inclined to shirk communion as often as he dares. Official reports show that frequently, in parishes of three or four thousand inhabitants, not more than two or three hundred partake of it. There is, moreover, in the Russian Church no first communion, properly so called; infants are admitted to the holy table, in accordance with the practice of the primitive Church. There is no long preliminary preparation for this initiation to the body of the elect, filling the youthful mind with religious awe and reverence, and which, among Catholics, and many Protestant sects, marks the event as one ever to be remembered. Religion thus becomes a less important element of early education, and loses much of its practical influence on after-life.

The sacrament of the holy chrism replaces confirmation, but it does not correspond to the similar ceremony of the Catholic Church; always following the custom of the early Christians, it is, by Russians, conferred immediately after baptism, and may be administered by a priest, not necessarily by the bishop.

Auricular confession exists, and in Russia, as among Catholics, the inviolability of its secret is protected by law, save in cases of political conspiracies. It is, however, held in very different estimation, and practised in a different manner; it is shorter and more general, less explicit, less exacting, and less frequent; it is restricted to sins of a grave and serious nature, without entering into matters of thought or conscience, or the minute specific detail of daily life; it is free from the inquisitorial, suggestive, often repugnant, investigation into personal and family affairs by the priest, and is, to a far less degree, an instrument of power and authority for the clergy. A few general questions, and the stereotype reply, "I am a sinner," comprise all that is usually necessary for absolution; there is no confessional or privacy; the priest and the penitent stand face to face, generally, but not always, separated from the congregation by a screen. During Lent the Church is crowded by the faithful, who, ranged in long processions, press one upon another, with tapers in their hands, frequently bowing the head, and, in accordance with Russian custom, making repeated signs of the cross; each one, advancing in turn, answers the priest's questions with the usual formula, receives absolution, and, passing on, lights his taper, and, with renewed genuflexions and crossings, places it before the holy images; a few days afterwards he returns for communion. The confessional rite thus reduced to the utmost simplicity may, for the piously inclined, be full of solemn meaning; but for the multitude it is only a duty ordained by law, and to be performed at stated intervals. That the holiest and most spiritual of the sacraments should, in the estimation of a people naturally of so devout a temperament, have degenerated into mere formal and external observances, and have lost their vivifying influence, is capable of various explanations. Their obligatory nature has much to do with it. The State has here lent its aid to enforce the commands of the Church; it is an article of the code that every Russian subject shall make confession, and partake of communion, at least once in every year; and the civil and military authorities are, with the clergy, charged with the execution of the law. These enactments have fallen into partial disuse; the progress of civilization, and of liberal ideas, render their universal application impracticable; still they exist for the intimidation of some, a stimulus to the indiscreet zeal of others. Certificates of confession are given with absolution; lists of the communicants of each parish are sent annually to the bishop, and, by him, those of the diocese are sent to the Synod, to be embodied in the tabular statistics submitted to the emperor. Compulsion is seldom employed, but the "moujik"[1] wishes to avoid the vexation of official supervision; petty employees seek to curry favor with their superiors, and the law affords an opportunity for them to display their alacrity. Religious duties, thus degraded to the level of police regulations, are performed in the same spirit as that in which the latter are obeyed.

Another explanation is found in the poverty of the clergy, and the inadequate provision by the State for their maintenance. They depend, for their support, upon the contributions they can levy upon their parishioners, and expect payment for the duties they discharge. Every sacrament—confession and communion, as well as baptism, marriage, and burying—is a matter of bargain; no recognized tariff exists, but a gift is exacted, of which only the amount is voluntary. The sinner compounds with the Church, and his penance is in inverse proportion to his liberality. The authority and influence of the priesthood suffer; the sacred office, and he who holds it, are degraded by this chaffering over a price for the highest privileges of the Christian faith.

The position of a Russian pope towards his flock differs greatly from that of the Catholic priest. Not celibacy, but marriage, is obligatory for him; the common existence of family ties draws him and his parishioners more nearly together, and makes their interests analogous. They create, as with the Protestant clergy, a stronger feeling of mutual sympathy, a greater community of ideas and sentiments; while they also tend to diminish pastoral authority, and to check the reverential respect involuntarily shown to those who, from noble and lofty motives, make the sacrifice of the purest joys

---

[1] *Moujik* is the diminutive of the Russian word "*mouje*," man, the Latin *vir*, and designates the peasant or serf.

granted to mankind. Ordination in the Russian Church is not necessarily for life; a priest may be relieved of his vows by the Holy Synod. If convicted of crime, he may, like any functionary, be degraded from his office; the death of his wife (a second marriage is not permitted) deprives him of his sacred character, and he can no longer officiate. In a word, the Russian pope is rather a minister at, and a servant of the altar, than the representative of the Deity.

The clergy of the Orthodox, like that of the Catholic, Church is divided into the regular and secular bodies; but here again wide differences prevail. In Russia there are monks and nuns under vows of celibacy, but there are no religious orders; there are numerous monasteries and convents, but they are isolated establishments, independent of one another. Great federated communities, united under central governments, constituting formidable spiritual powers within the State and the Church, do not exist.

As regards marriage, the Orthodox agree in many respects with the Catholic; they hold it to be a sacrament of the Church. There is, in Russia, no civil ceremony. They do not look with favor upon remarrying, and, while they tolerate a second and a third marriage, under penances, the Church canons prohibit a fourth. They declare the tie to be indissoluble, but the law considers physical defect, absence for five years, and adultery sufficient causes for separation; in the latter case, the innocent spouse may marry again, but the guilty one cannot.

From this comparison it is evident that, contrary to what is generally supposed, the differences between the Russian and other Churches, not of the Orthodox creed, are in reality fundamental, and not merely superficial; they do not consist simply in slight variations and divergences in the performance of similar rites and ceremonies, while the creed and the traditions, the hierarchy and the sacraments, remain the same; they go deeper; they affect the conception of Christian truth, and the spirit of Christian worship, and are manifest in the different influences exerted by the different Churches upon the government of nations, and upon the development of civilization.

The Catholic, by its concentration, by its regular hierarchy under a supreme head, by the spirit of obedience and submission which it inculcates, by the power and authority conferred upon its chief, and by its aim at universal dominion, tends to centralization, and favors the principle of absolute monarchy.

The Protestant, by its latitude in matters of faith, by its spirit of inquiry and freedom of interpretation, by the liberty of thought which it encourages, by its division into various sects and their independence of each other, tends to decentralization, and sympathizes with the principle of a representative, or republican form of government.

The Orthodox, fixed and immutable in its traditions and belief, although without any supreme authority over it, is conservative in its tendency; allowing wide scope, within defined limits, to individual opinion, it permits a certain freedom of thought; having no political proclivities, it neither advocates, nor favors, any special form of government, but accords with existing institutions, if they be not hostile to Christian truth. While not actually progressive, it is no enemy to progress, and allows the free development of the nations over which it holds sway, according to the national genius of each, and according to the influences which may surround it; it is equally at home in democratic Greece, and in autocratic Russia.

Orthodoxy appears to occupy an intermediate place between Catholicism and Protestantism, but it would be a grave error to suppose that it accepts this position in any timid or halting spirit, or as being in any wise one of transition, as if emanating from the former and gradually tending to the latter. On the contrary, it unhesitatingly asserts its claim to be the sole legitimate heir of the primitive Church, unchangeable and ever unchanging, immutable from the beginning, founded upon apostolic truth as upon a rock. Far from seeking alliance with either, it looks down upon them both, with pitying disdain, as wandering and estranged from Christ.

Christianity in Russia has, from its introduction, been subject to the principle of development peculiar and inherent to Orthodoxy. The Church has adapted itself to, and modelled itself upon, the political constitution of the nation; it has extended its jurisdiction as the geographical boundaries of the empire have been enlarged.

The degree of independence which it has enjoyed in its connection with the State, and the freedom it has allowed to those within its bosom, have been in harmony with the character of the national institutions; and the method of its administration has corresponded to that of the civil government. The autocratic principle, imposed upon the people by its rulers, did not have its rise in any timid subserviency on the part of the Church; it existed already in the nature of the governing power; it was recognized by the Church, as well as by the nation, and, under its influence, the one assumed its natural position of relative dependency, and the other was reduced to absolute subjection. In this result of dependency on the State the Church has never felt, nor acknowledged, any degradation of its sacred character; in its own estimation, and as its disciples declare, it has been guided by its universal practice, and by its early traditions, as exemplified in the relations which existed between the primitive Church and the first Byzantine emperors.

For a proper appreciation of this view of its position towards the State, it is necessary to follow the gradual development of the one alongside of the other, through the tolerably distinct phases, or periods, of Russian ecclesiastical history. These are, broadly: first, the period of the complete dependence of the Church upon the See of Constantinople; second, the transition period, during which it gradually acquired autonomy, and approached the time of its emancipation from foreign control; then, the period of the patriarchate, when its ecclesiastical independence had been definitively established, and it rose to its highest power; and finally, that of the Holy Synod, when it became subordinate to the State, and which still continues.

During the first period, the metropolitans of Russia had their seat primarily at Kiev, the capital of the great princes; they were almost invariably appointed, and sent thither, by the Patriarch of Constantinople; they were generally Greeks, ignorant of the language and customs of the people over whom they ruled; the Church was simply a diocese, a province of the Byzantine patriarchate.

The invasion of the Tatars, and the consequent removal of the seat of government from the banks of the Dnieper far to the interior of the country, separated the two Churches, and isolated them one from another; as the metropolitan accompanied the prince, the religious centre was displaced to follow the political. Communication became difficult, often impracticable, through immense wastes peopled with savage and warring tribes; a sense of independence on the part of the Russian Church was the natural result of rare intercourse, and this feeling was increased by the frequent necessity which arose of filling the ecclesiastical throne, when reference to, or waiting upon, Constantinople was an impossibility. It became a recognized principle that the primate should be of Russian blood, chosen by his clergy or named by the prince, and, although consecration by the Byzantine patriarch was still held to be essential, the idea of a national establishment was germinating. True to its origin and traditions, the Church was ever respectful to authority, and loyal to the legitimate sovereign. During long civil wars and foreign subjugation its influence expanded, and was less overshadowed by that of the State; it was favored and protected by Tatar khans, as well as by native princes. Conciliated by the former to strengthen and consolidate their dominion, by the latter to profit by its services as a mediator between themselves, or as an intercessor with their oppressors, it came to be the only bond which held the nation together—the safeguard and bulwark of the national existence. This was the most glorious age of the Russian Church, distinguished by unswerving patriotism, religious zeal, and intense nationality; the days of its great popular heroes and saints, and the epoch when its most celebrated institutions were founded. After the nation had issued triumphant from its tribulations, and the empire became independent and strong, the power of the Church dwindled before that of the State; it passively protested in the person of its only martyr, St. Philip, against the encroachments of the tsar, but it never rebelled against constituted authority, or strove to check the growth of autocratic government.

The ambition of Boris Godounov led to a recrudescence of its power; he encouraged the emancipation of the Church from foreign control, in order to win the sympathy of the clergy and profit by its influence over the people, precisely as he established, or consolidated, serfdom to conciliate the nobility and landed proprietors. The creation of the patriarchate exalted the Church, and increased the dignity and splendor of its position, but, at the same time, it severed its connection with the outer world and left it alone, exposed without allies abroad, without the hope of foreign succor, in the inevitable struggle which was to come for pre-eminence between the ecclesiastical and the civil powers. This struggle was postponed by the political occurrences of the years immediately succeeding. Again the Church proved the saviour of the national life, and rose, by the force of circumstances, and the patriotic devotion of its members, to almost undisputed supremacy in the reigns of Michael and Alexis Romanoff, and during the patriarchate of Nikon.

The fall of this mighty prelate meant the future predominance of the civil power, and the Church submitted with its wonted humility, accepted the interregnum ordered by Peter the Great, acquiesced in the abolition of the patriarchate, and consented to a final reorganization under the Holy Synod.

Its rise at different times, during the extraordinary vicissitudes of its fortunes, to almost supreme control in the body politic, was, on each occasion, the consequence of extraneous and fortuitous circumstances, rather than the result of any ambitious effort of its own. Its elevation was invariably followed, as the especial cause disappeared, by its submission to civil authority, and by harmonious co-operation with it. It is, however, to be observed that this submission related only to the administration of Church affairs, and never affected questions of dogma, nor of doctrine, raised high above the authority of the Church itself.

The synodical, or federative form, of government is the natural and logical one for churches of the Orthodox communion, as it adapts itself equally well to all political constitutions. In democratic Greece the Church has followed the example given by the Church of autocratic Russia, and its organization there, while differing in detail, is similar in principle. Whatever form among Orthodox Churches the higher, or governing power may have assumed, it has never made any pretence to be of divine origin, but, whether patriarchate or synod, has always been, and been held to be, of human institution; in either case entitled to respect, but with the advantage, on the part of the synod, of greater flexibility of adaptation.

In Russia, the composition of the synodical council is dependent almost entirely on the will of the emperor; nearly all the members, and their number is not limited, are appointed by him, but it would be an error to suppose that he is, in any spiritual sense, like the Pope of Rome, the head of the Church. If, in any legislative acts, he is so termed, it is only in his capacity of administrator of its affairs, and, as such, his authority is restricted by the canons, by tradition, and by œcumenical decrees. All questions of dogma and of discipline are beyond his control; never has a tsar, unless it be the demented Paul, claimed any rank in the clerical hierarchy; at the altar he yields homage to the priest, in common with the humblest of his subjects; he is simply, as he is designated in the catechism, the administrator and protector of the Church.

The Holy Synod takes precedence over all the other great bodies of the State; it replaces the patriarch, with all his rights and privileges; originally, it was more of a representative assembly, comprising the different ranks of the clergy, and bishops were in a numerical minority;

now, in accordance with the practice of the early Church, which placed authority in the hands of its bishops, the episcopal element predominates. The three metropolitans of Kiev, Moscow, and St. Petersburg are entitled to membership by right of their offices, and the latter is the presiding officer; the Exarch of Georgia is also admitted upon the same ground; the other members are appointed by the emperor—some for definite periods, others to hold office during his pleasure; some in full and regular standing, others as supernumeraries or assistants; they comprise four or five archbishops, bishops, or archimandrites, and two arch-priests of the secular clergy, one of whom usually is the chaplain and confessor of the emperor, the other the chaplain-general of the army. The Synod has its seat at St. Petersburg, and is permanently in session. The emperor is represented by a delegate bearing a title corresponding to attorney-general (ober-procurator), who assists at the meetings, but who is not, properly speaking, a member; this official is always a layman, frequently a military officer of high rank, and is the personification of the civil authority; he acts as the intermediary between the emperor and the Synod; all communications pass by his hands; he presents to the Synod all laws projected by the government, and submits all decisions of the Synod for imperial sanction; he proposes all measures, directs all business, and executes all decrees; no act is valid without his assent, and he has the right of veto, if any action of the Synod appears to him contrary to the laws of the State. Every year he prepares statements of the condition of the Church, of the clergy, and of religion generally throughout the empire.

The functions of the Synod are divided among several departments. Such of these as exercise supervision over clerical discipline, religious censorship, and all ecclesiastical matters, strictly speaking, come under the immediate direction of members of the Synod, while others, specially charged with care of the schools and of the finances of the Church, are placed under the attorney-general. All business is transacted in writing, without oral discussion, or deliberation in open assembly; bureaucracy or circumlocution, so generally prevalent throughout Russia, is carried to an extreme, and, as a consequence, the real direction of affairs devolves upon the various departments, and the members of the Synod do little else than sign what is put before them.

For the nomination of bishops the Synod submits three names to the emperor, who generally chooses and appoints the first one on the list; they are subject to the authority of the Synod, and each one, in his diocese, is assisted by a consistory or council, the members of which are named by the Synod, upon the recommendation of the bishop. This consistorial body acts chiefly as an ecclesiastical tribunal, and has jurisdiction over all cases of clerical discipline, or those in which the clergy are interested, and over matters relating to marriage and divorce; its acts require the episcopal sanction for their validity, and final appeal from its decisions lies to the Synod. The functions of this provincial council, within its jurisdiction, bear a general resemblance to those of the supreme governing body, and are, in like manner, shared by several departments; a lay secretary, appointed by the Synod, upon the nomination of the attorney-general, and subject to his orders, is charged with duties kindred to his own; the same bureaucratic, centralizing tendency exists as at the capital, and a similar controlling influence is exercised by the various departments.

From all the dioceses and provincial consistories constant reference must be made to the central head, whether it be for the erection of, or the removal of, a church edifice, for the employment of diocesan funds, for the distribution of charitable contributions, for the deposition of a priest, or his release from his vows. The bishop must present every year full reports upon the condition of his bishopric, upon its schools and institutions, upon the number of communicants, and of conversions from other religions or from dissenting sects; he cannot be absent from his diocese for more than a week without special authorization.

The prodigious centralization noticeable in the machinery of Church government in Russia is the inevitable result of the constant, close relations with each other enforced upon its component parts, and of the intimate connection maintained by the Church with the civil authority. This intimacy is enhanced by the rivalry between the regular and the secular clergy; ecclesiastical honors and preferments are monopolized by the former, and they are the more prone to subserviency towards the State as the source of all power and emolument, while for the latter there is no independent religious head at home, nor supreme pontiff abroad, to whom they may appeal, and they also turn to the civil authority as their natural, and only, protection against episcopal despotism.

While rejoicing in the favor of the State, the Church does not apprehend thereby serious danger to its independence as a Church; confident in the immutability of its dogma, which no authority can impugn, and in the pious devotion of its adherents, upon which the government dare not trespass, it is fully alive to the fact that the interference of the sovereign is limited by the unwritten law of tradition, and that, to undue encroachment, it has but to oppose its passive power of inertia, and to rely upon the fidelity of its followers.

CHAPTER VIII.

The Clergy, Black and White.—Monasticism and Monasteries.—Parish Priests.

In Russia, clerical life is not, as in other countries, simply a vocation or a profession, nor do the clergy there, as in France before the revolution of 1789, form one of the great bodies of the State; it is a distinct social class, set apart from the rest of the world; a separate caste, hereditary, and peculiar in its duties and privileges.

It is divided into monks, or the regular monastic clergy, and popes, or the secular parish clergy; the one is popularly termed the *black*, and the other the *white* clergy. The differences in their garb are hardly sufficient to explain these designations, for, while monks are always attired in black, and wear a long black veil hanging down behind from the cowl, the popes are not restricted to white, and often adopt brown, or other sombre colors; one peculiarity is common to them both—long hair and flowing beards.

The radical distinction between the two is marriage; the monks take vows of celibacy, but the popes must marry before they can have charge of a parish. In the Russian, as generally in Orthodox Churches, the episcopate and all offices of authority are reserved for the unmarried clergy, who are comparatively few in number, while the subordinate and more laborious positions only fall to the lot of the married clergy. From this custom arise diversity of interests, and a mutual spirit of rivalry and antagonism, the more intense in that marriage, absolutely forbidden to the one and equally obligatory upon the other, interposes an impassable barrier between the two bodies. A constant struggle, seldom openly avowed, but none the less ardent for that reason, is going on, the chosen few seeking to maintain their superiority, the others, who comprise the great body of the Church militant, striving to rise from their inferior condition, and be free from control. As a consequence of this species of dualism in the Church, there are influences and tendencies at work in opposite directions; the black clergy is the more conservative, sympathizing with the principle of authority and the maintenance of ancient customs and traditions, while the white is inclined to liberalism, and is more ready to yield to the spirit of innovation and progress.

Monasticism has, since its introduction into Russia, been a prominent feature in the history, and in the civilization of the empire and of the people, but in its nature and influence it has been, and is, widely different from the same institution in the rest of Europe. It has always been simple and primitive in its character, preserving still the same unity as at its origin, without change or variety in its development; in form, similar to that known in the West during the Middle Ages, prior to the days of St. Bernard, never branching out, nor subdividing, into many denominations or orders, each with a special object or mission. It has lacked enterprise, and mental, moral, or spiritual energy; it has aimed at a contemplative life, at asceticism, penitence, and the correction of the inner man; it has sought retirement for meditation and prayer; it has withdrawn from, and renounced, the world, and its ideal of the perfect life has been that of the anchorite in the desert, or of the Stylite on his pillar; its communities have not been created, as in the West, for union in the struggle with evil, nor for works of charity and benevolence, nor for earnest propagation of the faith, and they have never been centres of intellectual activity. The names given to the monasteries recall the ancient Thebaïd; the greater of them are termed "lavra" and "stavropigia;" the smaller are called "skeet" or "poustynia" (hermitages or deserts). The catacombs at Kiev, and the crypts of ancient churches were not tombs or receptacles for the dead, but were the dwellings of early saints.

This fondness for the solitary life of the anchorite is not yet extinct in Russia; although the government forbids the creation of hermitages, they are still found in distant, hidden places, the favorite refuges and resorts of the more fanatic among the dissenting sects.

With the conception of monastic life as it was understood in Russia, one simple rule has sufficed for all the different communities which have been founded. That of St. Basil, which does little more than establish the broad principles of conventual discipline, and is generally recognized throughout the East, was introduced into Russia by the Greeks with the Christian religion, and has remained in force, ever since, in all the monastic institutions of the country. As a consequence of the uniformity of organization, no separate orders have ever existed, and the Church has been spared the intestine struggle of powerful rival communities within its bosom. The larger institutions may have sent forth branches, or colonies, affiliated with the parent head, but these ramifications have disappeared, and the various establishments, under one common rule, are independent, each of the other.

Monastic life has been deficient in variety of development, in concentration and unity of purpose, and in diversity of results; it has exerted less influence upon the progress of society, but it has also been the cause of

MONASTICISM.

less embarrassment to both the Church and the State. Its action, though less multiform and varied than elsewhere in Europe, has been deeply felt. In Russia, as in Gaul and in Germany, monks have been the pioneers of civilization, as well as of Christianity. They penetrated the vast solitudes of the North and the East, converted barbarians and cleared forests, spread the Gospel among savage tribes and improved their material condition, and population followed after them as they advanced. Sympathizing and mingling freely with the people, they have had profound influence in forming national character, and have identified religion with national life. In the centuries of wars with Tatars, Lithuanians, Poles, and Swedes, monasteries have been the ramparts and bulwarks of the national existence, which owes both its origin and its preservation to the Church; in times of anarchy and subjugation its establishments have been the only havens of refuge for letters and learning brought from Byzantium; their only ark of safety in the deluge of barbaric invasion.

The history of the empire can be read in the annals of its great lavra. Those of the Petcherski, the convent of catacombs on the banks of the Dnieper, embrace the nation's youth, the age of Kiev, its ancient patrimony; while those of the Troïtsa cover its growth to maturity, the age of Moscow, its natural capital.

The great monasteries were, in reality, fortified cities of vast extent and dense population, grouping numerous churches around their shrines; in the Troïtsa there were fourteen, in the Solovetsk convent seven, in the Simonov and Donskoï five and six. Each name revives the memory of great deeds and heroic struggles, and appeals to both religious and patriotic sentiment. The walls of the Troïtsa exhausted the strength of the victorious Poles, and preserved the nation's life when Moscow and the empire were prostrate; Napoleon's armies stopped but a day's march from its gates, and resistance to his invasion was encouraged by what the people deemed divine interposition to save this sacred fortress; it gave shelter to tsars against domestic treachery, as well as against foreign foes. The Novospasski and Donskoï convents checked the Tatars at the entrance to Moscow. Solovetsk defied the Swedes.

Popular reverence for these holy citadels is enhanced by the natural beauties of their situations, the untold treasures and precious relics which they guard, and the hallowed spots which they commemorate. The Petcherski was the cradle of Russian monastic life, the home of Nestor and chroniclers of old; it is the shrine of innumerable saints, whose lives were passed in the mysterious caves where their bones are yet objects of pious veneration and worship; from the hillside of the Dnieper it looks out upon a broad expanse of meadow and stream as boundless as the ocean. The red-brick towers of the Troïtsa overhang picturesque ravines; its vaults are piled with incalculable riches, and its churches are sanctified by most sacred Icons. Iverski, upon an island of the beautiful Lake Valdai, is shrouded in magnificent forests. Voskresensk, the "New Jerusalem," is planned to reproduce the most revered sanctuaries of Palestine. Solovetsk, renowned for the austere piety of its brotherhood, is surrounded by scenery peculiarly impressive from its solitary and desolate grandeur, upon the bleak shores of the White Sea. Localities, fortunate in the presence and neighborhood of these holy shrines, are held by the people in especial veneration, and Peter the Great, in founding the city which bears his name, endeavored to invest it with similar title to popular regard by transporting thither, from Vladimir, the relics of the great hero and saint Alexander Nevski, and enshrining them in a vast convent, raised to rank with the famous lavra of the Petcherski and the Troïtsa.

At the great festivals of the Church these religious centres are still thronged by pilgrims, but their permanent inmates and regular votaries are now but few, and may be counted by scores, instead of by hundreds. The spirit of monasticism is less fervent than in former days, and the geographical distribution of existing monasteries marks the change. They are more numerous in the ancient cities, around the old capitals, Kiev and Moscow, and within the former republics, Novgorod and Pskov; less so in provinces recently colonized and peopled. Their numbers actually correspond to the antiquity, rather than to the density, of the population. In the empire there are in all about 550; in every bishopric there is at least one, the superior of which is, by right of his office, member of the diocesan council; they are served by about 5900 monks and 4900 nuns in full standing, with 4100 lay brethren, and 13,000 lay sisters and novices.

The causes of the noticeable decline in the monastic spirit, while religion retains firm hold upon the people, are both moral and political in their nature. Monasticism in Russia has never felt the renewing and vivifying influences springing from works of active charity and benevolence, while the more fervently devout and piously inclined of the population have been drawn away from the national Church, and from its institutions, by dissenting sects. The ready favor with which schismatic doctrines were received by the monks, as, for instance, at Solovetsk, brought them into direct antagonism with the authorities of the Church, who, determined to stamp out Dissent at any cost, subjected all religious institutions to strict supervision and severe regulations. The persistent opposition manifested by the monasteries to the reforms of Peter the Great aroused his anger, and arrayed all the power of the State against them. Every restriction, short of absolute suppression, was imposed; their property was sequestered, and their spiritual influence undermined by government interference, until the lower classes only held them in reverence; their number, and that of their inmates, was arbitrarily reduced; they were treated as institutions of the State, and in the choice of their superiors, as well as in all the detail of their administration, they were subjected to government control, exercised through the Synod; entrance to the monastic body was made difficult by stringent regulations, and the life made irksome by severe and vexatious discipline, calculated to repel and disgust the better class of those who felt a vocation for religious seclusion. By a singular contradiction, all high ecclesiastical dignities were reserved for the members of the monastic body, thus systematically degraded in general estimation. The effect of this policy, so fraught with danger to the standing and repute of the upper clergy, was counteracted by the practice of conferring these positions of responsibility only upon the elect, whose career in the seminaries and academies had been marked by ability. To graduates of brilliant promise every conceivable inducement to take the vows was offered; the limit of age was reduced from thirty years to twenty-five, and rapid promotion was assured. A superior class among the monks was thus formed, for whom monastic life was but a means for an end, an easy and certain path to power and influence; while for the great majority it was a dreary, monotonous routine of ceremonial religious rites, under rigid discipline strictly enforced.

A few only of the monasteries, and those are of minor importance, are dependent solely upon their own resources; by far the greater number, including the more celebrated, receive an allowance from the government as an indemnity for their sequestered estates.

First among these are the great lavra—the Petcherski at Kiev, the Troïtsa at Moscow, Alexander Nevski at St. Petersburg, and to these three there has recently been added Potchaïef, in Volhymnia, the chief monastery of the Uniates. Their appellation "lavra" is derived from the Greek "laura," a street or open place, which designation was applied in the East to communities of anchorites who lived in union, but occupied single and detached cells, in contradistinction to cœnobia, in which the inmates lived together under a common roof.[1] Each of these establishments depends upon the neighboring metropolitan, who makes it his official residence.

Next in rank are the "stavropigia,"[2] seven or eight in number, comprising several of the large monasteries in and around Moscow; they are exempted from the jurisdiction of the bishop of the diocese in which they are situated; formerly, they depended immediately upon the patriarch, who, at their foundation, took them under his special charge, and, at their consecration, sent the large double cross which surmounts them; from this circumstance is derived their name. Now they depend directly upon the Holy Synod, as succeeding to the rights of the patriarch. The remainder of the monasteries are divided into three classes, according to their importance.

The number of monks or nuns in each is fixed by statute; the lavra have about a hundred in full standing, and as many more lay brethren and novices; the Stav-

---

[1] Neander, vol. iii., p. 334.
[2] From σταυρός, a cross, and πηγνεῖν, to place.

pigia and the establishments of the first class have each thirty-three, the others still fewer; the regulations in this respect are relaxed according to the necessities of each locality; rural convents are allowed more inmates than those in cities, but the tendency of the reformatory measures now contemplated is, from motives of economy, to limit the number to the actual requirements of the service in each case, and to bring the monks strictly under the system of life in common, in order, by diminishing the expenses, to increase the funds that may be appropriated to the episcopal revenues, to the support of the poorer clergy, and to the maintenance of schools and hospitals.

The monasteries, as a body, are possessed of enormous wealth in immobilized property; they are rich in precious stones, pearls, and jewels, in vases of gold and silver, in furniture, ornaments, and objects of art of great value, the accumulations of centuries. These treasures, in many cases of fabulous amount, are unproductive and inalienable, sacred, as belonging to the altar. Some of these institutions have large incomes of their own, derived from lands formerly uncultivated, which, supposed to be of no value, escaped sequestration when their villages and serfs were taken by the State; from fisheries, and mills on streams formerly neglected, and from gifts and bequests sanctioned by special authorization. These revenues, where they exist, together with the government allowances, constitute but a portion of their actual resources. The sacred relics and miraculous pictures, which no convent is without, are objects of devout worship and superstitious veneration; they attract immense crowds of devotees, the aggregate of whose offerings is very large. At the Petcherski and the Troïtsa pilgrims are reckoned by hundreds of thousands, and none are so poor but leave their mite upon the altar. The holy images and wonder-working Madonnas are carried to the homes of the sick and infirm; Our Lady of Iberia, most revered of all, has horses and carriages kept for her service, and, it is said, brings in to her chapel at Moscow $50,000 a year. At stated periods, these sacred images are borne through the neighboring villages in solemn processions, and reap rich harvests from the contributions of the faithful, who eagerly vie for the honor of their visit. As, in the olden time, great princes and lords were wont to don the monkish garb at the approach of death, so now all Russians wish to be buried near the tomb of some one of the saints of the Church, and the privilege of reposing in ground hallowed by their near presence is made a prolific source of income to the convents or churches which possess some holy man's remains.

For women there are fewer retreats than for men, and, by published statistics, there would appear to be fewer nuns than monks; the official lists, however, do not give the total number of females within convent walls, as they include only those who, over forty years of age, have taken the veil. In point of fact, these institutions have more inmates than the monasteries; they are open to novices, and to lay sisters of any age; many young girls and women seek shelter within them, and remain there permanently, without consummating the act which would separate them definitively from the world, free, at any moment, to re-enter society, but generally content to pass their days in voluntary seclusion. An entirely different conception of monastic institutions, and of monastic life, whether for monks or nuns, prevails in Russia from that in Catholic countries. Charity, benevolence, or missionary enterprise are not the essential features, although they may be incident to the life.

Among the monks, for a few, it is the commencement of an ambitious career that may lead to power and station; for some others, more humble, yet devoutly inclined, it affords opportunity for meditation and prayer, and for growth in personal piety; for the many, it means freedom from military service and taxation, and escape from bodily punishment; for all, both monks and nuns, it is a sure refuge from poverty and want, a shelter for solitary or improvident old age.

The secular, married, or *white* clergy form the sacerdotal body; until recently it has been, by law as well as by practice, a close, hereditary corporation, a tribe, like that of Levi, consecrated to the service of the altar. This peculiarity of its condition arose by degrees, as a necessary consequence of serfdom and of the ancient constitution of society. The serf, bound to the soil, was prohibited from entering the Church, as, by so doing, he defrauded his master of his toil; and the noble proprietor was debarred, under penalty of the loss of his estates and of the privileges of his rank; the clergy could, therefore, be recruited only from among those of its own class, and a separate clerical body was thus gradually formed, bound to the altar, as the peasant was bound to the land. Sons of priests were compelled to attend the parish schools, and parish offices were filled by graduates of these schools. Custom, and Church law, had made marriage a condition of ordination, and as neither sons nor daughters of popes could marry out of the class to which they belonged, intermarriage of one with the other became obligatory, and this clerical class was thus further transformed, by degrees, into a distinct and special caste. The necessity for the existence of this peculiar order of things disappeared with the causes which gave rise to it. In 1861, serfdom was abolished; three years later, the ranks of the clergy were thrown open to all, and children of priests were freely admitted to other careers. While in theory, and before the law, these distinctions of class and caste have been abrogated, practically they still exist as a marked characteristic of Russian society, and their persistence springs from the difficulty of rapidly effecting radical changes among a people imbued, above all others, with regard for ancient usages; the long-continued Levitical organization of the parish clergy created habits of life and thought not to be easily eradicated, and, as a matter of fact, the clerical body still remains a class apart.

The inheritance of priestly rank tended to make the charges and the emoluments of the office also hereditary, and to establish, for the priest, a quasi vested right of proprietorship in the parish living. The pope endeavored to transmit his curacy to his children, not only as a legacy to a son, but also, when he had no son to succeed him in his charge, as a marriage portion for a daughter; and these pretensions, very generally realized in practice, came near securing the force of law. They were the more leniently considered by the authorities of both the State and the Church, from the necessity, devolving upon them at the death of a pope, of making provision for his family, and from their natural wish to impose this burden upon his successor; the situation was also further complicated by the circumstance that, usually, the parsonage and dwellings belonged, not to the parish, or to the village, which gave only the land necessary for the pope's support, but to the incumbent himself, and the new-comer was obliged to arrange with the heirs to obtain possession; as marriage was obligatory upon him, the simplest mode of settlement was for him to marry into the family; he could not espouse the widow, to whom, as well as to the pope, a second marriage is forbidden; so he took the daughter, whose dowry was the curacy, and pensioned off the rest of the relations when he entered upon his charge. This custom, sanctioned by the usage of centuries, was rendered unnecessary by the laws of 1864, but it still prevails, and is not likely to disappear until proper provision is made for the families of deceased popes.

The principle of heredity extended also to the subordinate offices of the parish church. After the priest and the deacon, who are received into holy orders, comes the great body of the minor white clergy, subdivided into many classes. In recent synodical reports the total number of popes is given as 37,300, of whom from 1400 to 1500 are proto-popes or arch-priests, the highest dignity to which a member of the white clergy may attain; they are the superiors in parishes having two priests; they are often appointed inspectors over the parish clergy, and are qualified for a seat in the Synod. Of deacons there are 11,500; they assist the pope at the altar, and may, at some ceremonies, as at funerals, replace him. The next, or third class, which is very numerous, nearly 600,000, comprises clerks, beadles, vergers, singers, sextons, bell-ringers, and all the minor officers; each of these subdivisions is separate from the others; its members intermarry, and its functions are practically hereditary. These three orders of popes, deacons, and the minor clergy are, and always remain, entirely distinct one from the other, and do not form successive grades in the parish hierarchy.

Educational institutions for the secular clergy are of three kinds—district or parish schools, seminaries, and academies. Graduates of the first-named, in which instruction is very elementary, are fitted only for the subordinate offices; the deacons, and the great majority of popes, issue from the second; the more distinguished members of the priesthood pass through the third, which correspond to the theological faculties of European universities. Merit is by no means ignored in conferring ecclesiastical appointments, and the student who fails in his examination for the priesthood cannot hope to rise above the diaconate. The course of study at the seminaries is varied and comprehensive; it includes ancient, or liturgical, Slavonic, Latin, Greek, Hebrew, and one modern language, mathematical and physical sciences, history, philosophy, and theology. The defect of the system is not in the extent of the field mapped out; its deficiencies, which are many and real, arise from the short time given to each department, and the consequent superficial nature of the knowledge imparted, from the use of antiquated text-books, from the absence of a catholic and liberal spirit in the method of instruction, caused by Russian isolation and want of intercourse with the Western world, and by neglect of modern progress in ideas and sciences; they are aggravated by the youth and inexperience of the instructors, who are frequently changed, and seldom adopt teaching as a profession, but accept a tutor's post temporarily, merely as a step in their career of official preferment.

The Russian pope, notwithstanding the imperfect nature of his education, is, intellectually, much superior to the community in which he lives, and if the influence which he exerts be less than might be expected of him, this must be attributed to the depressing and demoralizing conditions of his life, to his want of means, and to his social ostracism.

He is wretchedly paid: in cities, and where the presence of clergy of other denominations renders it desirable, from motives of policy, that his position should be decent, and more befitting his sacred office, the salary may reach 300 roubles [1] (at present about $150), but on the average, his annual stipend does not exceed 100 roubles ($50), a miserable pittance which cannot support him and his family in respectability. He becomes, therefore, dependent upon, and is at the mercy of, his parishioners; for the cultivation of the land allotted for his support the labor of his own hands cannot suffice, and he must rely upon the gratuitous and grudgingly-given assistance of the peasants, who can, themselves, barely keep body and soul together; he must eke out his meagre existence by gifts and offerings of his poor and scanty flock; these contributions might afford a decent livelihood, were not the larger part reclaimed by the Synod or the diocese, and the slender portion remaining still to be shared by him with the minor clergy of his parish. Necessity compels him to wring, or cajole, all that is possible from his congregation; his daily bread depends upon it, and every ceremony he performs, every sacrament he confers, is bargained for and haggled over as it can only be done in Russia; bridal-couples have left the altar unmarried, and bodies have been buried secretly, because the pope and the peasant could not agree upon a price; the pious and the indifferent, the foreign Jew and the native Christian, the Orthodox believer and the Dissenter, are all under contribution, and the pope's most engrossing occupation is to watch greedily over every member of his parish, to see that none evade the payment of dues he may rightfully exact, or beg. The task is arduous, for the occasions are many, and of diverse

---

[1] The mint value of the rouble is 65.8 cents, but in recent years, by depreciation, it has fallen to about 50 cents.

nature. Religion enters very largely into Russian daily life: at every important event, at every festival or anniversary, when starting upon, or returning from, a journey, at the inception, or completion, of every undertaking, a blessing is invoked, or thanks are rendered; and these domestic incidents, as well as ceremonies performed within the church doors, are made remunerative to the parish officers. At Christmas, Easter, and Twelfth-day the pope and his clergy, in their sacerdotal robes, loudly chanting the hymn "*Gospodi pomilui!*" (Lord, have mercy upon us!), go their rounds, from house to house, to bless, and sprinkle with holy water, the homes of their parishioners; they sometimes meet with but scant courtesy, and are dismissed from the gate with alms, as troublesome beggars, but, generally, they are welcomed with the free hospitality that characterizes the Russian people, and are expected to do justice to the viands and liquors set before them; to refuse to drink would be an affront, and often, before the day is over, these holy men are in most lamentable condition. The peasant, for whom drunkenness is a venial sin, is more amused than scandalized by the exhibition; but, when the time for feasting has gone by, the gluttony and intemperance he merrily encouraged are made a reproach. "Am I a pope, that I should dine twice?" is a popular saying, significant of the light esteem in which the people hold their pastors; they deem it even a sign of ill-luck to meet a pope by the wayside, while the better classes do not hesitate to show openly their want of regard. The priest's ecclesiastical superiors are not more considerate; he is seldom admitted to his bishop's presence, and he dreads the pastoral visitation. He is treated with contumely, deprived of all independence, and drilled to passive submission; his mental culture ceases, perforce, when he leaves the seminary, and he is as incapable of responding to the religious wants of the devout as he is of withstanding the progress of infidelity. Despised by, and isolated from, the community upon which he is dependent, his whole life is a ceaseless, wretched struggle for material existence; all devotional feeling is crushed out of his soul, and religion, for him, is debased to mere form and ceremonial, by which to earn a precarious subsistence.

The obligation of marriage weighs heavily upon him. While great advantages may result from it in many points of view, and in communities where, as in Protestant countries, the minister, properly remunerated, finds, in an intelligent, educated wife, a helpmate and co-worker, in Russia it is far otherwise. Even at the present day, the married pope may not aspire to the higher dignities of the Church; he cannot obtain a curacy without a wife; frequently she brings it to him as her dowry, and he loses it at her death. She feels, and makes him feel, her superiority as the moneyed partner in the association; she is generally without education, and, in her poverty-stricken household, is overwhelmed by domestic cares; she can neither afford him intellectual companionship, nor is she competent to share, or to encourage him, in pious and charitable work. Children come to increase his responsibilities and anxieties. Only recently have other careers than the priesthood been opened for them; and, while they are eager to embrace them, and escape from the sordid cares and degradations they have witnessed in their homes, they seldom find the opportunity; although they are raised, by education, above the laborer and the peasant, poverty, social prejudices, and want of influential relations check their aspirations; but too frequently they help to swell the multitude of disappointed, discontented, and ambitious youths who, hostile to the existing order of things, fretting under restrictions imposed by custom and habit, partially educated, and their minds filled with crude revolutionary ideas, are a serious danger in the body politic.

The welfare of the State and the good of the Church, alike, imperatively demand amelioration in the condition of the parish clergy. For twenty and more years past the question has been under examination, and important reforms have been commenced. The necessities of the government have restricted the appropriations for the clerical budget, but it has grown from one million of roubles in 1833 to ten millions in 1872, and the remuneration of the clergy has been raised. The number of parishes and of priests has been reduced, with, in each case, the same object in view—by diminishing the number of the recipients, to increase the share of each; but in this direction the measure of reform, limited by the immense extent of the empire and the sparseness of its population, has been pushed too far.

There are now in Russia about 43,000 churches and chapels, but while the cities, especially the more ancient, are abundantly supplied with religious edifices and an officiating clergy, the rural parishes are already too large. Of priests, in regular standing, there are less than 38,000, too few for the pastoral work. In Siberia, and in the frontier governments, the want of priests has been severely felt, and it has recently been necessary to ordain Seminarists, who had not completed their studies, and to recruit the clergy from students of lay institutions. When, as in these provinces, great distances separate the people from their places of worship, and the ministers of the altar are few, apathy and indifference are engendered, or schismatic and dissenting doctrines flourish without contradiction, and the prosperity of the Church is imperilled. The only reduction that may be yet safely made is among the multitudes of the minor clergy, the most ignorant and the most useless, whose services could, for the most part, be dispensed with without danger, and perhaps to advantage.

With efforts for the improvement of the material condition of the parish clergy, there is also a strong inclination to raise their social position. By marriage they are debarred from the episcopal dignity. Church discipline ordains that a bishop may not be married in the flesh; according to Timothy, he must be "the husband of one wife," and as, by a subtle interpretation of the text, he has already one spouse, the Church, he can have no other, and the episcopate remains the monopoly of the black clergy; but positions of trust and eminence are being brought within the reach of married priests, especially of those who are connected with the higher clerical education. A pope has recently been appointed rector of the ecclesiastical academy of St. Petersburg, an important post, hitherto always held by a monk. Measures of this nature, persistently pursued, would inaugurate a new era of reform, and, while instilling into the Church a more catholic and liberal spirit, would open, for the white clergy, a vast and hitherto closed sphere of usefulness.

CHAPTER IX.

The Raskol.—Early Heresies.—Attempted Reforms in Church.—Nikon.—Peter the Great.—The Popovtsi and the Bezpopovtsi.—Political Aspect of the Raskol.

The Orthodox Russian Church, for upwards of two hundred years, has been disturbed by numerous mysterious sects, almost wholly unknown abroad, and but partially understood at home. The religious movement from which they derive their being, generally designated as the "Raskol,"[1] or the "Schism," is peculiarly Russian and national in its origin and character. It has never extended beyond the limits of the empire, and, within them, it is restricted chiefly to the more ancient provinces, where the population is essentially Muscovite; it is of most diverse nature, absolutely without unity in its development, subdivided into a thousand different branches, separate and distinct one from the other, having only for their common object opposition to the established Church. It is exclusively a popular movement; it had its rise, and still exists, in the peasant's hut, and among the common multitude, without sympathy from, or affiliation with, the educated or upper classes of society, and it indicates a mental and social condition of the people which has no parallel in other lands.

Both German Protestantism and Russian Raskol preserve the stamp of their similar religious origin, as issuing each from an established State Church, but here the

---

[1] *Raskol* is a Russian word meaning the cleft, the rupture.

resemblance ceases, until it is again apparent in analogous results.

In the West, Dissent has generally proceeded from a spirit of investigation, doubt, and inquiry; from a desire for liberty, and from impatience of spiritual control; but in Russia it has sprung from diametrically opposite causes—the obstinacy of ignorance, persistent reverence for the past, and obedience to authority.

In the one case, the human soul has sought freedom from the trammels of form and ceremony to satisfy its aspirations towards an ideal, higher life; in the other, superstitious regard for ancient usages, devotion to external rites, have been the predominant influences. From a common starting-point the two movements have progressed in steadily diverging directions, but, while antagonistic in the principle of their development, they have arrived at similar results, inasmuch as the Raskol, rejecting the authority of the Church, by which alone unity of faith could be preserved, has recognized the right of free interpretation of mysterious, though immutable, dogmas, and accepted all the vagaries of individual opinions regarding them, thereby creating infinite variety of belief.

In the Middle Ages, during the constant wars between the appanaged princes, heresies and religious controversies were rife in Russia, as elsewhere. Each petty sovereign, as he arrived at power, endeavored to enlist the influence of the Church in his own behalf; three metropolitans, in the twelfth century, claimed, at the same time, the ecclesiastical throne at Kiev; and the disturbances within the Church, from their rival pretensions, permitted the growth of heretical doctrines, which related, however, not to fundamental dogmas, but only to external observances. Nestor, bishop of Rostov, accused of favoring them, was summoned to Constantinople for his justification, about 1162; and, during his absence, Leon, a neighboring prelate, usurped charge of his diocese. He openly professed and encouraged the practices laid to the charge of Nestor, and which, while at variance with canonical rule, aimed at stricter observance of Church discipline. He preached the necessity of abstaining from meat at the festivals of the Nativity and the Epiphany, whenever they should fall upon a Wednesday or a Friday. Nestor was acquitted and returned, but the heresy had meanwhile assumed such proportions as to necessitate further reference to the patriarch, before whom Leon was cited to appear, and by whom he was tried and condemned. This authoritative decision was set at naught by Constantine II., Metropolitan of Kiev, a native Russian, who shared the opinions advocated by Leon, and supported them by his authority.

This religious movement, the first of which any record exists within the Russian Church, is, in its ceremonial character, typical of the dissensions which arose in subsequent centuries; it was swallowed up and forgotten in the civil commotions distracting the country, but, in connection with it, the devotional disposition of the people was manifested in the popular belief that to divine displeasure, aroused by the defection of the head of the Church, was to be attributed the sack and ruin of Kiev, the holy city, in 1168, by a coalition of the appanaged princes, under Andrew Bogoloubsky of Souzdal.[1]

In 1370 the sect of the Strigolniki[2] appeared. They took their name from the craft of their founder, one

---

[1] Karamsin, vol. ii., p. 395; Mouravief, p. 39.
[2] Karamsin, vol. v., p. 130; Mouravief, p. 65, and note, p. 379. Strigolnik is derived from *streetch*, to shear.

Karp, a sheep or wool shearer, a man of the people, with whom was joined Nikita, a deacon of the Church. The movement was a popular protest against the greed, covetousness, and corruption of the clergy, and it spread rapidly among the lower classes at Pskov and Novgorod. Its founders commenced by railing at, and finally rejecting, the clergy altogether, as being a human institution, rendered despicable by the ignorance, degradation, and covetousness of its members; they alleged, by authority of St. Paul, that any Christian brother was empowered to teach the Gospel, and, for priests, they substituted leaders chosen freely among themselves. They denied the rite of episcopal ordination, and that the imposition of hands could endow the clergy with any divine power of imparting the grace of the Holy Ghost; this power they claimed for every believer, as an essential privilege of Church membership, by which all brethren were invested with the rights of spiritual priesthood. They renounced auricular confession and priestly absolution, as being contrary to God's commands to confess one's sins to Him, and to bow before Him alone; they rejected the priest's office in baptism and communion, and administered these sacraments one to another. To chant psalms over the dead, and to offer up prayers and oblations for their souls, they declared to be an innovation of the devil, practised by his agents, the priests, to satisfy their greed and covetousness, by the fees they earned. Nikita, degraded from his office, was thrown into prison, and Karp, victim of the fickleness of popular favor, was, at the instigation of his enemies, the priests, drowned by a mob in the river Volkov. The sect was suppressed, so far as outward manifestations went, but the leaven of its teachings remained fermenting in the popular mind.

A century later, about 1470, a heresy, known as that of

THE SECT OF THE JUDAIZERS.

the "Jedovstchina,"[1] or the sect of the Judaizers, was discovered at Novgorod. It was introduced from Lithuania by a learned Jew, Zachariah, a man profoundly versed in the cabalistic arts, generally believed, in those days, to be the peculiar inheritance of his race, and the source of Solomon's fabled wisdom. Taught in secret, it had already acquired formidable proportions before it was detected. It was supposed to have been grafted upon the former errors of the Strigolniki, which, not yet entirely forgotten, still remained latent in the mysterious undercurrents of popular belief; there was, however, no apparent affiliation or resemblance, save as regards a common hatred of the priesthood and opposition to clerical authority. This new sect rejected entirely the doctrines of the Christian religion; it denied the divinity, and even the existence of the Saviour, proclaiming that the Messiah was yet to come. Apart from circumcision, it inculcated the tenets of the Jewish faith; promulgated in mystery, it was readily received by a credulous, ignorant people, chafing under the onerous exactions of a grasping, covetous priesthood, which it despised more heartily than it feared. The adherents of this sect were scrupulously observant of all the rites and ceremonies of the Orthodox Church, and, by their crafty dissimulation, for a long period they escaped discovery. Among Zachariah's early proselytes were two priests of Novgorod, Alexis and Dionysius, who, while secretly spreading error, maintained unblemished reputations as faithful ministers of the Church; by their apparent zeal and devotion they gained the confidence of the great prince Ivan III., and were summoned by him to Moscow;

---

[1] Karamsin, vol. vi., p. 242; Mouravief, p. 89, and note, p. 383. See above, p. 43. From *Jedovstvo*—Judaism.

there he installed them as archpriests or deans, one in the Cathedral of the Assumption, the other in the Church of the Archangel. At the capital their efforts were, for a while, crowned with success; many in high position, among them Feodor Kouritsin, secretary of the prince, Helena, his daughter-in-law, and Zosimus, an archimandrite, became their disciples. The latter, by the influence of Alexis over the tsar, was, by him, arbitrarily appointed metropolitan of Moscow in 1491. Gennadius, Bishop of Novgorod, was the first whose suspicions were aroused; his representations were unheeded by Gerontius, then metropolitan, an aged and indolent prelate; but subsequent and more earnest appeals to the tsar, as defender of the faith, induced him to convene a council of the Church in 1505. Notwithstanding the protection and connivance of Zosimos, who presided as metropolitan, this assembly, moved by the vehement denunciations of Gennadius, aided by the hegumen of the Volokamsk monastery, St. Joseph, one of the most learned and enlightened men of his day, anathematized these schismatic and dangerous doctrines.

Alexis, meanwhile, had died, but Dionysius, with the tsar's secretary, and many of their adherents in high ecclesiastic and civil office, were condemned and handed over to the secular arm for punishment at the stake; Zosimos was deposed, but his deposition was attributed to intemperance and incapacity, in order to avert from the Church the scandal of punishing the apostasy of its head. The heresy was stifled, if not thoroughly eradicated.

Popular sympathy with these early religious movements seems to have been excited, both by the dislike and contempt felt for an ignorant, greedy, and rapacious priesthood, and by a preference, already manifested, for ancient and primitive forms of worship, as more akin to, and in harmony with, the earliest, and consequently the most reliable, revelations of divine truth. Already, in these obscure dissensions of the Middle Ages, the fundamental principle of the Raskol—that is to say, scrupulous regard for the letter of the law, formalism—begins to assert itself. An annalist of Novgorod, in the fifteenth century, mournfully complains that some of the clergy have impiously changed the ancient invocation of, "Lord! have pity upon us!" for "O Lord! have pity upon us!"

The manner in which the Russian people were converted to Christianity, suddenly, by order, as it were, made religion appear to them as consisting in form, in words, rites, and ceremonies. There had been among them no gradual assimilation of the truth; they had received no previous preparation by long-continued teaching, as in the West; they still retained their former customs, were still imbued with their ancient superstitions, and were too ignorant to fully comprehend, or appreciate, the pure and elevated morality of the Christian faith. Their rulers commanded, and they obeyed, submissively transferring their allegiance from the idol to the cross, worshipping at the altar in the same spirit as before their pagan shrines. The clergy were hardly more enlightened than the people; for them, also, the letter replaced the spirit, and they deemed their functions limited to the exact repetition of external observances.

By the ignorance and carelessness of scribes and copyists, the liturgy, and the Church-books were soon filled with errors, which, hallowed by constant use, passed into general acceptation, and were held in superstitious veneration by both the minister and the worshipper. The strange interpolations, the contradictions, the capricious readings of the text, seemed the more worthy of reverence as they were the more obscure. They were sacred formulas, full of hidden, mysterious meanings, and, from being capable of divers interpretations, were the source of many singular theories and eccentric teachings, based on what was received as revealed of God.

The necessity of careful revision and correction of the books, the ritual, and the service of the Church was, at an early period, felt to be imperative by many having authority in both Church and State. In the sixteenth century Vassili IV. appealed to Constantinople for competent assistance. Maximus, a Greek theologian of vast erudition and earnest piety, was sent from Mount Athos, and assumed direction of the work. He was favorably received by the tsar, and supported by the more enlightened prelates of the Church, but his efforts were rendered futile by the unreasoning fanaticism of the people and the bigotry of most of the clergy, envious of honors shown to a foreigner. The metropolitan Daniel, an ambitious and intolerant Churchman, was a bitter opponent of the contemplated changes, and his hostility was increased by jealousy of Maximus's influence with the monarch; this mild and pious monk, an uncompromising defender of the laws and canons of the Church, soon fell a victim to court and clerical intrigue, and was condemned by a council for daring to tamper with the ancient and sacred formulas and rites.

Ivan IV., the "terrible" tsar, was deeply read in theological learning, and in early life evinced great solicitude for the Church. He resumed the task, commenced by his father, of correcting and purifying the books and ritual, and convened, for the purpose, the council known as that of the Hundred Chapters, in 1551. Its decisions, of which no authentic record remains, appear to have been tainted by the prejudices and the ignorance of the age; they sanctified by their authority the superstitious practices existing, which, thus approved, took deeper root among the people, while the errors in the books remaining unaltered acquired additional confirmation. The introduction of the printing-press at the same period served to disseminate more widely the books and missals in their ancient form, and this was generally accepted as definitively the true and canonical version.

It was reserved for Nikon, in the middle of the seventeenth century, to accomplish a fundamental reform. This extraordinary man was well fitted for the task. His learning was, for the age and the country, varied and profound, his genius vast and enterprising, his piety and devotion to the Church sincere, his zeal and energy unbounded, and his determination inflexible. He possessed the entire confidence of his sovereign, and wielded over the State a power and influence commensurate with that he exercised over the Church. At his command Greek and Slavonic manuscripts were collected and collated, monks were summoned from Byzantium and from the holy sanctuaries of Palestine, and the work of expurgation and correction was vigorously pursued. The rites and ceremonies were restored in their primitive purity, and invested with all the pomp and splendor of the Oriental Church. The liturgy and missals, freed from interpolations and erroneous readings, were approved by a council, and the use of the amended version forcibly imposed throughout the empire. These radical measures, received with stupefaction and amazement, were at first apparently successful, but soon aroused a storm of popular indignation and revolt; resistance was organized and encouraged by a large portion of the clergy, especially by those of the lower ranks, who came in more immediate contact with the people; they denounced the alterations as a new-fangled religion, akin to Romanism or Lutheranism, and as a deadly attack upon the ancient Orthodox faith. The Church appealed to the State to enforce its edicts, and persecution increased fanaticism. Ten years later Nikon fell from his high estate, and, although the council which condemned him ratified the reforms he had inaugurated, his deposition seemed, to the people, a full justification for their opposition. The sanction and approval of the Eastern patriarchs served only to increase and intensify the popular feeling, by arousing the general hatred of foreign intervention, and added to the bitter contest the element of national jealousy and prejudice. What was, at first, merely an outbreak of religious discontent assumed by degrees the aspect of a political revolution. Dissent rapidly developed into schism; it became the Raskol, or the Rupture, and, once firmly established, was a power no longer to be summarily dealt with.

In all religious history no movement so serious and lasting has ever issued from such futile and trivial causes. The way of making the sign of the cross, its form, whether processions should march towards the East or towards the West, an additional letter in the name Jesus, the repetition of Halleluia twice or three times, the number of loaves upon the Holy Table, constituted the principal points of the controversy. Servile respect for the letter of the law, for the form only, was the very essence of its origin; but it must be remembered that, for the old Muscovite, Orthodoxy, Christianity, Religion itself was but ceremony and symbol, as embodiments of the fundamental dogmas of the faith.

The Dissenters, hitherto known as the Staroobriadtsi,[1] or Old Ritualists, assumed the name of Staroveri,[2] or Old

---

[1] From *starii*, old, and *obriad*, ceremonial.
[2] From *starii*, old, and *vera*, truth.

Believers; that is, true believers, and, by a singular contradiction, founded their claim to this designation upon the alleged antiquity of their practices, stubbornly ignoring the fact that the innovations, against which they rebelled, in reality restored the ancient worship in its primitive purity, while they were the innovators.

The principle underlying the Raskol is essentially realistic and materialistic, pushed to its extreme limits. Notwithstanding the extravagance of its deductions and the moral barrenness of its results, it is, in the singleness of purpose and fanatical sincerity of its adherents, entitled to respect, if not to sympathy. Reverence for the letter of the law is, for the Old Believer, a consequence of his regard for its spirit; in his mind the two are inseparably united; the form and the essence are one; both necessary elements of faith, both equally of divine origin, essential parts of a complete and perfect whole, revealed by God to man, as the only way of salvation; nothing in it is trivial, nothing superfluous; all is profound, mysterious, holy; one jot or one tittle may not pass from the law, and the words of St. John, set as a seal to close the Apocalypse, are, for him, a real and awful curse.

In this scrupulous regard for form the Raskol is in direct opposition to Protestantism, impatient of all fetters and restraint; it is allied to it in the free interpretation it allows to the text of the Word and in the many explanations it permits of the symbols of the faith. It seeks constantly a hidden, allegorical signification, not only in the expressions used, but also in the events narrated by the sacred writers; for instance, the story of Lazarus has been explained as a parable, and not a miracle performed by the Saviour; Lazarus was the human soul, his death the state of sin; Martha and Mary were, one the body, the other the soul; the grave was the cares of life, the resurrection of Lazarus the conversion of the soul. Christ's entrance into Jerusalem was not an incident in his career, but was a typical description of the entrance of the Holy Spirit into the heart of man. From this freedom of interpretation, indulged in by a superstitious, ignorant, and imaginative people, has arisen division into innumerable sects, with almost infinite variations of belief, as extraordinary and fantastic as they are numerous.

The strength and sacredness of family ties, together with the respect for ancient usages, at all times characteristic of the Muscovite race, have intensified their attachment to parental teachings and to doctrines inherited from their ancestors. "This was the religion of our fathers," they replied to remonstrances and menaces; "punish us, exile us, if you will, but leave us free to worship as our fathers did."

Nikon's changes attacked directly this reverential regard for what they deemed the past; the child remembered its mother's teachings, and refused to surrender the belief she relied upon; the peasant knew nothing of alterations or corruptions introduced centuries ago. Ancient usages, for him, were the usages of his forefathers, and the traditions of the village elders; he had heard vaguely of Romanism as an impious heresy, of his brethren in Poland seduced and forced by Catholic influence to a mongrel belief, hateful in his eyes, and he clung the closer to his father's creed. Both people and clergy were suspicious of every importation from abroad, whether it came from Western Europe, from the shores of the Bosphorus, or even from ancient Kiev, where priests studied "that thrice-accursed language, Latin;" they held it a mortal sin to call God "Deus," or the Father "Pater;" his only name was their own Slavonic "Bogh." A letter written by a Raskolnik, during the reign of Catherine II., relates " that in those days a violent persecution arose against us, pious Christians, dwelling peaceably among Little Russian perverts who eat pigeons and hares, and soil their mouths with the thrice-accursed plants coffee and tobacco; they have dragged some of us into their errors, but these were among us, though not of us; they were led by Satan himself—Satan, son of Beelzebub, offspring of the Serpent; they do not even think it a sin to call God Deus, and his Father, who got him, Pater."[1] The Raskolniks, who called themselves "spiritual," or "true" Christians, deemed themselves to be the only Orthodox believers, the elect, chosen vessels to preserve the purity of the faith; and classed all foreigners as heretics sure of damnation. The Raskol was the expression of national and popular prejudices, as well as that of earnest religious enthusiasm.

Not long after Nikon, Peter the Great appeared, the chief cause of the schism, the head and front of the offending.

It is difficult, at the present day, to realize the impression this monarch made upon his subjects. It was more than wonder and amazement; they were scandalized by his acts. He trampled under foot their most cherished customs and traditions; openly and brutally assailed ancient and venerable institutions, held in tenderest respect; meddled with private affairs, and invaded the sanctity of domestic life; enforced regulations which shocked their national prejudices and religious belief; revolutionized the form of government; degraded the dignity of his kingly office, and dared even raise a sacrilegious hand upon the holy Church.

---

[1] "Le Raskol," p. 50.

In the new Russia which he created the bewildered Muscovite could no longer recognize his native land; strange names were dinned in his ears, foreign habits and habiliments offended his gaze; the calendar and the alphabet were altered, saints' days and holy days were shifted; men's chins were shaven, women appeared unveiled in the streets; Moscow became Babylon; old Russia was shaken as by an earthquake, and chaos seemed come again. The memory of Nikon's innovations was revived; Peter walked in his footsteps, and was, by popular indignation, accused of being his adulterous offspring.

The civil revolution inaugurated by the tsar gave fresh vigor to the discontent aroused by the old patriarch's attempt to reform the Church; Old Russians, opposed to civic and social changes, sympathized with Old Ritualists, intolerant of clerical innovation. National prejudices were stimulated by religious fanaticism, and religious hostility was excited by respect for ancient customs and institutions.

The complicated machinery of a modern form of government was irksome to a primitive people, strongly attached to simple and long-inherited usages; it was vexatious and repugnant to their habits. They rebelled against heavy imposts, made necessary by the new requirements of the State; against novel duties and obligations imposed upon them; against recruitment and enforced military service. They were impatient of restrictions upon personal freedom, of passports, and rules for dress; they were conscientiously opposed to regulations offending their religious scruples, to the census, to the registration of births and deaths, to the capitation tax, or tax " on souls " (" podouchenoï oklad "); " making them pay," as they said, " for their immortal souls, which God had given;" and they invoked the punishment of David for numbering the people of Israel.

The inflexible determination of the tsar was met with equally persistent opposition from these enthusiasts. They were astounded by his conduct, and, in their amazement, began to question his identity and to deny his authority. Fabulous stories were secretly circulated, some to the effect that he was the son of Nikon; others that the true "white tsar," Peter, had perished at sea; and that a Jew of the accursed race, a son of Satan, had usurped the throne, slain the imperial family, and married a German adventuress, who brought with her into Russia myriads of her countrymen. He was the Antichrist, whose coming had been foretold by the prophets, and his reign was the reign of Satan.

In the presumptuous efforts of Nikon Old Believers had seen portents of impending evil; and in the impious acts of Peter, levelling the venerable institutions of the past, insulting religion and morality, they realized the fulfilment of the prophetic vision of St. John; the last days had come, and the end of the world was at hand. The tsar's abolition of the patriarchate, the restrictions he imposed upon the Church, his attacks upon the rights and privileges of the clergy, the war he waged upon ancient customs, his persecution of true Orthodoxy, his fondness for the hated heretical foreigner, his wonderful triumphs after repeated and crushing defeats, the irregularities and wild excesses of his private life, even his gigantic stature, his strength, and his striking personal appearance, designated him as the Beast of the Apocalypse. Fanatical ingenuity found ample confirmation in the prophecies for this popular belief. He abandoned the national and sacred title of tsar for the infidel appellation of imperator, and as therein, by the suppression of the second letter, they deciphered the apocalyptic number 666, they said he concealed his accursed name under the letter M.[1] The council at Moscow, which, while condemning Nikon, had anathematized the Raskol, was convoked in 1666; from this number, by dropping the thousand, in accordance with the old Russian custom of reckoning dates, they had 666; and as this was the number of the "beast," they read the date of the council as marking the commencement of Satan's reign. They found in the word Russia (Russa or Roussa) an anagram of Assur, or Assour of the Bible, and averred that the curses of the prophets against the Assyrian cities of Nineveh and Babylon were aimed at their own unhappy land. With their country thus given over to the powers of hell, and the devil sitting on the throne, surrounded by his imps, in the persons of the tsar's ministers and favorites, the Raskolniks felt it to be a religious duty to reject every innovation introduced, and every change made, under this Satanic rule, suffering with patient endurance, even unto death, rather than yield compliance to unrighteous behests. They carried their resistance into all the detail of daily life; as matters of conscience, they eschewed the use of tobacco, for "the things which come out of him, those are they that defile the man" (Mark vii. 15); of sugar, as it is refined with blood, and, by the Scriptures, man may not eat of the blood of beasts; of tea and coffee, as of foreign production; of the potato, as being the fruit with which the serpent tempted Eve. They objected to the paving of the streets, as a foreign invention. They submitted to double taxation, deprivation of civil rights, and to exile

---

[1] The Slav letters of the alphabet were, like the Greek, used for figures; and imperator, without the m, figured thus: i=10, p=80, e=5, r=100, a=1, t=300, o=70, r=100; total, 666.

even, rather than change their dress or crop their hair. They gloried in the red badge they were compelled to wear, as it pointed them out to the sympathy and commiseration of the people as the suffering, yet uncomplaining, defenders of national traditions and the ancient faith. Long hair and beards are still, as then, their distinguishing feature; and popular obstinacy, in this particular, proved stronger than the will of the autocrat. The more exalted and fanatic among them, called Stranniki,[1] or Fugitives, threw off all allegiance, and arrayed themselves in open opposition to the government, proclaiming resistance to constituted authority as their profession of faith.

Apart from the religious character of the Raskol, it thus assumed another aspect, social and political, equally important as a popular protestation against new or foreign habits, customs, and laws. In its origin and inception it was but a blind attachment to errors born of ignorance, prejudice, and superstition, essentially a religious movement, and upon this, its first principle, was engrafted, during Peter's reign, that of hostility to the existing government, and to constituted authority. The reforms inaugurated by him were generally accepted by the nobles and by the upper classes, but were repudiated by the people; the lines of demarcation between the two sections of society were more strongly drawn, and the Raskol became concentrated, almost entirely, in the lower ranks, which remained persistently faithful to the ancient order of things. It was conservative and reactionary, hostile as well to civil as to religious reform, a powful and dangerous element, frequently availed of by unscrupulous and designing men for the furtherance of

---

[1] From *strannik*, a traveller, or wanderer.

their ambitious ends. The Old Believers were, and are still, upholders of ancient usages, as well as of ancient creeds; they are old Russians, Slavophiles, in the fullest sense, Asiatic, Oriental in their opposition to change or progress; they still look back to the days of their fathers as the golden age, and see no hope nor encouragement in what the future may have to offer. This spirit, which has always been a characteristic of the Russian people generally, has, nurtured and fostered by religious enthusiasm, been one of the strongest influences against which modern civilization, aided by government support, has had to contend. It explains in some degree the crude revolutionary movements which have at times temporarily disturbed the empire. Ignorant and fanatical opposition to authority has frequently led to impatience of all control, political or moral, and given rise to the wildest theories of socialism and communism.

There is a liberal and democratic tendency in the Raskol, notwithstanding its stationary and reactionary character. It sprang into existence not long after the establishment of serfdom; its lowly origin won for it early unconscious sympathy among an enslaved population, to whom it appealed the more strongly from its rejection by their masters. The people, in their material condition, were but little better than the beasts of the field, and the aspirations natural to the heart of man found solace in the prospect of spiritual independence. Their souls, if not their bodies, were their own; and, in the sphere of religious belief, they unwittingly found the opportunity for self-assertion which raised them in their own estimation, and enabled them, in some degree, to realize the dignity of their manhood. Doctrines, to which they were already inclined, met with more hearty response from being at variance with those of their superiors; sympathy for their brethren, oppressed on religious grounds, inspired sympathy for all victims of authority. The Raskol opened its ranks, and afforded protection to the fugitive from justice, as well as to the sufferer from religious persecution. Its many sects, hostile and warring each with the other, were united in opposition, not only to the established Church, but also to the newly constituted order of things throughout; and the spirit of resistance to clerical intolerance was in close accord with resistance to civil authority, each, by mutual reaction, supporting and sustaining the other.

In the vast field of theological discussion there is but slight hinderance to the wildest efforts of the imagination; no material facts, no perfectly ascertained nor minutely defined beliefs arrest the speculative flights of thought, or direct them to positive and necessary conclusions. They may wander on indefinitely, developing most contradictory, yet logical, consequences; and the excitable, imaginative disposition of the Russian people, their devout and superstitious temperament, render them especially prone to indulge in ratiocinations of this nature; while the methodical, argumentative bent of their mind leads them on, from deduction to deduction, to the utmost extremes, which, however irrational, or even absurd, they are boldly prepared to accept. The fundamental dogmas of Orthodoxy, moreover, while being immutable, are simple and elementary, conveyed in language often vague and mysterious, capable of divers interpretations; consequently an inclination to refine and speculate is developed as a means of satisfying a spiritual craving. From this proclivity, freely exercised by an illiterate but intelligent people, untrammelled by any restraint, without guidance from any recognized authority, has arisen the multiplicity of sects in the Raskol, the widely diverging doctrines, the extraordinary, often contradictory, but apparently logical results arrived at from a common starting-point.

From its inception the Raskol seemed doomed to early extinction. The Old Believers originally rebelled in support of ancient rites and ceremonies, and from the first they were confronted by an obstacle fitted to deter men of less enthusiasm or of weaker faith. The only bishop who shared their views, when they rejected Nikon's reforms, was Paul of Kolomna; he was exiled, and died without having consecrated any successor in his episcopal office. The Raskol, thus left without a head, without a bishop to renew and perpetuate its priesthood, without officers to administer the rites which it had been created to defend, seemed paralyzed from its birth. In the opinion of its adherents the Raskol was not merely a doctrinal system that could be propagated by ordinary teachers, it was the true original Church of divine institution, now purified of error, establishing the connection between man and God by the intermediary of a divinely appointed priesthood, capable of transmitting, in regular apostolic succession, the powers received from its Great High Priest. By the bereavement it suffered at the death of its only bishop, all connection with Christ was severed; its mission was frustrated before it had commenced; the reason for its existence and the possibility of its continuance were destroyed by the loss of the sacred authority, without which, as they themselves at first believed, there could be neither Church nor clergy. The difficulty seemed insurmountable, but they had gone too far to recede, and religious enthusiasm stimulated their ingenuity. Two paths only were open; the more exalted and extreme of their number chose the one, the more conservative followed the other, and schism arose within the schism almost at its inception.

DIVISION OF THE RASKOL.

The Raskol was divided into two sects, which have ever remained, each hostile to the other. The adherents of one retained the belief that Christianity, or a Church, could not exist without a priesthood of regular apostolic descent; they held that the Church of Russia had not necessarily, by adopting Nikon's heresy, lost its sacred character, that ordination of priests by its bishops was still valid, and, consequently, that to have a clergy in regular standing they had but to convert and draw to their ranks ministers of the national establishment. These sectarians took the name of "Popovtsi,"[1] or Priest-possessing.

The adherents of the other declared that, by anathematizing true believers, by rejecting ancient traditions, books, and ritual, the National Church had become heretical, and lost all claim to divine power or authority; it was accursed, and its ministers were children of the Evil One; any communication with them was a sin, and consecration or ordination by them was pollution. The Eastern patriarchs shared in the condemnation, and no relief could come from them. Orthodoxy was extinct, apostolic succession and priesthood had perished with it. These fanatics were designated as "Bezpopovtsi,"[2] or those without priests.

The existence of a sacerdotal class, although it was small in number, and composed chiefly of ignorant, venal, or unfrocked popes, prevented the complete separation of the Popovtsi from the established Church, and the utter rejection by them of all Orthodox doctrines. They recognize, and still accept, the sacraments, and have, as will be explained, managed to revive the episcopate and to establish a regular hierarchy of their own.

---

[1] From *pope*, a priest of the Russian Church.
[2] From *bez*, without, and *pope*, a priest.

The Bezpopovtsi, on the contrary, with no stable foundation on which to stay their belief, no guiding authority to direct their steps, have wandered from Christian truth and ordinary morality, ramifying in every conceivable direction, following out, with inexorable logic, to their most extravagant and absurd conclusions the vagaries and eccentricities of individual opinion.

Renouncing the priesthood, they have abandoned all recognized forms of Orthodox or Christian worship; of the seven channels of divine grace, they have rejected all save baptism, which may be administered by lay brethren; the others are closed forever. Most extraordinary and conflicting ideas prevail among them, and each one is free to adopt and to follow such as may seem good in his own eyes. The more timid and superstitious among them, reluctant to accept as final their utter deprivation of all Christian ordinances, and their complete severance from all Church organization, have ransacked their imaginations to devise substitutes for the one and the other wherewith to appease their spiritual cravings. Without priests to hear confession and grant absolution, some confess to elders, some to sisters, as partaking by their sex of the blessing pronounced on Mary, "blessed among women," whom "all generations shall call blessed," and are fain to be content with promises of pardon. Without communion, these famished souls, hungering for holy food, resort to divers ceremonies which are, according to their moods and disposition, either fanciful and touching, or cruel and revolting: dried fruits, distributed by young girls, or flesh cut from a virgin's breast, are partaken of for spiritual refreshment. Amid their extravagances the ludicrous blends with the lugubrious. During the service of Holy Thursday certain of them, known as "gapers" or "yawners," sit for hours with their mouths wide open, waiting for ministering angels to quench their spiritual thirst from invisible chalices. While in constant and patient expectation of a miracle that shall again unite the body of the faithful upon earth with their Father in heaven, the great number of these enthusiasts rub tranquilly along through life, restrained by the engrossing difficulties of an arduous existence and the natural kindliness of the Russian character, from many of the aberrations that should logically follow upon their theories; but the more exalted and fanatic recoil from no consequences, however painful. Their dead are buried without prayer, as they have lived, in sickness and in trouble, without religious consolation; marriage is ignored, family ties and obligations are disregarded, and all the bonds and reciprocal duties upon which society is based are repudiated. This question of marriage is the chief stumbling-block in their path, the principal and fruitful cause of dissension and division among them. The moderate and more practical of their number consider conjugal relations as merely a personal and conventional association, convenient, entitled to respect even, but with nothing sacred or inviolable in its character. The more rigid affirm celibacy to be obligatory, and marriage to be a state of continual sin. Between these two extremes there is room for the wildest and most repulsive theories. Carnal sensuality is allied in monstrous union with religious mysticism. Free love, independence of the sexes, possession of women in common, have been preached and practised. Debauchery, as an incidental weakness of human nature, has been advocated as the lesser evil; libertinism as preferable to concubinage, and the latter as better than marriage. One of their most austere teachers cynically declares that "it is wiser to live with beasts than to be joined to a wife; to frequent many women in secret, rather than live with one openly."[1]

Such are some of the results at which the most scrupulous defenders of ancient rites have arrived from their modest starting-point. In order to preserve intact a few venerable ceremonies, they entered upon their blind and perilous undertaking, and have been led, step by step, to abandon, not merely the doctrines of the Orthodox Church, but all principles of religion and morality. It was not without evident trepidation that even the most fanatic were brought to accept conclusions so abhorrent, however logical in appearance. They have felt the necessity of justifying their course, and as their apology have argued that Christ had abandoned His Church and His people; that the triumph of sin and iniquity was the fulfilment of the prophecies; that the evil days had come when the saints should be troubled and given over to the adversary; that the Church, deprived of its priesthood, was the desolate sanctuary described by Daniel; that Antichrist had come, and the end of all things was drawing nigh. "Why, then," said they, "should the faithful be disquieted within themselves, or sorrow over a ruined Church; why mourn the social wreck, or be concerned for the mortal destinies of the race, when the last trump is about to sound?"

The reign of Antichrist and the coming of the judgment-day is the ever-recurring cry of the Raskolniks generally, but especially of the Bezpopovtsi. Like all religious fanatics, they differ widely among themselves as to the explication and as to the application of their belief in these events. Many of them hold that this period of tribulation may endure for centuries; that it is a third

---

[1] Kavyline, quoted by N. Popof, v. *Revue des Deux Mondes*, Nov. 1er, 1874; article by A. Leroy-Beaulieu.

Dispensation, similar to the old and the new, which both have passed away. The more moderate, together with the Popovtsi, understand them in a spiritual sense; they look more kindly on the civil government and on the established Church, as having been unwittingly made ministers of the powers of darkness, and as being capable of regeneration. The more rabid and extreme of the Bezpopovtsi comprehend them literally. Peter was Antichrist in person, who, in Peter's successors, still sits upon the throne, and the Holy Synod is the ministerial council of His Satanic Majesty. Herein lies a wide difference between the extreme branches of the Raskol, less important in its religious aspect, but more so in its political bearing and consequences. With those who regard the Church and the State as merely wandering from the faith, blind, it may be, to the truth, but not irredeemably perverse, some degree of harmony and some hope of eventual reconciliation are possible; but with the others, for whom all existing institutions, civil and religious, are the incarnation of evil, the handiwork of the devil, no understanding, truce, or peace can be expected.

The general belief in the actual advent of Antichrist has given rise, among the more extreme, who are at the same time the more ignorant and credulous, to the wildest vagaries, subversive of all law, government, and society.

Inasmuch as the tsar was the personification of evil, and his counsellors were imps of Satan, obedience to his decrees was sinful and infamous, and all communication with him or them was pollution. To escape from contamination they fled to desert places and shut themselves up in hidden retreats. Many deemed death preferable to life amid error and iniquity, and shortened their probation in an accursed world by murder and suicide. Certain fanatics, called "Dieto-oubiisti," or Child-killers, felt it a religious duty to slay new-born infants, in order that their souls, innocent of sin, might be sure of heaven without risk of damnation; some known as Stranglers, or Fellers (Doushilstchiki, or Tioukalstchiki), conceived that a violent death was the true way of salvation, pleading in grim earnestness that "the kingdom of heaven suffereth violence; the violent take it by force" (Matthew xi., 12), and piously despatched their relatives and friends by strangulation or blows, in case of mortal illness; others, who were very numerous in the early days of the Raskol, the Philipovtsi, disciples of one Philip, who were also called Burners (Sojigateli), preached redemption by suicide and purification by fire. In the wilds of Siberia and in the Ural Mountains hundreds, whole families at a time, threw themselves into the flames of their burning houses, kindled by their own hands, or offered themselves up on funeral pyres, with prayers and songs, as a holocaust unto the Lord.

Belief in Antichrist and in the triumph of iniquity induced expectation of the millennium and of the second coming of Christ to reign with the faithful for a thousand years. Vehement exhortations of crazed enthusiasts, interpreting literally the prophecies of the Apocalypse, excited the imaginations of the ignorant and superstitious with wild dreams of material happiness soon to be enjoyed by the elect. Even in recent days, in spite of strict laws and prohibitive enactments, impostors have played upon the credulity of the simple and devout population. Accompanied by women, whom they presented for adoration as the Mother of God, or as the Mystic Spouse of the Church, they have asserted themselves to be the promised Messiah, or the "voice of one crying in the wilderness," foretelling the coming of the

THE MILLENNIUM.—WILD ECCENTRICITIES. 205

Lord, and have sent forth their followers as "seekers after Christ" ("iskateli Christa"), to search through the world for the Redeemer. No prediction was too improbable, no extravagance too wild, for credence. Simple peasants, princes of national and foreign lineage, mighty warriors, have been announced as the long-expected Saviour. Napoleon, destroyer of kings, avenger of oppressed nationalities, was hailed as the victorious conqueror who was to put all things under his feet. There are still worshippers in secret at his shrine—his death is denied; he escaped from captivity and found refuge in the depths of Siberia, on the shores of Lake Baikal, from whence he shall come, in the fulness of time, to trample upon Satan and establish the kingdom of peace and righteousness. The ready acceptance of doctrines so strange and fanciful must be ascribed in great measure to the existence among the people of vague aspirations, similar to those among the ancient Jews, to ardent desire for freedom and for relief from slavery, to a universal longing for emancipation from serfdom and its burdens, to the hope and expectation of a future repartition of the soil. Promises of coming liberty and assurances of participation in the wealth of their masters, based on Biblical prophecies, were welcome to an oppressed and suffering population.

The abolition of serfdom was enthusiastically hailed as the commencement of the final revolution, the beginning of the end so eagerly desired and so long waited for. It deprived, for a while, the preachers of revolt and resistance of their most formidable arguments, and checked the growth of the extreme and fanatical sects of the Raskol. As, however, this benevolent measure failed to immediately realize their extravagant anticipations, in their ignorance and impatience, incapable of comprehending its operation or of appreciating the beneficent results destined to flow from it, they have made the tardy realization of its blessings a fresh departure for denunciation of the authorities, who, as they aver, ever seek to defraud the people of their rights. The influence of these apostles of disorder and evil is still sorely felt, but it has diminished, and must eventually yield to the era of progress and enlightenment inaugurated by Alexander the Emancipator.

Russia is not alone subject to the reproach of extraordinary and extravagant ideas, nor may their existence be solely attributed to the ignorance and degradation of her people; they have had their counterpart in England and in America, under very different conditions. The Ironsides of Cromwell, the Puritans of New England, bear strong resemblance to the Old Believers, and for originality, eccentricity, and multiplicity of religious creeds, the Anglo-Saxon is in no whit inferior to the Muscovite of White Russia. The great republic of the New World and the vast empire of the North complacently find many points of contact, and this one is, perhaps, of all, the most remarkable. Prophets and prophetesses of divers revelations have rallied around them, in America, disciples by thousands; no doctrine has been too absurd, no creed too subversive of order or of morality, to find acceptance and gather adherents there among Mormons, Millerites, advocates of free love, and multitudinous sects of similar description.

This singular analogy between two people of such different antecedents and character, surrounded by influences so opposite and antagonistic, is susceptible, in some degree at least, of explanation. In one case there has been extraordinary exuberance of ideas, excessive individuality of opinion, a vigorous spirit of initiative and innovation, independence of thought, and impatience of authority; these characteristics, combined with strong devotional tendencies inherited from a Puritan ancestry, have overflowed the natural channels of politics and industry into those of religious speculation and creeds. In the other, the domain of religious thought was the only one open to the aspirations and struggling efforts of the popular mind, the only sphere in which the intelligence of the people could move freely and without repression, or find opportunity for its expression and development. Mournful as have been the results attained in Russia, they bear, in their vigor, fecundity, and originality, strong proof of intellectual energy and vitality in the Russian people, of singleness of purpose, and of deep sense of religious obligation; great qualities in themselves, which are, if rightly directed, essential elements in the growth of a great nation.

CHAPTER X.

The Raskol Socially and Politically.—Praobrajenski and Rogojski.—Organization of Popovtsism and Bezpopovtsism.—Attempts at Reconciliation with the Church.—The Edinovertsi.—Modification of Raskol; its Extreme Sects.

THE Raskol has, during its existence of more than two centuries, exerted a wide, varied, and deeply-felt influence upon the Russian nation, and has, in its turn, undergone great changes and modifications from the pressure of surrounding circumstances.

Having considered it in its spiritual and religious bearing upon the mental and moral condition of the people, and upon the progress of civilization in Russia, and having traced the results flowing from it in this direction, it is necessary, for a full comprehension of the influence it has had, and still exercises, to view it in its social and political aspect; this is not less important, and it presents for investigation phenomena of an equally complex and peculiar nature; it will also be interesting to examine the counter effect produced upon it in the gradual development of the nation during a long series of years, and its present position, as an essential element of the Russian social fabric.

Any attempt to estimate the power and the influence of the Raskol, by ascertaining the extent of its sway and the number of its adherents, can give but vague and indefinite results, from the want of sufficient data whereupon to base an opinion. Official reports profess to exhibit the statistics of all the sects within the empire; the Raskolniks are included, and, by the census of 1871, they number about eleven hundred thousand. This figure is, by all competent authority, rejected as much below the actual truth, and the estimates made by those most capable of judging vary from two to fifteen millions. The Raskolniks do not themselves pretend to know with any degree of accuracy, and only affirm that "they are very numerous."

The government lists embrace only those who have, generation after generation, refused to be enrolled upon the parish registers, and who openly profess to be schismatics. Besides these there are the many who either timidly shun the avowal of their affiliation or who belong secretly to prohibited sects, and they comprise a very numerous class. A Russian writer, about twelve years ago, basing his calculation upon a careful examination of the reports of the Holy Synod regarding the religious condition of the people, arrived at a total of from nine to ten millions. Competent specialists of recent date[1] reckon them at fifteen millions. These latter figures may be excessive, but an estimate of ten or eleven millions is probably not an exaggerated one to-day (1886), and it agrees substantially with such information as can be derived from the Raskolniks themselves. It is certain that their number is rapidly increasing. Figures, however, give but a partial and inadequate idea of the extent and influence of the movement. Apart from those who may be said to be enrolled in its ranks, whether as public professors or as secret adherents, there is a very much larger number who, without actively joining, are in sympathy, more or less earnest, with it. As a general rule,

---

[1] Schédo-Ferroti, "La tolérance et le Schisme religieux en Russie," p. 153, cited by Leroy-Beaulieu, in an article of *La Revue des Deux Mondes,* Mai 1er, 1875.

the peasant or laborer who remains true to the Orthodox Church does not look down upon the Raskolniks as heretics to be hated or despised. On the contrary, he feels, rather, respect for them as holy men, more pious and devout than himself, ready, like the early Christians, to brave obloquy and reproach for the ancient faith. Until recent ameliorations in the morals and condition of the official clergy removed from it the well-merited charge of greed, ignorance, and indolence, it compared unfavorably with the often disinterested, always active and energetic, propagators of Dissent; the Church suffered in popular estimation from the comparison, even among its own children, while the Raskol gained. This feeling of sympathy for it is general; it is evinced in constant willingness to befriend, or screen, its adherents; it is deep-rooted and persistent. By many, even of the more liberal members of the Orthodox communion, it is believed and feared that a very large portion of the nation would lapse into Dissent if all restraint were removed, and grave apprehensions of the consequences to the Church of any radical measures of relief are a serious obstacle to the recognition of perfect freedom of conscience.

The strength of the schism is not to be measured by the number of its adherents or by the extent of popular sympathy with it; there is an additional element to be considered, which is the character of that portion of the nation in which it arose, and where it still exists in its fullest development.

Ridiculed and despised by the educated and the noble, it flourished especially among the people, and was recruited almost wholly among the laboring classes, peasants and mechanics, shop-keepers and petty merchants. In its origin a religious movement, it became a social and political one when the violent reforms of Peter the Great divided the nation, and created two hostile camps, with no feeling of reciprocal obligations or any common bond of union. Partisans of the ancient faith were upholders of ancient customs, and rallied to their side the opponents of social innovations and of civil changes. Religious enthusiasts sympathized with Old Muscovites, and the national party with Old Believers. This union was, however, a union among the lower classes; the noble, the wealthy, the ambitious, with few exceptions, followed the emperor's lead, and looked, with all the haughty superciliousness of that age, upon the people and upon popular opinion. The contempt of the great world was an effectual protection to the Raskol, and exercised its adherents in habits of meekness and patience. When, as it frequently happened, attention was drawn to them, and persecution followed, their common sufferings cemented their union and strengthened their endurance; but their lowly estate was their best safeguard in the early days; the movement prospered in obscurity, and attained formidable proportions before it was deemed of consequence or inspired apprehension. Although, at times, assailed at the instance of the Church, or, ignorantly serving as a tool in the hands of ambitious and unsuccessful schemers, it shared their fate and punishment, the crisis past, it fell back again into the shadow of its insignificance, and, with occasional vicissitudes, was, for a century and a half, alike ignored and neglected. Burrowing in the lower strata of social life, protected by its seclusion, it steadily increased and ramified. Strong devotional feeling and earnest convictions developed the moral sense among its adherents to a high degree. Every member of a community, the character of which may be affected by the behavior of the persons who compose it, is interested to watch carefully over his own demeanor and over that of his brethren, and the mutual support which results therefrom contributed, in the case of the Raskolniks, to raise the standard of morality among them. Their religious belief and practices encouraged sobriety and frugality; habit of free inquiry, and attempt at independence of thought upon spiritual matters, were followed by general increase of intelligence, and, under these influences, the Raskolniks, gradually and justly, won the reputation of being the most honest, the most capable, and the most reliable portion of the population. They were also banded together by a species of free-masonry, a common feeling of necessary co-operation and resistance to their powerful adversaries, while constant fear of persecution kept their zeal alive. To the vigor imparted by these causes, of a moral nature, are to be added the energy and independence resulting from the accumulation of wealth. Besides the special influence of the teachings of their creed, which preserved them from the besetting sins of the Russian people, self-indulgence and intemperance, they felt the impulse of other agencies, more general and more practical in their character.

Sects and races oppressed by persecution, excluded from all part or interest in public or national affairs, find vent for their activity, and for the exercise of their intelligence, in industrial, financial, or commercial enterprises. This has been the case with the Jews throughout the world, with the Armenians in the East and the Parsees in India; and the pursuit of wealth or of material prosperity, as the principal object in life for generations, has usually developed an hereditary and peculiar aptitude for its acquisition. This result is also true of the Raskolniks, although, doubtless, from the circumstances of their situation, to a less extent and degree. At the same time, instinctively, and in view of the universal corruption of the administration, they realized that wealth was for them a tower of strength against their oppressors. At Moscow, many of the finest houses and the largest factories belong to Old Believers; at Perm, and in the mining districts of the Ural, they are the most substantial capitalists. Their success has been sufficiently marked to excite the envy of their competitors, and to arouse clamorous complaints of a threatened monopoly by them of industrial and financial undertakings. Their system of mutual assistance and support is another secret of their prosperity, and many, indifferent to their principles, have joined their ranks to profit by their tacitly recognized co-operative organization.

Among them, as in every community, there are intriguing and ambitious men, ready to make use of the enthusiasm of their more simple brethren, and to advance their own ends at the expense of their neighbors; but the Raskolniks cannot, as a body, be accused of being actuated entirely by selfish motives; they are liberal and charitable, and many of them dispense their wealth freely and generously in the endowment of schools and benevolent institutions; some, even, in the encouragement of art and literature, although, in this respect, their munificence is generally, and in conformity with their prejudices, confined to what is national and Russian.

With increasing riches, and the accompanying tendency to luxury of living, there has been considerable relaxation in the severity of their habits and practices, more inclination to mingle with the outer world and share in its duties and pleasures. Deficient education has limited the influence of this temptation, but, in the nature of things, it is destined to continue and to extend with the progress of enlightenment and of modern civilization, and will introduce greater changes and modifications in the character and principles of the Raskol.

The healthy development which might have been expected from its habit of free inquiry, and from the freedom accorded to individual opinion, has been effectually hampered, not only by actual want of education, but also by the cramping and restricted nature of the few studies permitted.

The Raskolniks were, and are, strongly opposed to all modern, and especially to all foreign, ideas; their ears are closed to what they deem new-fangled notions, whether of domestic or foreign origin, as being tainted with impiety and heresy; they rest content with their ancient Slavonic literature, with the Scriptures, with old devotional books; they deliberately shut themselves up in a world of their own, fenced about by inveterate prejudices; they turn round and round within a narrow circle, the bounds of which their thoughts, however unrestrained therein, may never pass. Here lies the essential difference between Russian Raskol and German Protestantism: the one is sectional, narrow-minded, bigoted, jealous, and pharasaical; the other is universal, whole-souled, liberal, generous, and tolerant.

A geographical and ethnological chart of the Raskol would show it to be very unevenly distributed over the land. It flourishes best among the most energetic and vigorous of the population, in and around the ancient cities, among the peasants of the North, the miners of the Ural, the pioneers of Siberia, and the Cossacks of the Southeast. It is indigenous to Great Russia, and while its adherents are found in other provinces throughout the whole empire, amid Orthodox, Roman Catholic, and Protestant communities, they are generally colonists from Great Russia, who live apart from their neighbors, and, making few proselytes, are recruited from their original homes.

It is a natural and distinctive product of the old Muscovite race, which, although obstinate, full of prejudices, and not inclined to change, is realistic and superstitious, better satisfied with the form and outward symbol than curious to investigate the essence, or foundation, of its belief, and, above all, is intensely national.

Outward surroundings have had great influence, and the predominance of Old Believers in the most distant and less populous districts is not accidental, but is a natural result of the condition of the people who are thus isolated; they have little intercourse with one another, and still less with the outer world; they remain more primitive in their habits, and cling more persistently and more reverently to ancient customs.

The distribution of the two great branches of the Raskol is in harmony with historic precedent. The lay element of religious communities is ever apt to assert itself more boldly in the cold and rude regions of the North than in milder and more genial climes, and accordingly the Popovtsi, who retain a priesthood, are found chiefly towards the South, among the Cossacks of the Don, along the banks of the lower Volga, and of the river Ural; while the Bezpopovtsi, who reject priests and all Church government, occupy the shores of the White Sea, the neighborhood of the great lakes, the slopes of the Ural Mountains, and the solitudes of Siberia; the convent of Vygoretsk, in the wild and desolate region through which flows the river Vyg, was their most important centre. These northern governments are of prodigious extent: Archangel equals France and Italy together; Vologda and Perm are each as large as England. But few churches, and these distant many days' journey one from the other, are scattered over these vast territories; the number of priests is small, as it is fixed according to the population, which is scanty. The inhabitants do not congregate in villages of any size, but are sparsely distributed over the whole region; roads, where any exist, are bad, often impassable, and the climate is inclement and stormy. Attendance at church is, perforce, limited to rare occasions, and pastoral visits are almost unknown. From want of intercourse with their parishioners the clergy lost authority and influence over them; the peasant, isolated in his isba,[1] learned to suffice for his own needs, and became independent of priestly aid, even on the most solemn occasions. Left to himself, he looked to the Scriptures for his guide, and interpreted them according to his feeble and limited light; he had not the resources of the Protestant Puritan in education, nor in the accumulated wisdom of the Christian fathers and ancient philosophers. Were he capable of, and did he care for investigation, he could, at best, rely only on the bewildering scholastic treatises of Byzantine theologians; a little learning is dangerous, and his mind was starved with indigestible food, filled with crude or false ideas, erroneously comprehended, and his imagination was fired by mystical sophisms.

Some Russian writers have attributed the preponderance of the Bezpopovtsi, in the north of Russia, to the influence of the neighboring Protestant nations of the north of Europe, but this hypothesis is unnecessary for the explanation of the fact, and it is not in accordance with the peculiarly indigenous, national character of the movement, whether it be considered at its inception or in its most radical development.

---

[1] *Isba* is the hut, or cabin, of the Russian peasant.

Geographically speaking, the ancient metropolis, Moscow, is the religious centre of the Raskol, from whence its missions, or colonies, went forth, either voluntarily or driven out by persecution.

The Old Believers could cross no ocean, like the English Puritans, to bar pursuit, but they could find refuge against oppression in the vast solitudes of their native land, or over the borders among the neighboring people. As exiles, or as emigrants, they carried their doctrines and their nationality beyond the great lakes, over the Ural Mountains, and into the Caucasus; they sought safety and peace among the Protestants of the Baltic provinces, the Catholics of Poland, and the Mussulmans of the East. Vetka, a village of ancient Poland, in the province of Mogilev, became, at an early day, the headquarters of the Popovtsi; there, rapid increase in their numbers and in their wealth, activity in the propagation of their doctrines, aroused the suspicions and the jealousy of the Russian government. Twice, in 1735, under Anna Ivanovna, and in 1764, under Catherine II., Russian troops violated Polish territory to attack and suppress them. On the first occasion Vetka was destroyed, and its 40,000 inhabitants, forced back into Russia, were distributed through the southern provinces. They obtained permission to settle among their co-religionists of Russian Ukraine, near Staradoub,[1] and gathered there, within a few years, over fifty thousand adherents around the new sanctuary. Vetka also soon regained nearly its former importance, and was, a second time, destroyed by Catherine II.

Many colonies of Raskolniks were established just beyond what were then the boundaries of the empire; some

---

[1] *Staradoub* means the old oak.

were induced to return to their native land by the liberal promises of Catherine II.; others have again come under Russian sway by the conquest of the countries in which they were settled. A number still remain on foreign soil; one at Gumbinnen, in Prussia; several in Bukovina, an Austrian province; others in European Turkey and Asia Minor. They have always held aloof from the people about them, and retained strong traces of their Muscovite nationality and origin. The safety they thus secured, and their liberation from Russian control, have proved of signal advantage to the Raskol, and enabled it to arrive subsequently at a regular and independent organization, such as, if kept totally within the empire, it never could have realized.

A complete and comprehensive system of organization for the Raskol, as a whole, in a religious sense, was rendered impossible by insuperable difficulties.

The absence of any well-defined theological creed or standard, the free exercise allowed to individual opinion, have given rise to innumerable sects. Upwards of two hundred were reckoned in the eighteenth century; many have disappeared, and are disappearing; more have arisen, and are constantly arising, harmonizing, like the denominations of Protestantism, to a certain extent, but without having a similarly stable, definite, and universally accepted basis of belief, and expressing every conceivable variety of doctrine.

As a social or political institution, in which the religious element enters to a large degree, the consolidation of the Raskol, accomplished with very considerable, if not entire, success, was facilitated by the peculiar spirit of association, and by the aptitude for self-government which are characteristics of the Russian people.

The leaders, succeeding to the inflammatory enthusiasts who originated the movement—the Denissoffs and Koveline, with many others—have generally been men of action and practical sense, evincing great administrative ability. They have, by their energy and skilful management, given a material unity and solidity to the Raskol which it could never have attained if it had continued to be, as at the first, simply a religious manifestation.

For one of the two great branches of the Raskol, for Popovtsism, the difficulties in the way of a religious organization arose chiefly from circumstance, and not from principle, and they were consequently far less formidable than the obstacles encountered by the other branch, Bezpopovtsism. The former has recently arrived at a solution of the problem which proves apparently satisfactory, and is accepted by the great majority of its adherents, though not by all; before treating of this event, however, it will be interesting to review the vicissitudes through which it passed.

The recognition of the necessity of a priesthood for the existence of a Church maintained, among the Popovtsi, the ancient dogmas of Orthodoxy, and preserved the unity of the faith. Indulgence in freedom of interpretation was more circumscribed, and division into sects, by differences of individual opinion, was less frequent than among the Bezpopovtsi. Almost the only element of controversy was the conditions requisite for the admission of popes. As their clergy was recruited among refugees from the established Church, they were contemptuously styled "Beglopopovtsi,"[1] or "Community of runaway priests." These popes, before reception, were subjected to humiliating ordeals of abjuration, purification, and penitence; they were rebaptized; some-

---

[1] From *beglii*, runaway, and *pope*, priest.

times immersed in full canonicals, lest, by a prior removal of their insignia, their sacred attributes should be washed away.

Not much respect could be felt for men thrust forth from their own Church for misconduct, or tempted from it by cupidity. Generally they were well remunerated, but held in light esteem as mere hirelings, in accidental possession of certain exclusive powers. They were treated with increasing indifference in process of time, and deacons, or even unordained persons, were accepted and allowed to officiate; they were kept in strict dependence, and had but little influence over the congregations who paid their stipend, chose or rejected them at pleasure, and retained all power and authority in their own hands. This predominance of the lay element in the administration of Church affairs was a common feature of both branches of the Raskol.

From their early days the Raskolniks of both divisions favored the establishment of "skeets," or hermitages, convents, and similar institutions, in remote districts, or over the border in an adjacent country, to serve as places of refuge and religious centres. Dissensions, rivalries, differences of opinion, creating numerous sects, constantly arose, and no one establishment among them all rose to any pre-eminence, or was able to impose its authority as supreme over either the one or the other branch.

A terrible public calamity afforded them both an opportunity, of which they cleverly availed, to remedy this grievous want of a central head.

The plague broke out at Moscow during the reign of Catherine II., and raged with unparalleled fury; all efforts of the government to stay its ravages or to afford adequate relief were insufficient. In this appalling crisis the empress made appeal to the charity and generosity of all her subjects for the general good. Great public misfortunes level minor distinctions and draw together communities suffering from a common evil; the people responded heartily to their sovereign's call, regardless of class or creed, and among the first to offer their services were the Feodocians.

This sect, named from its founder, Feodoceï, was an offshoot from the Pomortsi, or Dwellers by the seashore, a very numerous branch of the Bezpopovtsi, inhabiting the region between the great lakes and the White Sea. It seceded from the main body, whose centre was at Vygoretsk, on the river Vyg, early in the eighteenth century, on account of the extreme violence and ultra nature of the opinions of its adherents and their fanatical enthusiasm.

About 1737 it first appeared at Moscow, where it labored secretly, but most earnestly, to propagate its doctrines, which were eminently hostile to the government, and maintained the principle of resistance to the tsar as Antichrist. Its efforts were crowned with such measure of success as to render it one of the most influential of the many sects of the Bezpopovtsi.

Its leaders, shrewd and astute men, saw their opportunity in the public distress, and, masking an ulterior purpose under the guise of solicitude for the general welfare, begged permission to contribute to the measures of relief, and offered to create, at their own expense, hospitals for their sick, and to give burial to their dead. Other sects of the Bezpopovtsi joined with them, and the Popovtsi followed the example. Charitable impulses, always strong and easily aroused among the Russian people, were stimulated by the evident contingent advantages likely to accrue, and which the Raskolniks, from their greater spirit of initiative and intelligence, were quick to realize. Their request was granted in 1771, and immediately the Bezpopovtsi at Praobrajenski, and the Popovtsi at Rogojski, outlying and desert suburbs of Moscow, founded the establishments which became, each respectively for its own branch, the headquarters of the Raskol. They were under the direction of men animated by fervent religious enthusiasm, but possessed also of sound practical sense, knowledge of business, and great sagacity; they could, moreover, depend implicitly upon the obedience and devotion of their followers, and were amply supplied by them with the necessary funds.

At first they were content with what the emergencies of the times demanded, having, however, wise forethought for the future. Very extensive grounds were surrounded by high walls, within which cemeteries were set apart and hospitals erected, secluded from public curiosity. Acting with consummate prudence and circumspection, they sedulously seized upon every favorable opportunity to extend their privileges, insisting upon the charitable nature and purpose of their work, but always humble and avoiding attention, quietly profiting by the general disdain which they inspired, and skilfully availing themselves of their wealth to influence the venal and corrupt officials of the government.

Under Alexander I., Koveline, a leader of the Feodocians, a very adroit and able manager, succeeded in obtaining a very much larger measure of independence, with permission to create homes for the destitute and similar benevolent institutions. Concessions accorded to one branch were extended to the other, and, within comparatively few years, these modest establishments had grown to be great and powerful communities, had acquired official recognition under regular charters, secured the right of self-organization and government, with authority to manage their property and affairs free from clerical or official supervision; they had each a corporate seal, a treasury, their own laws and regulations, administered by a council or governing body almost totally without control.

Around these centres the Raskolniks gathered in great numbers, building houses, establishing shops and factories, until these once deserted suburbs were transformed into flourishing and populous districts. Thus within the ancient capital, the stronghold of Orthodoxy, despised and persecuted followers of a proscribed creed finally secured foothold, and found safe refuge under the ægis of government protection.

From these headquarters their influence radiated forth over the whole land; they created subsidiary branches, subject to the central authority, and gathered in abundant wealth from gifts and bequests; at the height of their prosperity they were said to have had in their treasuries the enormous sum of ten millions of roubles (about £1,300,000).[1] Their leaders, combining to a remarkable degree worldly shrewdness with religious enthusiasm, made these establishments, not merely centres for the propagation of their doctrines, but also centres of trade, of manufactures, and of commerce. They offered, not only a home for their destitute and suffering brethren, but a refuge for all fugitives, outlaws, deserters, and wanderers, who, under pretence of religious sympathy, claimed protection and succor, and in this motley army of followers they found cheap and willing tools, ignorant but zealous emissaries. During the tolerant reigns of Catherine II. and Alexander I. these institutions had

---

[1] See note, page 174.

grown to such proportions as to excite popular jealousy and government suspicions; their leaders were accused of illicit and underhand machinations, of secret plotting, dangerous to public welfare and to the authority of the State; they became involved in lawsuits and disputes regarding property alleged to have been obtained under false pretences, or by bequests under pressure of improper influences. An inquiry was ordered by Nicholas, which resulted in the confiscation of their riches, the sequestration of their buildings and estates, and, gravest calamity of all, in the loss of their independence. The hospitals and cemeteries were left to their charge, but an imperial commissioner was added to their board of administration. Their religious services were prohibited, and their churches were closed or handed over to priests appointed by the Holy Synod.

By this last measure the Popovtsi suffered equally with their radical brethren of the other branch, inasmuch as their clergy, although of Orthodox ordination, were, as renegades from the established Church, forbidden to officiate.

Rogojski, the headquarters of Popovtsism, had provided means for its social organization, but it never had possessed any sacred authority, and had not, nor could it have, satisfied the eager aspirations of its disciples for an ecclesiastical government of divine origin.

For many long and weary years they had endeavored to find an escape from their only, but humiliating, method of recruiting the priesthood, and to establish a hierarchy of their own of regular apostolic descent. Some among them had advocated as efficacious the imposition of hands by a deceased prelate, present at least in the flesh, but the ceremony was incomplete; a corpse could not, and no one present could for it, pronounce the sacramental words. Every effort, for well-nigh two hundred years, had proved futile, but a solution of this grave problem was reached at last during the troubled revolutionary period towards the middle of the present century, and it came from a quarter as strange as it was unexpected.

These old Muscovites, the most conservative and reactionary of the population, "Russians, sons of Russians," were, by a singular contradiction, indebted for it to men with whom they had nothing in common, who were bitterly opposed to what they held in deepest reverence. Their new auxiliaries were, primarily, political exiles from Russia, who were in open revolt against their sovereign. They were aided by the emissaries of radicalism and revolution throughout Europe, who saw in the Russian emperor the chief opponent of their schemes.

The Raskol seemed to offer a fertile field for their operations; its multitudinous ramifications and hidden affiliations all over the land afforded every opportunity for secret plotting and intrigue. Its millions of adepts, although intelligent and prosperous, were ignorant and credulous, enthusiastic and easily excited; they were, for the most part, from precept and education, at heart hostile to the government, and would, if their sympathies could be aroused, prove a terrible foe to the authoritative and autocratic principle personified by the tsar. Actuated by these ideas, the revolutionary leaders endeavored to unite the liberal progressive party of young Russia with the old Muscovite conservatives, but these antagonistic elements could not harmonize; they were too widely at variance; the modern scepticism, or atheism, of the radicals shocked the profoundly religious sentiments of the Old Believers; while, from a political point of view, they could never agree, and the attempt failed. The effort was, however, suggestive, and shortly afterwards, partisans of Polish nationality seized upon the idea which prompted it as a means of arousing powerful opposition to the oppressor of their country's liberties. With wider views and a better comprehension of the situation, they not only saw a possible nucleus of resistance among the Old Believers, but they also devised a way of rendering it available for their purposes. They conceived the bold plan of creating, for these schismatics, a religious centre beyond the boundaries of the empire; of consolidating the various elements of opposition existing in the numerous discontented and disaffected sects scattered throughout the land, by providing for them a supreme pontiff whom they would all recognize and obey. They expected, by thus satisfying their ardent and long-deferred aspirations for a spiritual head, to insure their sympathy and connivance. In order to render their co-operation effectual, and to make it subservient to the aims of the Polish party, it was essential that this pontiff should have his seat where he would be safe from all attempts of the imperial government; and that, while apparently free to exercise independent action, he should be under the influence and control of the insurrectionary leaders.

They commenced operations among a colony of Cossack Old Believers, situated in the Dobrutscha, near the Russian frontier, who had emigrated in the eighteenth century, and who still maintained close and frequent relations with their co-religionists within the empire. By exciting hopes of a re-establishment of their ancient faith, by vague and illusory promises of Cossack independence, as naturally following the restoration of Polish nationality, their confidence was gained, and, through them, the expectations of their brethren in Russia were aroused.

After many long and fruitless researches a personage,

endowed with the necessary qualifications and willing to accept the position, was discovered among the Eastern prelates. Ambrosius, formerly Primate of Bosnia, recently deposed by the Patriarch of Constantinople, consented to adopt the creed of the Old Believers, and to become their head. In 1846 he was formally installed as metropolitan, and established his official residence in an important convent of their community at Belo-Krinitsa (Fontana-alba), in Bukovina, a province of Gallicia. The situation, at a point where the three great Slavonic empires meet, was well chosen. It lies within Austrian territory, and Austria was not sorry to have within its grasp this thorn in the Russian side, wherewith to counteract or retaliate for Russian intrigues among her Slavonic population. After many vicissitudes, depending on the shifting political relations of the two empires, Ambrosius finally secured tranquil possession of his eccclesiastical throne. His authority was speedily acknowledged by the Old Believers in Austria and Turkey; in Russia there was more hesitation, but, notwithstanding the repugnance of some of the more conservative to accept a foreigner, or, as they styled him, "a priest from beyond the sea," as their spiritual chief, he was formally so recognized by the leaders of the Raskol at Rogojski, and by the great body of their followers.

His first step was the creation of a regular episcopate. He divided the empire into dioceses, and appointed bishops subject to his authority, as in England the pope of Rome established a Catholic hierarchy, independent of the English government.

These schismatic prelates and their priests, known to the initiated only, are active and zealous emissaries; they officiate in secret and in disguise, wander freely over the land, protected by the devotion of their adherents, or, if detected, easily purchasing immunity from venal officials with the abundant resources at their command.

Danger to Russia was apprehended from the existence, beyond the control of its government, of an irresponsible power, wielding such extensive authority over a large portion of the population, and it formed the subject of frequent remonstrance and of much diplomatic correspondence with Austria. It was a constant annoyance to the Emperor Nicholas, whose haughty spirit could ill brook the slight to his authority. He was angered that his determination to stamp out Dissent should be thwarted by this insignificant chief of a despised sect, whose adherents were an ignorant mob of peasants and serfs. Opposition on their part to his attempts to Russianize Poland was feared by him, and expected by the Poles, but both were disappointed; the loyalty of the Old Believers to the tsar proved stronger than their gratitude to the Polish patriots, and, as apprehensions from this source disappeared, the existence of a schismatic pontiff was disregarded. Ambrosius, alternately suppressed, ignored, and tolerated by Austria, as circumstances dictated, died in possession of his ecclesiastical dignity. Cyril, a Russian, succeeded, and, during the Crimean war, disaffection, possibly overt resistance to imperial authority, was feared, but again patriotism and national sentiment rose superior to ceremonial differences, and the Old Believers recognized in the Turks the traditional enemy of Orthodoxy and holy Russia.

The accession of Alexander II. aroused hopes of a brighter future. The elders of Rogojski induced their metropolitan to visit his flock; he came to Russia in 1863, disguised and secretly, but probably with the connivance of the government.

A council, under his direction, established regulations for the Popovtsi, and this branch of the Raskol, thus provided with a regular hierarchy and a complete organization, seemed definitively constituted as an independent and united Church. Dissensions, however, soon arose; the new clergy, less docile than their renegade predecessors, resented the domination of the lay element in the community, and arrogated to themselves an authority which the congregations were reluctant to acknowledge. The council, from prudential motives, maintained Belo-Krinitsa as the seat of the pontiff, but appointed a vicar to reside in Russia as his representative; the metropolitan, suspicious, and apprehensive of diminution of his dignity, refused to delegate his powers to a vicegerent. By this conflict of authority Popovtsism was, ere its organization had attained full maturity, threatened with internal divisions.

In the midst of these dissensions the Polish insurrection of 1863 broke out, and the Old Believers again fell under suspicion, and were threatened with the harsh treatment which doubtful allegiance would merit. They indignantly repudiated the charges of treachery and treason, and eagerly offered pledges of their loyalty "to God and the Tsar." They sent Cyril back to his foreign home, and the council proposed to cease, for a time, all relations with him. Their leaders at Rogojski addressed the emperor with assurances of their fidelity, and issued an encyclical letter to all members of the "Holy Catholic Apostolic Church of the Old Believers," with an exposition of their doctrines calculated to conciliate the authorities of the established Church and of the State, declaring that "the Old Believers who recognize the necessity of a priesthood agree in all questions of dogma with the Greco-Russian Church; they worship the same God, believe in the same Jesus Christ, and are truly more in accord with the national Church than are all sects who reject the priesthood." They anathematized revolutionists as "enemies of religion and of country," as "children of the impious Voltaire;" and affirmed that the official Church and that of the Old Believers, being in harmony on all fundamental points, may exist, side by side, in mutual toleration and Christian brotherhood.

These declarations at this critical period were gladly welcomed by the emperor and the Holy Synod, and aroused hopes of eventual agreement and reunion.

Language of this tenor, held by the descendants of the stern enthusiasts who, two centuries previously, had held both Church and State to be accursed, indicates the great change that had taken place among the members of this branch of the Raskol.

There were still among them some who fanatically adhered to their ancient prejudices, and, on the subject of the circular published by their leaders, the Popovtsi were divided; by far the greater number, and the more intelligent, known as the "Okroujniki," or "Circularists," approved of it; the minority, comprising the more ignorant and obstinate, called the "Razdorniki," or "those who quarrel," maintained the primitive doctrines of the schism, and renewed the controversy upon the spelling of the name Jesus, stoutly averring that the "Christ Iissous" of the State Church could not be the same divine person as the "Christ Issous" of the Old Believers, and must be Antichrist.

A second council, convened at Belo-Krinitsa, served only to further embitter the discussion, to weaken the authority of their primate, and to detach from their body many of its influential partisans.

Under these circumstances, with an evident desire on

either side for reconciliation, a speedy end to Popovtsism, by its absorption into the Mother Church, might seem probable, but many obstacles still intervene, and chief among them is the difficulty of satisfying their rival pretensions.

Old Believers insist upon the ancient rites; they further demand that, having been condemned by a council, they shall, with equal solemnity, be absolved by a council, and acknowledged to have ever been steadfast in the Orthodox faith; the Holy Synod might yield, as regards ceremonies and verbal differences, but, as to the graver question of doctrine, it exacts submission, recognition of error in the past, and repentance, before it can allow the Church to receive them back into full communion.

A similar desire on the part of the State and of the Synod to end and heal the schism in the Church was evinced during the tolerant reign of Catherine II., towards the close of the eighteenth century. In order to restore unity and bring Dissenters back to their allegiance, they were ready with every concession possible. The ritual in use before the days of Nikon was acknowledged to be canonical, and priests were specially ordained to officiate in accordance with it. Some of the Old Believers, less imbued with prejudice, or more tolerant in matters of conscience, yielded to the earnest appeals and exhortations of the clergy, supported by the influence and authority of the government, and were enrolled alongside, as it were, of the Orthodox in regular standing, as belonging to a branch of the established Church, under the appellation of "Edinovertsi," or "Uniate Believers."[1]

Had a similar step been taken when Alexis was on

---

[1] From *edin*, one, and *vera*, faith.

the throne it might have stifled the Raskol at its birth; nearly all that had been demanded originally was accorded, but it could no longer suffice. A century and more had passed—long years of struggling, persecution, and suffering; Dissent had crystallized and hardened into schism, with habits of independence and of free inquiry; it had become impatient of control, with an individuality of its own, social and political, as well as religious, and a deeper principle than one of mere ceremony was at stake. The sincerity of those in power was doubted; Old Ritualists, now Old Believers and schismatics, feared the Church and the gifts it proffered.

Catherine's plan was in many respects akin to that of the pope when he created the Greek Uniate Church as a middle ground between the creeds of Moscow and Rome, with the jesuitical hope, in either case, that, having traversed half the distance separating Catholicism, or the Raskol, from Orthodoxy, the semi-convert might be easily induced to complete the journey.

The restrictions imposed upon the Edinovertsi were the most obvious hinderances to the prosperity of the sect. It could not be recruited from among the members of the established Church, of whom many were in secret sympathy with Dissent, but might have been satisfied with this intermediate creed, inasmuch as secession from the Orthodox communion was absolutely prohibited; it was not acceptable to the great body of those who openly professed to be Old Believers, on account of its halting, temporizing character, and of the incompleteness of its organization. The Greek Uniate Church, to which it has been compared above, had owed its success in a large degree not merely to a special liturgy and ritual, but also to the possession of a regular and independent hierarchy; to Edinovertsism no episcopate was allowed, and its priests were ordained by, and subordinate to, the bishops of the established Church; they consequently inspired neither confidence nor respect, but rather suspicion and dislike, as the paid functionaries of an alien, if not a hostile, authority, and the denomination itself occupied an inferior, uncertain, and humiliating position, being neither one thing nor the other.

The real and most serious obstacle to its success was the radical change wrought by time in the principle and spirit of this branch of the Raskol, and which also affords an explanation of its persistent vitality. It was no longer a mere stickling for ancient form and ceremony; it had become, what it now actually is, the expression of popular resistance to the enforced union of civil and religious government, to the absolute dependence of the Church upon the State.

Old Believers, accustomed by long habit to freedom from clerical authority, favor the separation of the spiritual from the temporal. While they demand the ancient rites and former ecclesiastical constitution, with a national patriarch as supreme head of the Church, they do so with a keen sense of the importance of restricting clerical power within due bounds, and of giving the lay portion of the community its just and proportionate share in the administration of the Church.

Their ideal would seem to be a national, popular, and democratic establishment, united and strong, but independent and free from government interference; its affairs under the charge of, and its clergy chosen by, all its members acting in concert.

With these aspirations, and from this point of view, Popovtsism, or the Raskol of the priestly branch, can no longer be deemed a petty, sectarian, or unreasonable movement; it becomes an object of universal interest, and is entitled to respectful consideration and earnest study from all who, without as well as within the empire, sympathize with the progress of liberal ideas.

It has been and is vastly more difficult, if it be not impossible, for the Bezpopovtsi than for the Popovtsi to arrive at any definite ecclesiastical organization. The fundamental principle of their doctrine, by destroying all faith in the sacerdotal character of the clergy and in the existence of a priesthood, or of a Church upon earth, seems to preclude all hope of any such result.

They are deprived of all spiritual bond of union among themselves, acknowledge no authority as guide, nor any restraint upon individual opinion. They claim for each the right of free interpretation of the Scriptures, and the exercise of this liberty, together with the habit of inquiry which it engenders, has led them to wander from the dogmas of Orthodox belief, or, if retaining them in theory, to accept such explanations of them as suit the wildest fancies and vagaries of the imagination.

Their sects have become innumerable, ever shifting and varying, undergoing constant change and transformation, with incessant divisions and subdivisions; new ones spring into existence as the old die out, affording evidence of the vitality and energy animating the movement. They recognize no ministers save their elders or "readers," who, chosen by themselves, are generally virtuous and worthy men, well, and sometimes deeply, versed in Scriptural knowledge; but frequently most extraordinary, even monstrous, caprice governs their selection. Vulgar, loudly self-asserting fanatics impose themselves upon a congregation, or, under the influence of sensual and erotic excitement, which, among ignorant communities where self-indulgence is unrestrained, often accompanies excessive religious exaltation, females of vile and profligate character are accepted as inspired prophetesses.

Their leaders have considerable influence over their followers, but exercise no priestly functions save baptism. Their form of worship is simple and elementary; the Bible is read and expounded, or, in the absence of a teacher, the congregation awaits in silence and obscurity for a manifestation of the spirit. To this Quakerlike simplicity and absence of ceremony the Bezpopovtsi join scrupulous regard for the devotional practices of the primitive Church; they strictly observe the fasts, and hold the holy images and relics in superstitious veneration; they retain the sign of the cross, repeating it in their prayers very many times, according to the ancient Russian method, and they perform assiduously the "pokloni," or saluations before the Icons.

Inasmuch as their service is stripped of most of the ceremonies of the Church, they attach the more importance to such as they have retained, investing them with peculiar significance. Certain sects ordain the performance of a hundred "pokloni," for the purification of food, two hundred at a funeral; they impose upon a neophyte two thousand a day for six weeks, with the addition of twenty full prostrations each week. They have a holy horror of tobacco, sugar, and coffee, and avoid certain dishes, the flesh of unclean animals, such as the hare and the pigeon. They seem thus to find compensation for the rejection of the spiritual rites of the Church in slavish and exaggerated compliance with the more gross and materialistic.

Although they have no priests, they have monks and nuns, who dwell in "skeets," or hermitages, under strict and rigorous rules, holding their property in common, and are subject to the authority of a superior, charged with the administration of the interests of the community. Their first important establishment of this nature, and from which most of the others issued, was the convent of Vygoretsk, founded in 1694, near Lake Onega. From the earliest days of the Raskol the Bezpopovtsi have been very numerous in the region of the great lakes and along the shores of the White Sea. When, in the reign of Alexis, they were dislodged from their stronghold at Solovetsk, they spread throughout the country to the north and east under the general designation of "Pomortsi," or "Dwellers by the sea-shore;" at the end of the seventeenth century several of their detached colonies settled along the banks of the river Vyg, and within a few years they were united in one community by the efforts of two brothers named Denisoff, men of great administrative ability and earnestness, under whose wise government and direction they rapidly increased in numbers and wealth until their establishment at Vygoretsk became the most important centre of this branch of the Raskol. Divisions soon arose among them, as the inevitable result of the freedom they accord to personal opinion, and about 1732 a small number seceded from the main body under Feodoceï, formerly a deacon of the Church, and who died soon afterwards in prison. The immediate cause of the secession was a partial reconciliation of the majority with the State government during the reign of the empress Anna; they consented to acknowledge her imperial authority, and to make mention of her as tsarina in their prayers. This concession shocked the principles of the more fanatic, who withdrew, anathematized their weaker brethren, and maintained their opposition to the sovereign as Antichrist.

The stern enthusiasm of these Feodocians, so called

after their leader, gave them pre-eminence among the Bezpopovtsi; about 1772 they founded the establishment of Praobrajenski at Moscow, which, under their skilful and energetic administration, became even more powerful than the neighboring institution of the Popovtsi at Rogojski. The more dangerous doctrines of these violent sectarians, and the greater prosperity attending their efforts, rendered them more liable to the jealous hostility of the public and to the suspicions of the government. Praobrajenski fell, as did Rogojski immediately afterwards; its funds were confiscated; its council was placed under official supervision; its religious edifices were purified and handed over to the clergy of the national Church; only the hospitals and cemeteries were left to the schismatics.

Reconciliation between the Bezpopovtsi on the one side, and the established Church and imperial government on the other, is still, as in the past, rendered more difficult than for the Popovtsi, by the double antagonism which exists, by apparently insurmountable obstacles of both a religious and political character.

Rejection of the priesthood and of the sacraments means utter condemnation of the whole Church, and leads to consequences totally at variance with Christianity, and subversive of all moral principle. Belief in the advent of Antichrist, and in his personal reign, inevitably results in hostility to existing institutions, in revolution, and in anarchy.

How to rightly comprehend the two-sided nature of their own doctrines, and to adjust them to the duties and exigencies of daily life, is the great problem which agitates and divides the numerous sects of the Bezpopovtsi, and the question for the government is not less grave or embarrassing. How can heretics and rebels, of whom some, like the Philippovtsi, have preferred self-immolation in flames to submission, or, like the Stranniki, have abjured all civil restraints rather than risk contamination with an accursed world, and who, all, have for centuries denounced the Church, and preached resistance to the emperor, reviling him as the impersonation of Satan, ever be rendered peaceful, law-abiding subjects, or be even tolerated in a civilized community?

Time, however, softens asperities, and diminishes moral distances and differences; common interests suggest compromises; necessity imposes restraints; the bitter passions, aroused by persecution, are soothed by the milder spirit of modern civilization; and the fierce logic of fanaticism yields to the persuasive influences of toleration and forbearance. There are but very few of the Bezpopovtsi of to-day who still cling to the strict letter of their creed, and regard their sovereign as the vicar of Satan, and the incarnation of evil. Some explain the reign of Antichrist in a spiritual sense, others wait for fuller manifestations of his presence, and all obey existing laws without troubling their consciences as to the source from which they emanate. The very men who profess to believe that the earth is under the dominion of the devil are, in point of fact, generally as orderly, sober, and discreet members of society as their neighbors, who acknowledge the ever-present power of the Lord, and an overruling divine Providence.

The government, desirous of reconciliation, satisfied with obedience to the laws and tacit recognition of its authority, became tolerant, and ceased to harass or vex peaceful subjects on abstract matters of belief; it required, however, as evidence of loyalty, and as acknowledgment of its supremacy, that schismatics should, like the Orthodox, make public mention of the sovereign in the prayers of their service. On this score it has been content with partial acquiescence. The supplication of the national Church for the emperor is long, minutely designating each member of the imperial family, with repeated invocations for the "very pious, very faithful" emperor, "Defender of Orthodoxy," "Head of the Church;" laying stress on his titles as spiritual chief as well as temporal lord. The recognition of his qualities, in this respect, has always been, and is, especially obnoxious to the Bezpopovtsi.

When Anna proposed to send a high commissioner to visit their colonies on the River Vyg, and bestow upon them marks of her imperial favor, they were desirous of evincing their sense of her gracious condescension, and agreed to comply with the custom of her other subjects, and introduce the name of the sovereign in their religious services. They could not, however, accept the established formula, or recognize the sacred appellations of "Orthodox" and "Head of the Church;" nor could they sanction the use of the foreign and impious designation of "Emperor;" but they consented to offer up prayers for their ruler under the national and venerated title of "Tsar." A minority of their number refused to make even this concession, and, headed by Feodoceï, seceded from the main body and maintained their opposition to imperial authority. Time has, however, for the great majority, triumphed over the severity of their principles, as well as over their prejudices; and the elders of Praobrajenski, the headquarters of the obstinate Feodocians, have, like the Old Believers of Rogojski, sent loyal addresses and presents to the emperor and his children.

The loyalty of these sectarians has been severely tried in more recent days, during the Nihilist movement, but it has never wavered. Nihilist writers acknowledge that "there is no way to influence them to active revolutionary protest against their oppressors."

There yet remains between the civil authority, or rather between society at large and the Bezpopovtsi, the question of marriage and of family ties. With the rejection of the sacerdotal class the sacrament of marriage was abrogated; this doctrine is common to all the sects, and its conception and application is the chief source of differences among them.

Is marriage absolutely prohibited, and celibacy obligatory upon all, or may not some remedy be devised? Every conceivable variety of opinion has found advocates. The most reasonable and moderate recognize a conjugal tie, which may be created by the blessing of parents, and sanctified by kissing the cross and the Bible in presence of the family and of each other. This form of oath is, for the Russian, the most solemn that can be administered. Others hold that the mutual assent of the bridegroom and bride constitutes a marriage which is valid, but only while this mutual assent exists. Love being in its essence divine, union of hearts can alone authorize union of lives; and this estate is holy so long only as it is consecrated by mutual affection. Ties, thus easily formed, are often durable, for the reason that they are so fragile. A simple mode of life, earnest moral and religious convictions, the force of habit, and the existence of interests in common, tend greatly to mitigate the evils attendant upon a union which mere caprice may dissolve; but, notwithstanding this, and in spite of the glamour of fine phrases and of eloquent disquisitions upon the elevating and purifying influences of free love, such a condition of things is in itself vicious and the cause of vice. Human nature is weak, and carnal passions are strong among simple peasants, as well as in more civilized communities, and give rise to similar abuses.

MARRIAGE AMONG THE BEZPOPOVTSI.

While Raskolniks are justly considered as the most honest, frugal, sober, and industrious of the Russian people, in all the ordinary avocations of life, they are, in all that relates to the intercourse of the sexes, held, with equal justice, to be the most immoral. But this is not the worst feature of the case; free love and free divorce are among the lesser evils which flow from their opinions; more deplorable still are the consequences arising from doctrines which have been inculcated by the more rigid of their sects, especially by the Feodocians of Praobrajenski, who have held that all connection of the sexes is unlawful, inasmuch as nothing can replace the lost sacrament. Their creed is concisely enunciated, "Zshenaty, raz zshenis; ne zshenaty, ne zshenis"—"Being married, get unmarried; not married, never marry." Or, as a popular catechism states it, "The youth should never take wife, the husband should never possess the wife; the maiden should never marry, the wife should never bear children." Those who infringed this commandment, and were convicted of having had children, were ignominiously expelled from the community, or were subjected to severe and humiliating penance. Adherence to such maxims was, in the nature of things, impossible, and those who sinned had strong inducement to conceal or suppress the evidence of their guilt. Infanticide was a frequent reproach, substantiated by the discovery of bodies of newly-born children in draining ponds, and by the bribery of officials to prevent similar measures when they were contemplated.[1] Occurrences of this nature were recorded often in provinces where the Bezpopovtsi were numerous. Although these accusations were strenuously denied, they were natural

---

[1] "Le Raskol," p. 66; Haxthausen, vol. i., p. 263.

consequences of the ferocious doctrine that "when a child is conceived, its soul comes not from God the Creator, but from the Devil."

No community, of steadily increasing numbers, could, while professing such abominable principles, remain united. Many sects seceded from the main body to adopt more rational views of the married state, hardly advancing, however, beyond an authorized concubinage; the weaker brethren, called "Novozsheny," or the "Remarrying," were driven forth from the fold with contumely and insult; the rigid apostles of celibacy, condoners of libertinism, severed all intercourse with them, and would neither sit at the same table nor sleep under the same roof.

Under the modifying influences of time and civilization these demoralizing and horrible doctrines, relics of a barbarous age, are no longer openly espoused. At Praobrajenski, the ancient stronghold of radical Dissent, they are rejected, and that they have ever been advocated, is indignantly denied. While there is ample evidence of the contrary in the past, their repudiation at the present day is indicative of the moral regeneration in progress.

Unhappily the purification of the empire is not complete, and the strange, unnatural heresies of the old Feodocians still retain their hold upon a few extreme sects, who find recruits among the most abject of the population. The most numerous of these deluded fanatics are the "Stranniki," or "Wanderers," also called the "Begouni," or "Fugitives," who assume, themselves, the name of "Pilgrims." Belief in the actual personal reign of Antichrist, and in the bodily presence of Satan upon earth, is the base and corner-stone of their doctrine.

This sect sprang into existence during a spasmodic revival of Bezpopovtsism, kindled by the vigorous repressive measures of the government at the time of Pougatchev's rebellion, towards the end of the eighteenth century. Its founder was a soldier named Efim, who deserted from the army and found refuge in a convent of the Feodocians, situated in the wilds of Olonetz. He turned monk, became involved in disputes with his superiors, and appealed to Praobrajenski for redress; his complaint was rejected, whereupon he announced himself as the apostle of a new creed, and went forth preaching the absolute renunciation of all social ties and obligations, taking for his text the words of the Saviour, "to leave father and mother, son and daughter, to take up the cross and follow me" (Matthew x., 36-38). Practical application of this allegorical precept soon degenerated into vagrancy, and worse. His followers, absolved from all restraint, social and moral, in open warfare with all constituted authority, shunning all manner of work as sinful, lived by mendicancy, and, when that failed, by theft; their ranks were swelled by vagabonds and ruffians, ready to embrace a faith so much in accordance with their ideas. Pillage, robbery, even murder, to secure means of subsistence, were sanctioned, or inculcated as religious duties. They made friends and proselytes among the ignorant and superstitious population, chiefly in Kostroma and Yaroslav, where they terrified the peasantry by their threats, or imposed upon them by claims of peculiar sanctity and self-abnegation. Their mode of procedure was calculated to impress the excitable imaginations of the country people dwelling in the solitary depths of the forest; they would mysteriously, at night, gather round a lonely hut and, unseen in the darkness, chant devotional hymns in a solemn, melancholy strain, and appeal to ancient Slavonic hospitality, invoking curses upon the household that should deny them charity. Often the simple-minded boor, carried away by his fears and crazed fancies, would abandon home, family, and all, to join these self-appointed saints.[1]

They gave a literal interpretation to the words of the Gospel, and renounced the world; they would have no abode, own no property, acknowledge no law, no allegiance, no obligation, and justified their rupture with society on the plea that Satan ruled supreme. They would carry no passports nor papers to establish their identity, and defaced the imperial arms as the seal of the "Beast;" they prohibited marriage, held all things in common, and called each other "brother and sister."

In this co-fraternity there are two degrees of affiliation—that of "pilgrims," or "fugitives," under vows of vagrancy and poverty, and that of "entertainers," or "hospitallers," "strannopreeïmtsi."[2] The latter are novices, who, secretly adhering to their tenets, continue to pursue their ordinary avocations, and whose duty is, pending complete initiation, to afford refuge and help to their brethren. The Pilgrims only are received into full communion by a baptismal rite, which imposes utter renunciation of the world and a mendicant life. This ceremony is performed at night, in desert places, and, in preference, with freshly-fallen rain, or the water of some distant pool, as the rivers and lakes are contaminated by the use of the unrighteous.

They have no churches, but worship in secret retreats, in the depths of the forest, around trees, on which they hang the holy images. The hospitallers, in consideration for human frailty, are allowed a time of probation, but before death they must enter into full communion

---

[1] "Le Raskol," p. 59.

[2] From *stranno*, a stranger, and *preeïmets*, welcoming, receiving.

by holy baptism. Each pilgrim bears his wooden platter and spoon; they will neither pray nor eat in the presence of the worldly, or of their own novices; they surround themselves with mystery, and recognize each other by secret signs; their adepts are trained to strict obedience, and may, or, if so bid, must, without question, minister to the wants of a pilgrim without seeing his face or hearing his voice. By their extensive ramifications, by the blind devotion of their adherents, and by the secrecy that shrouds their movements, they are assured of immunity from detection, and of freedom in the propagation of their doctrines.

The reign of Nicholas was the period of their greatest prosperity. This monarch, the impersonation of absolute power, implacable enemy of liberalism and progress, was hostile to spiritual as well as to civil freedom. He believed that heretics who differed from his opinions were guilty of criminal obstinacy, and merited the harsh severity he conceived it to be his duty to exercise; unity of faith he deemed essential for the State; he would have but one Church, one creed, and one will in his dominions; his subjects should not only obey the laws he proclaimed, they should worship as he directed; the celebrated maxim of Count Ouvarov that "Autocracy, Orthodoxy, and Nationality are the three principles upon which the social fabric of the empire rests,"[1] was the basis of his policy; he grudgingly accorded a measure of toleration to the mongrel Church of the "Edinovertsi," but pursued all dissenting sects with relentless and persistent severity.

The people were miserable and discontented, their condition pitiable, their desire for relief intense, and they

---

[1] "Le Raskol," p. 36.

listened with willing ears to advocates of resistance to their oppressors; they welcomed those who offered a hope of escape from the tyranny which made their lives a burden. These missionaries of revolt taught secretly in barracks and in prisons, as well as among the suffering and wretched peasantry. Runaway serfs, outlaws, escaped convicts, fugitives from Siberia, deserters fleeing from the terrible life-long military service, were received among them; they encouraged mendicancy as a meritorious profession, and to all vagabonds without papers, "brodiagi," as they were called, they offered a refuge from police pursuit.

This extreme sect, recruited among the dregs of the people, is the illustration and logical result of the Raskol pushed to its farthest limit; it is the final and most energetic expression of popular opposition to the exactions of an all-pervading despotism, to the worries of an insatiable, vexatious bureaucracy, to the dreaded military conscription, to hopeless servitude of body and soul. Its adherents could offer only passive resistance, but their exalted fanaticism welcomed punishment, and even death, in evidence of their determination and sincerity; like the martyrs of old, in a nobler cause, their blood and their sufferings were the seed of their faith.

Where rigor and severity have failed, reform, liberal measures, relief from cruel and crushing abuses, the abolition of serfdom and its attendant evils, with the consequent amelioration in the social and moral condition of the people, are gradually eradicating these extravagant and monstrous ideas by forcing their last refuge among the lowest and most degraded of the population.

The anomalous position of children born among Raskolniks, how to determine their civil rights and settle questions of property and inheritance, has long been a puzzling problem for the government. The only marriage that had hitherto been recognized by the Russian code was the religious ceremony, celebrated by the clergy of the established Church, which alone has had authority to keep the official registers of births and deaths.

The Bezpopovtsi disavowed marriage altogether, and the clergy of the Popovtsi had no legal standing, so that the ceremony performed by them was of no effect. In the eye of the law all children born among the Raskolniks of either branch were illegitimate, incapable of inheriting.

Custom, and the patriarchal habits of the people, aided by the connivance of a venal administration, afforded in practice a partial relief; but a complete and satisfactory solution of the difficulty seemed beyond reach. The only possible remedies appeared to be recognition of the various sects and giving the force of law to the ceremonies adopted by them, or the institution of a civil marriage.

The first method suggested seriously affected the Church and the interests of the official clergy, and was, moreover, insufficient, inasmuch as many sects recognized no religious ceremony nor any form of marriage; the second was totally at variance with the precepts of the Orthodox creed, and equally repugnant to the Raskolniks, who, on that point, agreed with the Church, and who also strongly objected to the registration which it required.

Finally, in 1874, an expedient was devised which promises to satisfy present emergencies, and conciliates conflicting opinions. Special registers for Raskolniks are placed in charge of the police and district authorities, and they are empowered, after publication of the bans for a week, to receive and enter therein the declaration of the bridal couple, and of the witnesses, to the effect that a marriage has taken place; they may thereupon, without inquiry as to the performance of any ceremony, grant a certificate which is valid in law as evidence of marriage, confers upon the contracting parties the same rights as a regular marriage before a priest, and subjects them, in like manner, to the jurisdiction of the ordinary tribunals in all matters appertaining to marriage and divorce.

This measure is as yet limited in its application to the million or more schismatics enrolled upon the official lists; its benefit for them is very great; it regularizes their social position and that of their children, relieves them from grievous humiliation, and elevates them, both in their own estimation and before the law, to an equality with their fellow-subjects. Restricted as it yet is, it may well rank high among the many wise reforms of the late reign, and affords palpable evidence of the spirit animating both State and Church in dealing with the momentous problems which the religious question presents.

For a full comprehension of the many and great difficulties encountered in the attempt to arrive at a full solution of this complicated and perplexing subject, it is necessary to pursue the inquiry further, to descend to the lower strata of Russian Dissent, and to extend investigation alongside of and below the Raskol, properly so called, with its many branches and ramifications. In these depths of popular superstition, underneath the Old Believers, who are in partial harmony with the Church, and the No Priests, who reject Church and clergy, there are numerous obscure and mysterious sects; some indigenous, evolved from the excitable, prolific imagination of the Russian people, without direct affiliation with the Raskol; others of foreign origin, either disseminating rationalistic and communistic theories, which have analogy with Western ideas, or presenting strange and fantastic doctrines, which, in their extravagance, rival and seem to revive the wildest vagaries of ancient Eastern fanaticism.

CHAPTER XI.

Sects not Belonging to the Raskol.—Mystical and Rationalistic Sects.—Erratic Sects.—Recent Sects.—Vitality of Sectarian Spirit.—Attitude of Government towards Dissent.

THERE are in Russia, apart from, and independent of, the Raskol, strictly speaking, numerous other sects, harmonizing in some degree with its extreme ramifications, but drawing their inspiration from different sources, and, in most respects, separate and distinct from it. They did not originate in any rupture between ancient tradition and modern innovation, but in rejection of all Orthodox, in many instances of all Christian, doctrine or tradition.

Viewed as a whole, Russian sects exhibit singular contrasts: those which pertain to the Raskol are distinguished for scrupulous adherence to form and ceremonial, and are imbued with a rigidly conservative, reactionary spirit; while the others, making clean sweep of dogma and ritual, rush to the contrary extreme, and espouse the most advanced, novel, and revolutionary ideas.

This wide divergence is due to the character of the people, excessive in all things, in revolt as in submission, and also to the constitution of the Eastern Church. In it, as in the Church of Rome, the various elements are so combined, and are so mutually dependent, that difference of opinion on fundamental principles is inadmissible, and denial of one article of belief involves rejection of them all; minor questions of ritual and discipline only are open for discussion.

Amid the divers and contradictory characteristics of

sects foreign to the Raskol, one feature is common to them all—disregard of form and ceremony, of tradition and authority. They proclaim contempt for the letter of the law, but pretend to cling to its essence; they boast the possession of spiritual religion, pure and undefiled. Freed from all trammels, independent of all control, exercising full liberty of opinion, they pursue their ratiocinations to their logical but, frequently, extravagant and absurd conclusions.

The original sources from which these various creeds arose cannot be accurately determined; they must be sought beyond the limits of the Russian race, both in the West and in the East, and are Oriental as well as European. Of these sects some are tinged with the forgotten Christian heresies of the first centuries, others are blindly groping in and about the theories which form the subject of modern thought and inquiry. Many, which appear to exhibit results emanating from contact with the west of Europe, are, from this possible historic affiliation, and a certain assimilation in their teachings, collectively designated by native authors as Russian Quakerism. But the term is not exact; their doctrines are too varied, too peculiar, notwithstanding some points of accord, for so comprehensive a classification. Others might, with more propriety, be called Gnostic; they present a curious mixture of realism and mysticism, of pagan and Christian ideas, and offer such strange analogies with notable heresies of the early Church that Russian writers have revived for them the ancient names, as, for instance, the "Montani," so called, probably, from the "Montanists," heretics of the third century, who, like their modern prototypes, "maintained an enthusiastic succession of prophecy."

They all proclaim the spiritual nature of their belief,

and may be classed in two categories, according as they trust to inspiration, or as they rely upon reason and free inquiry.

The former are mystical, inoculated with Gnostic heresies, reproducing and exaggerating the eccentricities and aberrations of ancient fanaticism. The latter are rationalistic, proclaiming a reformatory, higher, more philosophic doctrine; they aim at a religion free from dogmas and ceremonies, similar to that of the more advanced denominations of Protestantism.

In the sombre and mysterious recesses of the Russian mind, in the constantly active workings of popular thought, there is a strange admixture of the fantastic and monstrous heresies of the early and middle ages fermenting with modern progressive ideas, crudely conceived and partially understood; the grossest and most materialistic impostures of the past are revived in presence of vague and indefinite aspirations for a better knowledge of the truth, as seen in the clearer light of the present day. These two groups of sects, antagonistic in the nature of their doctrines, the one appealing to the senses and the imagination, the other to reason and reflection, both claim to be striving after a purer, more elevated, and more spiritual religion.

The mystic sects all accept and depend upon prophecy; their adherents believe in constant communications with the Deity; they are instructed and led by inspiration, comforted and sustained by visions, and feel a deep conviction of supernatural guidance, which fills their souls with faith, the evidence of things not seen. The period of revelation has never been closed, or, if closed, has been reopened for them. Prophets still walk the earth; personal manifestations and incarnations of the Divinity still occur. Judæa is not the only country that has been blessed by the presence of the Son of God; there are Bethlehems on the banks of the Volga and of the Oka, where new Christs have been born "to bring glad tidings of good things."

"I am the God announced by the prophets, descended a second time upon earth for the salvation of mankind, and there is no other God but Me," is the first commandment of Daniel Philippovitch, the incarnate God of the Khlysti.

In no other country, among no other civilized people, would such cynical blasphemies be listened to, much less reverently accepted; and their success denotes a mental state as primitive, as credulous, and as expectant of divine revelation as was that of the Eastern world when Christ appeared.

The two most important of the mystic sects, the "Khlysti" and the "Skoptsi," or the "Flagellants" and the "Eunuchs," are generally considered to be closely connected; the latter to be, perhaps, an extension or a continuation of the former.

The "Khlysti" are so called from khlyst, a whip, in allusion to the practice common among them of self-flagellation; they take themselves the name of "Khrystovschina," or the "Community of Disciples of Christ," which, by a sarcastic play on words, is transformed into "Khlystovschina," or "Community of the Whip." The appellation they prefer is "Lioudi Bojii"—"Men of God," and they address each other as "brother" and "sister."

The origin of the sect is uncertain; it is supposed to have arisen about the middle of the seventeenth century, and to have been introduced into Russia by foreign traders. Some authorities give as its founder one Kullmann, a disciple of Jacob Boehm. This visionary came to Russia as the apostle of a new revelation; announced himself to be the Messiah, and preached the coming of the kingdom of the Holy Spirit. Accused and convicted of heresy, he was burned at the stake in 1689 at Moscow.

The Khlysti themselves claim to be of national, and also of divine origin; they have their traditions and a gospel, orally transmitted, for it is a principle of their creed, scrupulously observed, never to reduce their doctrines to writing. When their God appeared on earth he cast aside the Scriptures and prohibited all written testimony, in order that his disciples might never be disturbed by conflicting statements, or by disputes and differences of opinion such as distract the Orthodox and the Old Believers; by this precaution they hide the mysteries of their faith and the secrets of their worship, and give to personal inspiration its widest, freest scope, unfettered by any previously recorded revelation.

According to their traditions, the true faith was revealed during the reign of Peter the Great by the Father Almighty, who descended from heaven in clouds of fire, upon Mount Gorodine, in the government of Vladimir, and was incarnate in the person of Daniel Philippovitch, a peasant of Kostroma, and a deserter from the army, to whom his adorers gave the appellation of the God "Sabaoth."

By union with a woman a hundred years old, he begat a son named Ivan Timofeievitch Souslov, whom, before reascending into heaven, he proclaimed to be the Christ. His followers called themselves the "worshippers of the living God," and, like the Brahmins of India, who teach the constantly-recurring birth of Vishnu, they seem to have felt the need of a frequent re-apparition of the Divinity to keep alive the faith; and they have had a procession of Christs, succeeding one the other, by adoption or filiation, each reverenced as the living Saviour, the representative of the first incarnation.

Ivan Souslov, who was a serf of the Nariskyne family, chose twelve apostles, and with them preached the twelve commandments of his father, Sabaoth. He was arrested by the police, scourged, branded, and tortured without revealing the mysteries of his creed, and was crucified near the holy gate of the Kremlin; buried on Friday, he rose again on the night of Saturday, and reappeared among his disciples. The legend, so far drawn from the Biblical narrative, was not sufficient to satisfy the cravings of his followers for miracles; and it goes on to relate that he was again seized and crucified, and his skin flayed from his body; that over the bloody and palpitating limbs a woman spread a sheet, which formed a new skin, and Christ, resuscitated again, lived many years on earth, and finally ascended into heaven to be joined with the Father.

Every relic of their incarnate deities, the villages where they were born, the dwellings they inhabited, their places of burial before ascending on high, are held in special veneration. Although the Khlysti rejected marriage as unclean, an exception was made for the families of Daniel Philippovitch and Ivan Souslov, in order that the blood of the first Redeemer might not die out from among men. Towards the close of the reign of Nicholas there lived in the hamlet of Staroë, thirty versts from Kostroma, a woman named Ouliana Vassiliev, to whom they rendered divine honors, as the last lineal descendant of Philippovitch. To put an end to the pilgrimages and manifestations of which she was the object, the government placed her in an Orthodox convent, but the house she had occupied is still venerated as a holy shrine, as "God's house," and Staroë has become their Nazareth; a well in the village furnishes the water used to make the bread for their communion, and is forwarded during winter in frozen blocks to their different communities.

The moral law of the twelve commandments issued by Philippovitch is rigid and austere; the use of spirits, marriage, and presence at wedding-feasts or similar festivals, incontinency, theft,[1] and swearing, are forbidden; brotherly love, belief in the Holy Ghost, and secrecy upon matters of faith are enjoined.

It is not possible to ascribe the rapid increase of this sect to the silly legends related of its founders, or to any special influence of its moral code, which is in itself neither new nor in any wise remarkable; its success and popularity must rather be attributed to the doctrine of personal inspiration, which it persistently inculcated.

Its adherents were taught to believe in the spirit as made manifest in themselves, to trust to the promptings of their own souls, to accept the effervescence of their own imaginations as evidence of the Holy Ghost working within them; added to this was the powerful stimulant of imposed secrecy; the ignorant and credulous love the unknown, and the mysteries of the faith and worship were concealed from strangers with a jealous care, which excited wonder and curiosity. "Keep my precepts secret," says their dodecalogue; "reveal them neither to father nor mother; though thou be scourged with the knout, or burned with fire, suffer without opening thy mouth;" and the proselyte, at his initiation, swears to preserve silence upon all he may see or hear, "without impatience

---

[1] The commandment forbidding theft, a very common weakness of the Russian peasant, is conveyed in figurative and singularly impressive language: "Thou shalt not steal: whoever shall have stolen even a kopeck shall bear it upon his head at the judgment day, and his sin shall not be forgiven him until the kopeck shall be melted in the flames of hell." A kopeck is a large copper coin, of less value than a cent.

and without fear of the knout, of the stake, or of the sword."

These injunctions to secrecy, common to all the mystical sects, together with the absence of all written testimony, explain why the existence of these communities remained so long unknown, and why, when it was first suspected, so little could be ascertained regarding them; the difficulty of detection was moreover enhanced by the fact that their disciples were ostensibly members of the established Church, and conformed strictly to its rites and regulations.

As has been the case with other secret bodies, the Khlysti have been accused of immoral and licentious practices; most probably, in recent days, these accusations are not unfounded, but when reprehensible excesses exist they are an incidental, not a necessary, consequence of their teachings, and may not be adduced as the attraction to which is due the rapid extension of the sect. In meetings of mystic enthusiasts there are always appeals to sensuous excitement, and appearances are often deceitful; similar suspicions were aroused against the agapæ of the early Christians. Exuberance of language and gesture, ardent and voluptuous expressions, tender and affectionate imagery, are resorted to, often involuntarily, as a means of quickening mental perceptions, kindling the imagination, and awakening the soul to holy ecstasy; even when the bounds of decency are passed it is with ulterior purpose, and not as an end.

Many of these Russian sectaries have, like their prototypes of old, or their modern Anglo-Saxon brethren, adopted violent and continuous corporal exercise as a part of their ritual. Dancing in some form, as well as singing, is an habitual ceremony. With the Khlysti a whirling rotatory movement, similar to that of Mahometan dervishes, or of American Shakers, is practised. The meeting is opened with hymns and invocations to the God Sabaoth and to the Christ Ivan; after which the chief elder reads from Acts the words of the prophet Joel: "And it shall come to pass in the last days, saith God, I will pour out of my Spirit upon all flesh, and your sons and your daughters shall prophesy, and your young men shall see visions, and your old men shall dream dreams" (Acts ii., 17). Then follows a spectacle, such as may be seen among the dervishes of the East; the hearers commence the sacred dance, at first in solemn measure, turning in slow cadence, then with quickly increasing rapidity, until the whole congregation is revolving round in a bewildering, giddy maze; men and women, old and young, in transports of contagious frenzy, are borne away in the crazy whirl with frantic distortions and gesticulations to imitate the flutter of an angel's wings, and lost to all sense of time or place. Each follows his own fancy, according to the devotional inspiration of the moment; one, seized with convulsive trembling, stands rooted to the spot in ecstatic rapture; another, with wild cries and sobs, stamps and bounds in the air; one goes whizzing round the room in a furious waltz; another spins upon his heels like a teetotum, with arms extended and closed eyes, rapt in inward contemplation; the veteran performers are so skilled in this holy exercise and gyrate with such rapidity that they seem more like whirling phantoms than human beings; their long dresses swell out around them, their hair stands erect, they are dead to all surroundings, and spin and twist and twirl until they fall exhausted, almost insensible, breathing out broken sighs and unintelligible exclamations from their parched and panting lips. Their faintness and the perspiration pouring from their bodies they liken to the agony and bloody sweat of Christ in the garden of Gethsemane. These religious dances are provocative of intense sensual enjoyment; they act upon the nervous system like strong liquors or narcotics, and intoxicate like opium or hashish. The Khlysti call them their spiritual beer, "doukhovnoe pivo," and frequently stimulate their effect by scourging with rods; hence the name applied to the sect.

The crisis of supreme exaltation is the moment for prophesying; half-uttered phrases, frantic ejaculations, incoherent words, are accepted as revelations from on high, transmitted through their unconscious means, and if the message is incomprehensible, it is said to be in unknown tongues, which the elder may interpret at his pleasure.

The Raskol has, since the days of Peter the Great, been confined almost exclusively to the lower orders, but of these mystical sects some have penetrated into high places. Imperial ukases and official records show that their adepts were, in the eighteenth century, found at court in princely families, among foreigners of distinction and ecclesiastics of exalted rank, as well as among native Russians and laymen. Similar occurrences took place during the reigns of Alexander I. and of Nicholas. In 1817 a secret society of mystics was detected in the imperial palace of Michael, at St. Petersburg; it was dispersed by the police, and a few years later was again surprised in a neighboring suburb. Officers of the emperor's household, functionaries of high rank, both men and women, were among its members, all solemnly pledged to secrecy and possessed of the spirit of prophecy. To arouse the prophetic inspiration they had recourse to the whirling dance and scourging of the Khlysti; brotherly love, mystic union of the sexes, spiritual marriage, and the inward presence of the Holy Ghost were their favorite topics of discussion.

It is worthy of remark that their doctrines, although eminently hostile to the Christian religion, were received with especial favor by monks and nuns, and by the peasantry belonging to monasteries. This singular circumstance has been attributed to the antagonism existing between the lower and the upper clergy, and considered a species of protestation on the part of the inferior orders against the domineering and corruption laid to the charge of their superior brethren. Religious communities, as, for instance, the convent of the Dyevitchi, at Moscow, were infested with these heresies; in Orthodox churches their leaders, dying apparently in the odor of sanctity, were entombed in holy ground, and pilgrims worshipped at shrines polluted by their remains. To check this scandal and desecration, when it was discovered, their graves were opened and cleansed and their bodies committed to the flames.

Russian society of this period, weary of Voltairian scepticism and encyclopedic materialism, agitated by vague devotional aspirations, was awakening to the seductions of a spiritualistic faith. Philosophic theories, mystical ideas, inspired by Cagliostro, St. Germain, and Mesmer; Freemasonry, with its secret mysteries; religious Catholic influences, diffused by Joseph de Maistre and the Jesuits, were mingling and commingling, working together in mutual action and reaction. Circumstances were propitious for the reception, even in polished circles, of the dreamy, fanciful illuminism of earnest enthusiasts, although of low and vulgar origin. It was, however, but the fashion of the moment, and, speedily forgotten, fell back into the depths from which it sprang. There, by contact with the gross ignorance and sensual proclivities of the people, it rapidly became materialized and polluted by all the aberrations naturally resulting from unrestrained exercise of personal inspiration.

Apostles of asceticism, chastity, and self-denial were succeeded by demagogues preaching and practising self-indulgence and license. Pure spirituality could not suffice, abstract morality had no meaning, aroused no enthusiasm; sensual gratification was more alluring than mere pleasures of the imagination. Carnal appetites were appealed to, and their satisfaction encouraged, as a prelude and excitement to the ecstatic trance. Embraces, kisses, and the intercourse of the sexes became, among the mystics, as among barbarous tribes of old, a part of their religious service; the sacred names of charity and love were prostrated to ignoble use.

An offshoot of the Khlysti, known as the "Shakouni," or "Jumpers," openly professed debauchery and libertinism to excess, as an efficient means of conquering the flesh by exhaustion and satiety, and of hastening the moment of prophetic revelation.

This branch sect, which was detected at St. Petersburg during the reign of Alexander I., differs from its parent stock in the style of gymnastics adopted by its members, but also and especially in the abominable obscenities it preaches and practices as a religious duty. It is supposed to be of foreign origin, having been introduced into Russia from the Finnish provinces. Whatever may have been the intentions of its founders, it has degenerated into a secret society for the encouragement of vice and sensual indulgence.

Instead of a rotary motion, its exercise consists in leaping, springing from the ground in successive bounds, and hence the name applied to its adherents. They meet secretly at night, the leader chants the prayers, commencing in a low, monotonous tone, gradually increasing in rapidity and loudness, and, with the growing excitement of his hearers, he begins a slow jumping movement, modulated on his song, and becoming more and more violent as his voice rises higher and the chanting quickens; the audience, arranged in couples, engaged to each other in advance, imitate his example and join the strain; the bounds and the singing grow faster and louder as the frenzy spreads, until, at its height, the elder shouts that he hears the voices of angels; the lights are extinguished, the jumping ceases, and the scene that follows in the darkness defies description. Each one yields to his desires, born of inspiration, and therefore righteous, and to be gratified; all are brethren in Christ, all promptings of the inner spirit are holy; incest, even, is no sin. They repudiate marriage, and justify their abominations by the Biblical legends of Lot's daughters, Solomon's harem, and the like. Other of their rites are abject and disgusting; their chief is the living Christ, and their communion consists in embracing his body; ordinary disciples may kiss his hand or foot; to those of more fervent piety he offers his tongue!

These fanatics are vigorously pursued by the police, their meetings are dispersed, men are imprisoned and women confined in houses of correction, but, notwithstanding, they have spread from the capital to cities of the interior; their performances in their different communities have varied, but have been always of the same licentious nature.

At Riazan a prophetess assumed the title of "Mother of God;" chosen adepts performed the sacred dance in couples before her with blasphemous obscenities too horrible to name, while she exhorted them in the words addressed to the wise virgins whose lamps were trimmed;

and the congregation around repeated the sign of the cross and bowed in prayer.

At Smolensk they danced naked, and the people, in derision, nicknamed them "Cupids." All mystical and religious symbolism disappeared, and their meetings are simply disgusting orgies.

To the erotic and libidinous rites of these and similar sects were sometimes joined cruel and bloody ceremonies, which are relics of ancient paganism, preserved in popular tradition. Suffering and death, as well as voluptuousness and sensuality, the mysteries of the grave like the wonderful reproduction of life, appeal strongly to the imagination of a simple, childishly ignorant, and credulous race.

Human sacrifices and a species of devout cannibalism, exalted to religious significance, are alleged against some of these crazed fanatics. It is said they baptize and slay an infant born of an unmarried woman, and commune with its heart and blood, mixed with honey, as emblematic of the blood of the Lamb;[1] and that on Easter night, when they celebrate the worship of the Mother of God, they cut out pieces from the breast of a young girl, and share the morsels among them, while they sing and dance around her. The victim, who is persuaded by promises of glory in the life to come and honor in this world, to offer up herself a living sacrifice, is ever afterwards held as holy.[2] Ferocious and savage practices of this nature are totally at variance with the naturally mild and kindly character of the Russian peasant; but under the influence of religious exaltation he is transformed into a wild beast, reckless of consequences; ready in the past for murder

---

[1] Archbishop Philaret, "History of the Russian Church."
[2] Haxthausen, vol. i., p. 253.

or for self-immolation, as his frenzy might dictate, and capable at the present day of excesses as brutal and as extraordinary.

In no other country has a moral and religious system ever been based upon deliberate and degrading mutilation of the body. It were vain to seek a parallel during the darkest days of paganism, or in the most carefully hidden mysteries of Grecian mythology. Enthusiasts, like Origen, may have sacrificed their manhood in order to secure tranquillity of mind and perfect freedom of thought, but neither the priests of heathen deities nor Christian fanatics have ever raised the act to the height of a moral obligation, or endeavored to found upon it a creed and a religion. This has been reserved for Russian zealots.

The severity of the early fathers in whatever related to the connection of the sexes sprang from abhorrence of any enjoyment which might gratify the sensual, and degrade the spiritual, nature of man. They averred that if Adam had preserved his obedience to the Creator he would have lived a life of virgin purity, and, by some harmless mode of vegetation, Paradise would have been peopled with a race of innocent and immortal beings;[1] but they preached sobriety and continence, not mutilation. The "Skoptsi," or the "Eunuchs," with the inexorable logic of the Russian peasant, push their reasoning further.

Emasculation is, according to them, simply the most radical and effective form of asceticism, as it removes all incentive to indulgence, and therefore it should be practised. The surest way of attaining the holy gift of prophecy, and of being at one with God, is to free the

---

[1] Gibbon, vol. ii., p. 323.

soul from the influence of the senses, and, by destroying the carnal appetites, to make the mind independent of the body; this they inculcate as a solemn obligation. They teach that man should be like the angels, without sex and without desire. Their poetry and hymns are filled with allusions to this ideal excellence. They call themselves the "White Doves," "Belye Goloubi;" the "Holy Ones," the "Pure and Saintly" in a world of sinners; the "Virgins," who follow the Lamb whithersoever he goeth (Rev. xiv., 4).

Marriage and the relations of the sexes have in Russia given rise to the most contradictory opinions, with diametrically opposite results — unbridled license and enforced continency by mutilation.

The Skoptsi, on this question, agree with the most radical sects of the Raskol, and resemble them also in some other particulars, and in the tendencies of the doctrines they profess. Like the Feodocians and the Stranniki, they disregard consequences, and push their logical deductions, without faltering, to the end. They manifest the realism inherent to the Russian character, and, with it, the reverence for the letter of the law which distinguishes the Old Believer; they materialize asceticism, reducing it to a surgical operation, and giving a literal interpretation to scriptural injunctions. They lay great stress on the Saviour's commands: "If thy hand or thy foot offend thee, cut them off;" and, "if thine eye offend thee, pluck it out and cast it from thee" (Matt. xviii., 8, 9). They base their peculiar tenet on Christ's saying: "There are some eunuchs which were so born from their mother's womb, and there are some eunuchs which were made eunuchs of men, and there be eunuchs which have made themselves eunuchs for the kingdom of heaven's sake. He that is able to receive it, let him receive it"

(Matt. xix., 12). They believe in the millennium, and rely upon the prophecies and upon the Apocalypse for their authority.

For the consummation of their self-consecrating sacrifice, the "baptism of fire," they prefer that men should wait until they have passed the age of puberty; they are then capable of judging for themselves, and the operation, being then more dangerous to health, implies greater devotion; it is rarely inflicted on children. The mutilation may be complete or partial, and is designated, accordingly, either as the "Royal Seal," "Tsarskaïa Petchat," or as the "Second pureness," "Vtoraïa Tchistota." It is not obligatory upon women, although many voluntarily submit to it; for them the usual ceremony consists in deforming, or destroying the breasts.

While they repudiate marriage in principle, they do not, in the interest of their sect, ignore it altogether. Some among them, believing that they only are the elect of God and depositaries of the true faith, deem themselves authorized by a higher law to transgress this precept, in order to provide for the transmission of their doctrines; they delay the final sacrificial rite until they have begotten children, whom they train up in their belief and in expectation of its penalty. A son of theirs, who, arriving at manhood, should rebel, and endeavor to escape his fate, becomes a renegade and a traitor against whom every hand is raised, and whose life is in jeopardy.

They are zealous propagators of their creed, in order to attain, as speedily as possible, the full number of one hundred and forty-four thousand "of them which are sealed" (Rev. viii., 4), when they expect the Messiah will come to establish his kingdom, and give the empire of the world to his saints.

This heresy, which is the most modern of all, probably

THE SKOPTSI, OR EUNUCHS.

owes its origin to influences from the East, slowly filtering through the lower ranks of the population. It made its appearance as a distinct sect at St. Petersburg about 1770, the year of the plague at Moscow. Its founder, Andreï Selivanov, died, a centenarian, in 1832; his followers worship him as the incarnation of the Son of God. Their religious belief and their practices resemble those of the Khlysti, from whom they sprang, and are either an exaggeration of the doctrines of the parent sect, or the result of an attempt at reform; an ascetic reaction against the license and sensuality into which the votaries of Souslov had fallen.

The "White Doves," like the "Men of God," base their religious system upon personal inspiration and prophecy, and rely in a similar manner upon bodily exhaustion, caused by violent exertion, to produce the holy trance. At their meetings, which they call "Radenie," "Zeal," or "Earnestness," held in the evening or at early dawn, the disciples, clad in long linen robes, girded about the loins with girdles of peculiar make, worship their Lord seated upon a throne, and listen to the revelations of those whom the Spirit moves.

Proscribed and pursued by the police, they avoid detection by maintaining their membership of the Orthodox Church, and scrupulously conforming to its ordinances.

The peculiar rite enjoined by their creed is not merely an act of asceticism; it has a symbolic sense also, and is based upon a singular interpretation, not, however, originating with them, of the fall of Adam and Eve. They aver that the carnal union of our first parents was the original sin, which must be atoned for by mutilation; they acclaimed Selivanov as the Redeemer, and his emasculation as the scriptural atonement, in which all who would be saved must participate. While they rejected Jesus as the Saviour of mankind, and deny the efficacy of His death upon the cross, they recognize Him and His apostles as precursors of Selivanov, and assert that mutilation was taught by them in secret. This doctrine was the hidden Eleusinian mystery of Christ's teachings; as in time it became corrupt, or was forgotten, the redemption of the world demanded a new Saviour to preach and practice the true Gospel in all its purity and might, and the Son of God became again incarnate in the person of their prophet.

This impostor appeared during the reign of Catherine II.; of his previous history and antecedents nothing positive is known; he was ignorant and illiterate, unable to read or write, and was probably a peasant who had escaped military conscription by taking refuge with the Khlysti, among whom he became prominent. An aged prophetess, Akoulina Ivanovna, who presided over one of their communities, recognized him by inspiration, and proclaimed him to be the Son of God; his followers rapidly increased, and attracted suspicion; he was arrested, knouted, and exiled to Siberia, from whence he was allowed to return by Paul I. Besides his divine character, he assumed that of temporal lord, and like the Raskolnik Pougatchev, claimed to be Peter III., who had not been put to death, as supposed, but had escaped to Irkutsk, and a soldier had suffered in his place. Selivanov declared that Peter was the incarnation of Christ, who had never died, but was immortal, and wandered over the world, variously and at various times, manifest in the flesh, without sex, consecrated by God; the fulfilment of divine grace ("ispolnen blagodati"), speaking by inspiration; the Son of God, but not God; revealed in due season by the Father to His true children, and who now appeared again incarnate in his own person as Christ and Tsar.[1]

The history of Russia is full of similar impostures, which have always found ready acceptance among a people credulous and excitable, greedy for the marvellous, and ever wildly dreaming, in their degradation and misery, of a deliverer to come.

Selivanov doubtless thought to strengthen his spiritual pretensions by claiming to be the true "White Tsar," and his disciples, in their worship, addressed him as "King of Kings and Lord of Lords" (Rev. xix., 16).

According to the Skoptsi, Paul was curious to see the man who pretended to be his father, and recalled him from Siberia for that purpose, but his return was not triumphant; he was confined as a lunatic in an insane asylum, and recovered his liberty only under Alexander I., at the intercession of a Polish noble, Elinski, who, with a few others in high position, was, in secret, a convert to his creed.

For eighteen years longer, favored by the singular moral state of Russian society at that period, and protected by the influence of wealthy partisans, he lived at St. Petersburg, sedulously laboring to spread his doctrines, and worshipped by his patrons as God and Tsar. Finally, in 1820, he was confined in the monastery of Souzdal, where, imbecile from old age, he died in 1832.

The Skoptsi do not admit his death, but declare that he still lives in the depths of Siberia, whence he will come, at the appointed time, to establish the kingdom of righteousness. Some of them believe that Napoleon will marshal the angelic hosts who will surround their leader and will share his triumph. Napoleon's fame has left

---

[1] Haxthausen, vol. i., p. 249.

an indelible impression upon the Russian popular mind, and there are sects, obscure and little known, akin to the larger mystic bodies, still convinced that he was the true Messiah, who is to come again, and which worship before his image. His memory, and that of Peter III., who is confounded with Selivanov, are held in profound reverence by the Skoptsi, and portraits of the three replace among them the holy pictures of the Orthodox. They have other typical emblems of their faith, and chief among them are representations of King David dancing before the ark, and of the crucifixion, with the figure of a monk upon the cross instead of that of the Saviour.

Notwithstanding their precautions, the Skoptsi are betrayed by their pale, sallow complexion, their scanty beard, shrill voice, effeminate, peculiar gait, and hesitating, wavering look. They are numerous among the money-changers of the large towns; like the Jews, they have a marked predilection for pursuits that involve the handling of coin. Their probity and their financial skill are universally recognized; they possess, in a high degree, the practical spirit of the Great Russian, and the mercantile instincts of the Raskolnik; their eagerness for gain, and their success in its acquisition, are proverbial. To amass wealth is their engrossing preoccupation; severed from family ties and affections, passionless, not tempted as other men are, old before their time, they devote a life-long energy to the accumulation of property with keen, calculating, systematic perseverance. They are untiring in the propagation of their belief, and the lavish expenditure of the wealth they delight in acquiring accounts for the wide diffusion of their repulsive doctrines.

Imprisonment and exile are insufficient to repress their

proselyting zeal; they have been forced into the army; whole regiments have been formed of their adherents, and sent to garrison frontier posts; entire communities have been transported to the Caucasus and to Siberia, or driven to seek refuge beyond the border; but they remain steadfast in their faith, and ardent in their missionary labors, patiently awaiting the reappearance of their Lord and King, and their numbers increase rather than diminish. Although no longer molested, if they refrain from active propagation of their doctrines, they are under strict police supervision; their condition is inscribed on their passports, and all who lodge or employ them must notify the authorities.

It is a remarkable anomaly that the partisans of these unnatural and revolting practices are usually, in the ordinary avocations of life, the most respectable and honest of men.[1] They are frugal, sober, and industrious; they avoid meat and fish; use neither spirits nor tobacco; and the flesh of a white lamb, with bread made of white flour, consecrated by lying in the grave of one of their saints, serves for the communion feast, which they celebrate on the first day of Easter, their only festival. Their religious services are conducted with propriety and decorum; chaste and simple hymns are sung, of which the following, quoted by Haxthausen, is an example:

> "Hold fast ye mariners!
> Let not the ship perish in the storm!
> The Holy Spirit is with us!
> Fear not the breakers! fear not the storm!
> Our Father and Christ is with us!
> His mother Akoulina Ivanovna is with us!
> He will come! He will appear!

---

[1] W. H. Dixon, "Free Russia," p. 140.

> He will sound the great bell of the Uspenski.[1]
> He will collect all the true believers together!
> He will plant masts that will not fail!
> He will set sails that will not rend!
> He will give us a rudder that will steer us safely!
> He casts his anchor in a safe harbor!
> We are landed! we are landed!
> The Holy Spirit is with us!
> The Holy Spirit is among us!
> The Holy Spirit is in us!"[2]

This nautical phraseology is explained by the system of their organization, arranged with the remarkable aptitude for self-government displayed by Russian schismatics, from the "Old Believers" to the "Men of God" and the "White Doves."

They form themselves into "korabl," which may signify either "ships" or "naves of a church," and their confederation recalls that of Free-Masonry with its lodges; this latter institution was introduced into Russia at about the period of Selivanov's appearance.[3]

Each korabl comprises the disciples of a city, a town, or a district, and is under the charge of a prophet or prophetess, whose inspired revelations are its law and guide. That of St. Petersburg, ruled over by Selivanov in person, was, in their mystic language, the Royal Ship, having for its pilot and commander the living God, who directed the evolutions of the squadron of smaller vessels.

---

[1] The "Uspenski Sabor," or Great Cathedral of the Assumption, at Moscow. *Uspenie*, the Assumption.

[2] Haxthausen, vol. i., p. 249.

[3] Free-Masonry, founded in Russia by Schwartz and Novikov, was widely extended, and had considerable influence during the reigns of Catherine II., Paul I., and Alexander I. All secret societies, and Free-Masonry with them, were abolished by Nicholas in consequence of their connection with the insurrectionary movement of 1825.

The Skoptsi still form a close corporation with secret signs of recognition, one of which is said to be a red handkerchief spread over the knees, and which they strike with the right hand. This distinguishing mark is frequently seen in their portraits of Peter III. and of Selivanov.[1]

The Khlysti and the Skoptsi, with their various affiliations, can scarcely be termed Christian denominations, or even heresies, properly speaking; they are parodies of Christianity, with their special saving deities, their own dogmas and systems of morality, reproducing and exaggerating the heterogeneous teachings of the ancient Gnostic creeds.

In opposition to these mystic sects are the communities animated by advanced ideas and liberal tendencies, similar to those developed in modern times, among civilized nations.

In endeavoring to escape from the superstitions and trammels of ritualism, the Russian peasant has not been swayed solely by mystical symbolism, dreams, and chimeras; he has also felt the influence of intelligent reflection, and, by the exercise of his sober reasoning faculties, has evolved doctrines and beliefs of a highly philosophic and rationalistic nature.

The reformatory, Protestant aspirations of the Russian mind are exhibited in two sects of similar tendencies, connected together by the character of the creeds they profess, as also in their historic development, and each having many divisions and ramifications.

They are the " Doukhobortsi,"[2] or " Champions of the Holy Spirit," and the " Molokani,"[3] or " Milk Drinkers."

---

[1] Haxthausen, vol. i., p. 251.
[2] From *doukh*, spirit, and *borets*, a wrestler or champion.
[3] From *moloko*, milk.

The latter are probably so named because they refuse to keep the Lenten fasts, and partake freely of milk, and of food prepared from milk, on the days when its use is prohibited by the Orthodox Church; this designation, which is contemptuously applied to them, is also supposed to be derived from the name of the Molotchnaya, the Milky Stream, a river of the south of Russia, so called from the chalky white color of its waters, along the banks of which their first and principal communities were originally established.

The adherents of both these sects are distinguished for their utter disregard of all ritual, and of the traditionary religious festivals, fasts, and forms of which the Russian people generally are scrupulously observant. The lines of demarkation between them are not strictly drawn, and their members pass frequently from one to the other. They call themselves "Istinie Khristiane," "True" or "Spiritual Christians," and reject all external practices and ceremonies, as being, in their nature, materialistic and idolatrous.

The Doukhobortsi reject the sacraments, the Molokani receive them only in their spiritual sense. They both appeal to reason and to conscience as against the formalism and superstitions of the Orthodox and of the Raskolnik, empty sources of endless and vain disputes. "The Rasknolnik," they say, "will die a martyr for the right to make the sign of the cross with two fingers; we do not cross ourselves at all, either with two or with three fingers; we strive to attain to a better knowledge of God."

The Molokani, like the Bezpopovtsi, recognize no priesthood, but for a different reason; not because the Church has lost its sacerdotal power, but because, in the true Church, there is no need of a clergy. What the "No

Priest" deplores as a calamity, they acclaim as righteous doctrine. According to their belief there is no bishop, no pontiff, no master save Christ; their elders, who read and expound the Word, are appointed by themselves, as God-fearing men, whom they choose as directed by the apostle Peter, and who have no priestly character nor authority, and wear no special garb.

"God is a Spirit, and they that worship Him must worship Him in spirit and in truth" (John iv., 24); this is the fundamental maxim of their creed, which they apply and follow out with the inflexible logic of the Russian peasant. All ceremonious observances during prayer, the repeated cross-signing, the "pokloni," or genuflexions and prostrations, dear to the heart of the Raskolnik and the Orthodox, they abstain from; the holy images, which all, save the most fanatic of the Bezpopovtsi, worship and revere, they deny as useless, unmeaning symbols. "God is a Spirit," they repeat, "and images are but idols. A picture is not Christ; it is but a bit of painted board. We believe in Christ, not a Christ of brass, nor of silver, nor of gold, the work of men's hands, but in Christ, the Son of God, Saviour of the world."

Their idea of a Church is according to the words of Christ: "Where two or three are gathered together in My name, there am I in the midst of them." They have no sacred edifices. "Solomon built himself a house, but the Almighty dwells not in temples made by the hands of men;" "the heart of man is God's only temple."[1]

Their services are simple and plain; they meet at each other's houses to listen to the Scriptures, repeat the Lord's Prayer, and sing Psalms.

They acknowledge the sacraments only in their spirit-

---

[1] Haxthausen, vol. i., p. 283.

ual sense; while they meet and break bread together on the anniversary of the Last Supper, they do so in commemoration of the event, and attach no religious or mysterious significance to the act. "The true communion of the body and blood of Christ is," they say, "to read and meditate upon His Word; all else is vanity."

Of baptism they declare: "We understand, not the earthly water, but the spiritual cleansing of our souls from sin in faith, and the destruction of the old Adam within us, with all his works."

Of confession: "We hold by Paul; confess your sins one to another, and pray for one another; any thing further we do not allow."

Regarding prayers for the dead, they are silent.

These statements are taken from confessions of faith, drawn up, not for their own use, but for their justification with the government, and may be liable to suspicion in some particulars, but they are corroborated by what can be ascertained of their practices. The conclusion of their profession is thoroughly Protestant in its character. "Besides the Holy Sacraments, we accept the Word of God and inward faith as our guides. We do not consider ourselves as not sinful, nor as holy, but work out our own salvation with fear and trembling, in the hope of attaining it solely, and alone, through belief in Jesus Christ, the only begotten Son of God, and the fulfilment of the commands of the Lord; we have no power of ourselves to effect this, but obtain it only through living faith in our Intercessor and Redeemer, Jesus Christ."[1]

The origin of these rationalistic sects is obscure. Kullmann was burned at Moscow, in 1689, for teaching the philosophy of his master, Jacob Boehm; Procopius

---

[1] Haxthausen, vol. i., p. 284.

Lupkin was condemned, in 1710, for asserting that the Church had lost the true spirit of Christianity, and that he had been appointed to set it right; Dimitri Tvaritenev was convicted of spreading Calvinistic ideas, by a synod, in 1714. These various doctrines may have aided the development of new opinions, but the Molokani themselves pretend to date from the sixteenth century, when, in the reign of Ivan the Terrible, an English physician introduced among Muscovite friends the reading and study of the Bible. The seed fell on fertile soil, and from it sprang a reformation more radical in its principles than that of Luther and Calvin; a Protestantism of the most advanced type, rigid, rational, and unitarian, recognizing God as supreme, and His Word only as law, but withholding from Christ the full attributes of the Deity, and considering the Holy Ghost as simply a manifestation of Divine Grace.

These ignorant peasants, in reasoning out their faith, seem instinctively to have arrived at conclusions regarding the unity of the Godhead similar to the belief of Locke and Channing in later days.

The Doukhobortsi evince more of the Oriental spirit, and were, perhaps, somewhat influenced by the Bogomile heresies of the Middle Ages, some hints of which may have permeated into Russia with the Bulgarian colonies which settled in the neighborhood of Kiev prior to the thirteenth century, during the wars between the French empire of Constantinople, the Hungarians, and the Turks.[1]

---

[1] The Bogomiles were followers of a Bulgarian doctor named Basil, who rejected the Old Testament and most of the New; denied the resurrection of Christ and the mysteries of the Catholic faith, the sacraments, the necessity of a Church or a priesthood, prohibited marriage, and preached community of goods and of women, and utter reliance on the infinite mercy of God. The name of the sect is derived from the Sla-

The doctrines of the Molokani are more sober and practical, more positive and rational, while those of the Doukhobortsi have a strong tinge of mysticism and naturalism.

The broad principles which guide both these bodies of sectaries may be readily discerned, but the exact nature of their opinions, especially as regards the Doukhobortsi, is more difficult to comprehend. They are, for the most part, peasants, with little or no education, and in their own minds, doubtless, their belief does not assume the form of a complete or perfectly defined system of theology.

The Milk Drinkers base all religion upon the Bible. The Champions of the Spirit treat the Inspired Book with less respect, and look beyond its teachings; they aver that Christ preferred the spoken to the written word, and that every man is a gospel unto himself; "the letter killeth, but the spirit giveth life" (2 Cor. iii. 6), and they consequently pay less attention to the strict construction of the Scriptures; most of the Christian traditions and dogmas they either reject entirely or understand in a symbolic sense; they also reject a priesthood, but they go beyond the Milk Drinkers in ascribing divine powers to their leader, whom they acclaim as Christ. They seem to have vaguely forestalled Hegel's method of interpreting the sacred mysteries, and do not consider the incarnation as an isolated, solitary fact in human history, but as an ever-recurring miracle in the life of every Christian; in each one Christ lives, teaches, suffers, and is resuscitated, and the consequences which they drew from this allegorical method of explanation

---

vonic words "Bogh" ("God") and "Milotti" ("have pity upon me"). Basil was condemned by a council at Constantinople, in 1118, and burned at the stake.

inclined them to belief in metempsychosis. This doctrine of an ever-renewing presence of the Saviour was seized upon and advocated to his own advantage by Kapoustine, the most distinguished of their leaders, a man of genius, originality, and eloquence, who ruled like a prophet of old in Israel. He taught that Christ is born again in every believer, that God is in every one. When God descended into Jesus, as Christ, He chose Him because Jesus' soul was the purest and most perfect of human souls, and being favored by God above all human souls, it had, from generation to generation, animated new bodies, always retaining, by God's will, a remembrance of its former condition, and every man in whom it resided was conscious that Jesus' soul was within him. In the early days it lived in the persons of the popes and heads of the Church, who were, for this reason, universally acknowledged, but later the Church fell into error, and this divinely appointed chief was thrust aside by human passions and ambition; his place usurped, he wandered away, unrecognized by all save a chosen few, but always existing. "Thus," said he, "Sylvan Kolisnikov, whom the older among you knew, was Jesus, but now, as truly as the heaven is above me and the earth under my feet, I am the true Jesus Christ your Lord!" and his followers fell down and worshipped him.

He introduced among them the principle of community of goods, and under his firm and sagacious direction they rapidly increased in numbers and prosperity, their villages along the Molotchnaya river were named after the Christian virtues, as Terpenie (Patience), Bogdanovka (The Gift of God), Troïtchatka (The Trinity), Novospasskaya (The New Salvation), etc.; in 1833 they counted about four thousand inhabitants.[1] A small number

---

[1] Haxthausen, vol. i., p. 289.

among them, called "Obstchii," or "Communists," carried their theories to extremes, and advocated community of women, as well as of property, but their views were never generally accepted.

Like the Quakers and Moravians, both the Molokani and the Doukhobortsi are strongly prejudiced against all oaths and against military service. War is utterly opposed to their ideas of charity and brotherly love. The radical nature of their religious belief influences their opinions on social and political questions, and as their inclinations are democratic, even communistic, they have been accused of preaching resistance to all authority, temporal as well as spiritual, and of giving refuge in their villages to criminals and fugitives from justice; but while this is an exaggeration, socialistic opinions have aroused among them a general expectation of the millennium. They have dreams of a regenerated world, of an "empire of Ararat," soon to come, when peace and righteousness shall prevail. Although they passively submit to the present order of things, they do not sympathize with it, and cherish obscure traditions of a Western hero, the "lion of the valley of Jehoshaphat," destined to overthrow the false emperor and restore the throne of the White Tsar. The fame of Napoleon awakened their hopes, and it is said that, in 1812, they sent a deputation to inquire of him if indeed he were the deliverer announced by the prophets.

The adherents of both these sects have, by the testimony of all who, either in official or private capacity, have known them, always been distinguished for honesty, sobriety, industry, and peaceful obedience to the law. The government has frequently interfered to prevent the extension of their doctrines, and has transported their settlements hither and thither to isolate them, but, wherever established, they have invariably evinced the same docile submission and useful qualities. Agriculture is their favorite pursuit; they have been active pioneers in the southern steppes, making the wilderness to blossom like the rose, creating little republics, animated by a strong theocratic spirit, realizing, as it is possible only in small communities, imbued with ardent faith and under strict moral discipline, the utopian theories of practical socialism.

Their flourishing colonies on the Molotchnaya river fell into anarchy and disorder at the disappearance of their leader, Kapoustine, about 1814; he was accused of attempts at proselytizing, and thrown into prison. Although he was soon afterwards liberated, nothing positive is known of his subsequent career. His son and grandson, who succeeded him in turn as the Christ, were weak and inefficient, and all authority fell into the hands of a council of elders, who were accused of frightful and revolting practices, substantiated by a government investigation in 1834.[1] The emperor Nicholas, always intolerant of Dissent, seized upon this pretext to break up their settlements, and in 1840 ordered the transportation to the Caucasus of all, both Molokani and Doukhobortsi, who refused to join the established Church.

In their new home the Molokani, less extravagant than the others, have, by their frugality and industry, again built up thriving and prosperous villages.

Among the reformatory Protestant sects there is one with Jewish tendencies, recruited chiefly among the lower population, whose history is obscure, whose doctrines are but little known, but which merits notice from the singular fact of its existence amid a people obsti-

---

[1] Haxthausen, vol. i., p. 291.

nately and universally hostile to the Israelitish race. Its distinguishing characteristic is their substitution of Saturday, the Jewish Sabbath, for Sunday, and its adherents are accordingly designated as "Soubbotniki," or "Sabbatarians."

They do not pretend to know from whence they derive their belief, to which they are ardently attached, and, when questioned by the authorities, attempt no explanation, but, like the Raskolniks of old, take refuge in passive and obstinate resistance. "It is the creed of our fathers; leave us that, and we will submit to all else," is their reply.

Jews and Jewish sects have existed in Russia from time immemorial, and these Sabbatarians may be the successors of the Judaizing heretics of the fifteenth century, whose doctrines, at that period, penetrated among the upper clergy of Novgorod, and, for a moment, threatened the stability of the Orthodox Church; or possibly they may be descendants of Jewish families, converted long ago by force, or from selfish motives of interest, and who preserve among themselves the traditions of their ancestors. They are found chiefly in the southwest, near the Polish provinces, where Jews are numerous and Jewish influence is strong.

The denial of the Trinity, common to the reforming sects, has inclined some of them towards the Mosaic dispensation, and, in the study of the Bible, they have given preference to the Old Testament over the New. Notwithstanding the hatred and contempt felt by the common people for the Jews, this point of contact in their religious belief has inspired efforts for a reconciliation of the Jewish and the Christian creeds. Recently Nicholas Ilyne, a learned, eloquent, but visionary man, was confined in the Solovetsk monastery, on the White Sea, for the crime of preaching a gospel which, in suppressing alike the dogmas and rites peculiar to Church and Synagogue, should unite them both in one faith, based on belief in the Unity of God and on righteousness of life.[1]

The servile formalism of the Raskolnik, the extravagant mysticism of the Khlysti, the gross asceticism of the Skoptsi, the reformatory radicalism of the Protestant sects, all bear witness to the seething agitation and distressing anxieties which disturb the popular mind in Russia. In its groping after the truth it is borne hither and thither, towards ritualism, mysticism, or rationalism. However numerous and diverse the old paths indicated by religious enthusiasm, they have not sufficed to content the aspirations of an eager and imaginative race, still seeking, in questions of faith, as in other great problems, the true and final solution. Sects are constantly arising and disappearing. As old creeds die out new ones are being born. In the active effervescence of a vigorous people, young in civilization, freshly emancipated from ancient servitude, mental and corporeal, still inexperienced and undisciplined, brought into sudden contact with modern progress and ideas, while yet strongly imbued with old prejudices and superstitions, imposture and fanaticism assume the language of inspiration, favored by the religious instincts of the masses, and feebly opposed by the doubting spirit of the few. Popular credulousness and individual scepticism combined produce astonishing and contradictory results.

Striking characteristics of the Russian people, who, though ignorant, are naturally intelligent and quick, are their childish simplicity, their naïve enthusiasm, their facile credulity; they are still capable of welcoming false

---

[1] Dixon, "Free Russia," p. 124.

Christs and false tsars; the most fabulous stories yet have credence, and the most barefaced mystifications find dupes.

In 1874, scarcely at a day's journey from the capital, in the neighborhood of Pskov, it was currently reported, and actually believed, that the government had the intention of sending five thousand young girls to the Black Sea for distribution among the Arabs, and of bringing back as many swarthy maidens to fill their places. Marriage became an epidemic throughout the district, and every youth or damsel, of suitable years, was quickly provided with a mate to escape either deportation or a copper-colored wife. An inquiry established the fact that the tale originated with an innkeeper named Iakovlev, as an ingenious method of increasing his custom, inasmuch as, at a marriage ceremony, the tavern is as well patronized as the church.

If the fable have its religious side, it is the more readily believed. In the same vicinity a sect was discovered, in 1872, composed almost entirely of women, the creation of a runaway monk named Seraphim. Its proselytes were called the "Strijenisti," or the "Shorn," as at their initiation their hair was cropped, and the sale of their tresses was a source of income to its founder. His peculiar doctrine, which was the special allurement, taught that sin must precede, and is an indispensable preliminary to atonement; as their chief, he provided his disciples with the means of grace.

Similar instances abound, and explain the severity of the Russian code against false prophets and religious impostors.

Besides rogues and charlatans, there are many who sincerely believe in their mission, who have a devotional craze, which imposes upon a people whose emotions are easily aroused, and who share the belief, common throughout the East, that the insane are peculiarly blessed of God, and possess his Holy Spirit. Prophecy is the general characteristic of sects founded by these enthusiasts or demoniacs. The revelations are of diverse nature, enunciated in diverse ways. They pronounce the actual fulfilment of scriptural promises and threats, or, predicting the future, they deal with the mysteries of heaven and hell, and proclaim the approaching end of the world and the coming of Christ. Vague, incoherent, fluent declamations, clothed in ambiguous, but terse and Biblical, language, are devoutly received as inspired utterances, and are personally applied by credulous and imaginative listeners.

Women are especially endowed with the gifts of preaching and prophesying. The Russian peasant looks upon them as inferior beings in the usual avocations of life, but concedes to their feebler practical intelligence greater powers of comprehension of divine influences, and greater susceptibility to them. He considers religion as essentially a domestic matter, and, as such, especially within the domain of the weaker sex. These female leaders often bear the title of "Bogoroditsa"—"Holy Virgin," or "Mother of God," which is taken in a mystical sense, or sometimes literally, by those who are awaiting a new Messiah. These "Virgins," or "Mothers," are usually accompanied by a "Christ," but often exercise an authority equal to or superior to his. Souslov, among the Khlysti, and Selivanov, among the Skoptsi, each had a "Holy Mother," and their successors likewise. Akoulina Ivanovna, the first Bogoroditsa of the Skoptsi, is still invoked and worshipped with divine honors; their traditions declare her to have been the Empress Elizabeth, and, in defiance of history, the mother of Peter III., whom they confound with Selivanov.

Youth, beauty, or even virtue are secondary considerations; Akoulina was very aged when she proclaimed Selivanov, and of her successors many have been of mature years and of dubious reputations, owing their elevation to talent for intrigue, or gift of prophecy, or a fluent tongue.

The predominance of female influence in matters of religion cannot be attributed to indifference on the part of the men, nor is it peculiar either to Russia or to Russian sects. In England and America the Shakers and similar denominations have had at their head a "mother" or a "bride," the "Lamb's wife" (Rev. xxi., 9); and the practice seems a natural consequence of the more emotional, excitable temperament of the "pious" sex.

The ever-changing manifestations of the spirit of unrest pervading the Russian people present a dreary spectacle, as monotonous in its general character as it is diversified in its special aspects. They are as evanescent as clouds flitting over a landscape; scarcely more persistent or more definite. Every important crisis, every national event, evokes a corresponding spiritual movement to satisfy the aspirations or emotions of the moment.

It was natural to suppose that the abolition of serfdom, by removing the heaviest grievance bearing upon the people, would have been a fatal blow to sectarian protestations against existing evils, but, after a short lull of expectation, they were, on the contrary, aroused by it to new life and productive energy. The discontent of the peasantry at the conditions affixed to the purchase of land found vent in demonstrations taking religious form, and based on religious and Biblical grounds.

At Perm, in 1866, Pouschkine, a small burgher of unsound mind, became notorious by proclaiming that the "earth is the Lord's, and all that therein is" (Deut. x., 14); and that "the seed of the righteous shall inherit the earth" (Psa. xxv., 13). He thereupon founded a sect and preached the doctrine that enfranchised serfs were entitled to the land by right, without payment and without rent.[1] Elsewhere equal distribution of land was advocated as ordained by Scripture, and peasants refused to pay taxes, on the plea of revelations from St. John and St. Varvara in the seventh heaven; that the promised days had come when "God should wipe away all tears from their eyes," and the "former things had passed away" (Rev. xxi., 4).

Similar misconception of the emancipation led to opposition all over the empire to the new regulations regarding the tenure of land, and the peasant evinced a comprehension of his material interests as keen as it was unfounded, and as strong as was his reverence for divine injunctions.

Movements of this nature, however, which invariably assume a religious guise, need only police interference for their suppression, but they are, in their form of manifestation, indicative of the inveterate habit of the Russian peasant to connect every event with religion.

The sects that have come to light within the last few years are generally radical in both their political and moral aspect.

They may be generically classed under the two heads already specified, as either mystical or rationalistic, and whereas formerly the first named were the more prolific and prosperous, at present the latter are the more numerous and important. The recent manifestations are comparatively petty and obscure, limited in their extent

---

[1] Dixon, "Free Russia," p. 130.

and influence. A few illustrations will suffice to indicate their nature, which exhibits the singularly contradictory tendencies still existing among the people, ranging from gross materialism, combined with fanciful mysticism, to exalted spirituality and rationalism.

In 1866 the "Tchislenniki," the "Counters," or "Enumerators," proclaimed, in the government of Saratov, a new revelation contained in a book brought down from heaven by angels. Their leader was an illiterate peasant who preached a new gospel to the effect that God's people must be "counted" and set apart, that the order of time had been disturbed, holy festivals and fast days were wrongly calculated, and hours which should be sacred to the Lord were profaned by secular work. They kept Wednesday as the day of rest, instead of Sunday, and celebrated Easter on Ash-Wednesday. They rejected the priesthood, and held that every believer may administer the sacraments; they declared the established Church to be an institution of Satan's devising, ridiculed its ceremonies, and cursed it with all belonging to it. Their doctrines are said to resemble those of the renegade monk Seraphim, and teach that sin is the only way to salvation, the necessary prelude to pardon. In practice they seem to unite the ritualism of the Old Believers with the radicalism of the Milk Drinkers, and the license of the Jumpers.

In the government of Tambov a small burgher, named Panov, gave himself out as Christ, and collected a band of followers who claimed to be the only pure and righteous ones, and held themselves carefully aloof from a world of sinners doomed to hell-fire.

At Troïtsa and Zlotooust, the "Pliasouni," or "Dancers," appeared in 1870; ostensibly belonging to the Church, but following the lead of a male and a female prophet who preached doctrines similar to those of the Khlysti.

In 1872, at Belevski, an army officer proclaimed a creed based upon that of the Skoptsi.

Among the sects of the other category, which are both spiritualistic and rationalistic, there is greater variety of opinions; they range from the most abstract mysticism to negation of all religion.

The "Nyemolyaki," or "Prayerless People," content themselves with inward meditation, without any outward expression or ceremony. The "Bezslovestnie," or the "Dumb," abstain from speech altogether. The "Moltchalniki," or the "Taciturn," push their extravagance to denial of all religious belief; they reject the Bible and all traditions; recognize no priesthood nor Church; have no forms, ritual, nor prayer; disbelieve in a future life and in God, and carry their principle of negation to extremes. Every man is a revelation and an authority to himself, which suffice for the present day.

Another sect worship the portrait of the "Beatified" Redeemer, and give themselves up to the holy ecstasy which its fixed contemplation arouses. The object of their adoration is a picture in the Troïtsa monastery, of which the legend is that a very pious Byzantine emperor felt the greatest longing to behold the face of the Saviour, and wearied Heaven with his prayers, which at last were answered. In a dream Christ appeared to him in the glory of His Transfiguration; before vanishing from his sight He pressed to His face a cloth lying upon the emperor's bed, and in the morning, when the emperor awoke, he found upon the cloth the likeness which he had beheld in his vision.

It is the counterpart of the legend of the Western

Church, and of St. Veronica's napkin, upon which was reproduced the features of the "Suffering" Redeemer.[1]

The sect of the "Vozdoukhantsi," or the "Sighing Ones," was discovered about 1871, among the petty merchants and traders of the city of Kalouga. Their founder was Ivan Tirkhanov, a shoemaker, who preached the abrogation of all Church ceremonies and the ritual; he declared the sacraments to be vain and useless in themselves, and that they should be taken only in a figurative spiritual sense. Man needs no intermediary between himself and his Maker; real religion consists in mute adoration, in mental communion. Prayer uttered by the lips, the spoken word, is too gross and too material for the worship of God, who is a Spirit; in the heart alone should mortals draw near their Creator; the sighings of a contrite heart, the aspirations of a devout soul only are acceptable in His sight, and these sectaries, with the simple-minded, credulous realism of the Russian, appeal to the Deity, and adore Him by silent, long-drawn breathings and heavy sighs.

The "Stundists" appeared first in the neighborhood of Odessa, where there are many German Lutheran communities, and are probably the earliest, perhaps the only, sect of a distinctively foreign origin, and having direct affiliation with Western Protestantism; their name, as well as their doctrine, is German.

Among the Teutonic colonists were sectaries, under the leadership of Michael Ratuzhny, who called themselves the "Friends of God" ("Gottesfreunde"), and who met together for the reading of the Bible during their leisure hours ("Stunden"), whence their appellation of "Stundists." They endeavored to spread their doc-

---

[1] Haxthausen, vol. i., pp. 77 and 255.

trines and practices among Christians of all denominations, and, about 1870, their disciples were found in Little Russia. The dissemination of their teachings in this portion of the empire is remarkable, from the fact that Little-Russians have generally evinced but slight interest in religious movements without the pale of the Church, and feel no sympathy for the foreign population in their midst. From Odessa and the government of Kherson the Stundists spread into the adjoining provinces of Ekaterinoslav and Kiev. Their religion appears to be a Protestantism of a very decided type, and in the few church ceremonies which they retain, such as a second baptism for adults, they resemble the Anabaptists and Mennonites of Germany. They reject external observances, fasts, images, the invocation of the saints, and all the rites of Orthodox worship as simply useless and unnecessary; they seem to be animated more by a spirit of calculation and of economy, of indifference to outward form, rather than by religious scruples or any deep-seated repugnance to church ceremonies; they appear to regard them as unprofitable and a needless waste of time, rather than as being in themselves impious or idolatrous.

In private life they are distinguished for sobriety, frugality, and industry; they evince remarkable intelligence in the management of their affairs, are obedient to the laws, and exact in the payment of taxes and imposts, but, in spite of official pressure, they refuse to have recourse to the clergy, whom they consider to be a costly and useless parasitical excrescence. They advocate the equal repartition of the land, are inclined to socialistic opinions, and form a community of brothers and sisters, all enjoying equal rights.

The policy of the government towards them has been similar to that adopted with the Molokani, and has produced similar results. Instead of preventing the spread of their doctrines it has had rather the contrary effect, as, by breaking up their settlements and distributing them through the Caucasus and Siberia, it has sent forth, in the persons of the exiles, an army of zealous missionaries.

The sects of which mention has been made are but a few of the many recently brought to light. The vitality and persistent energy of the sectarian spirit are remarkable, inasmuch as most of the causes provoking its manifestation either exist no longer, or are rapidly disappearing. Effects, however, are often perceived after the first impulse has ceased to act. Sect begets sect, as the plant is reproduced by its yearly seed. It is hopeless to expect to stifle the spiritual aspirations of a vigorous, quick-witted, eager race, and to arrive at the dead level of unity of faith and obedience to one Church, which the emperor Nicholas conceived to be the consummation most devoutly to be wished; nor is such an achievement desirable; but to check the extravagances resulting from superstition and ignorance, to direct the restless spirit of the people to proper channels and towards a legitimate end, demands wide diffusion of education and knowledge, for "ignorance is the mother of devotion;" moreover the gap still yawning between the extremes of Russian society must be bridged over by liberal measures, in accordance with the spirit and requirements of the age. It is a work of time and patience, for the Russian people are tenacious and slow to change. The century and a half, since the days of Peter the Great, have not sufficed to cement the nation together as a homogeneous whole, and less than a generation has elapsed since the abolition of serfdom inaugurated the present era of reform.

In further explanation of the present mental state of

the Russian people, and for better comprehension of the continued eccentric, fantastic manifestations of a religious character, it may be observed that while the ultimate results of the thorough transformation of national life, still progressing, will be to calm and pacify the agitation which it excites, for the time being it tends to encourage and stimulate aspirations for new things, and these aspirations, in accordance with the character of the race, invariably assume religious guise and expression. Although socialistic ideas, and tendencies of an economic and practical nature, are engrafted upon the doctrinal teachings of many of the new sects, there is among the people a deep-seated, devotional craving which the formalism of the Raskol, and the rigidity of the State Church with its official clergy, fail to satisfy, which inevitably finds relief in new creeds and more spiritual religions, and to which education only can give intelligent direction.

The attitude of the State towards the Raskol and the various independent sects has varied according to the necessities of the times and the circumstances of the moment.

The tsar Alexis and his son, Feodor, persecuted dissenters as heretics and enemies of religion. Peter the Great pursued them as perturbators of the public peace and opponents of imperial reform, or he tolerated them as industrious, tax-paying subjects, sources of income for his impoverished exchequer. Catherine II. and her successors have treated them alternately with kindness or with severity, endeavoring at one time to allure them back into the Church, and at another solicitous only to bring them into submission to civil authority.

During this latter period, that is, since Catherine's accession to the throne, the policy of the government towards them has been fickle and changeable. They have been in turn persecuted and tolerated, threatened and encouraged, according to the whim of the sovereign or the prevailing influences of the moment. This shifting, fluctuating legislation, and the contradictory nature of the measures adopted are attributable to the general ignorance which existed regarding the different schismatic movements—ignorance the more gross, from the indifference and contempt felt for any popular manifestation of opinion, and which led to the careless and erroneous comprehension of all the various bodies, with their heterogeneous doctrines, under one head, the Raskol.

As a consequence of this grave misapprehension the same remedies were indiscriminately applied to them all. Orderly Old Believers, with a regular hierarchy, anarchical No Priests, with none, Flagellants and Champions of the Spirit, reactionary conservatives and revolutionary radicals—all confounded together with reckless disregard of reason or propriety—were treated alike.

As public opinion became by degrees more enlightened, and the apparition of eccentric and immoral sects rendered it necessary to make distinctions, insufficient classification again led to further confusion and error.

All Dissenters were included in two categories, "pernicious" sects and sects "less pernicious," as if the only difference between them consisted in the degree of evil.

The "pernicious," or dangerous sects, so called, comprised all whose doctrines appeared to threaten public or social order, to set at naught the moral law, or endanger the unity of the Orthodox Church. The peaceful Molokani and ignorant Sabbatarians figured in the official lists with the rebellious Stranniki, the fanatical Khlysti and Skoptsi.

In dealing with them the government seemed actuated

at different times by various motives, now acting simply in defence of political and social interests, and, again, solicitous for the welfare of the Church and the advancement of religion. It had no fixed, permanent policy, and adopted no clear or well-defined system of legislation. Authoritative enactments, dictated by the presumed necessities of the moment, or by the caprice of the sovereign, followed one upon another, the last abrogating or modifying the preceding. Such laws as did exist were arbitrarily applied, altered by special instructions, and tampered with by venal officials.

The emperor Nicholas, for the first time, ordered a special investigation of the subject, and was amazed at the extent and influence of the movement, which, with his accustomed energy and decision, he attempted to regulate with a view to its entire suppression. A secret commission was charged with the affairs appertaining to the Raskol, and administered them under ordinances framed by itself, but never publicly promulgated. Dissenters of every creed and denomination, subjected to regulations of which they were frequently left in ignorance until enforced, became a defenceless prey to the cupidity of government employees and to the rancorous hostility of the lower clergy. Such of them as belonged to the peasant class were inhibited from holding positions of trust in the rural districts; those who were traders or merchants were excluded from mercantile guilds, and deprived of the privileges of their order. A Raskolnik could not testify in courts of justice against an Orthodox; he was not allowed to change his residence without permission, and was forbidden to leave the empire; the erection of new churches and the repairing of the old ones were prohibited.

To these severe and legally authorized restrictions was

added the more grievous persecution of almost irresponsible government agents, the "tchinovniks," against which the only protection and means of redress was bribery.

This melancholy state of things could not fail to attract attention when Alexander II. commenced the era of reform which dates from his reign. Imperial commissions of able and distinguished men were appointed by him for the serious and impartial examination of the question of Dissent, and their efforts were encouraged by the assurance of his personal interest and co-operation. Their work is still in progress, but provisional enactments, applied with comparative justice by a more honest administration, have already greatly alleviated the condition of the Raskolniks.

A circular, issued in 1858, firmly established the principle of toleration by allowing to all Raskolniks, born such, the exercise of their religious faith; it is probable that this privilege will be eventually extended, and that similar provision will be made to guarantee their civil rights, which now exist by sufferance only. The measures contemplated will, it is believed, leave them free to change their residence at will, to travel abroad, to enter mercantile guilds, to create schools for their children, and, what is especially gratifying to Russian pride, to accept and wear decorations or honorary distinctions. The marriage difficulty has been already solved by the edict of 1874.

The old classification of the sects is still preserved in theory, but while such as are reputed dangerous will probably be kept under rigid supervision, active persecution has ceased; their meetings in private may be tolerated, so long as they do nothing to violate public decency or to offend against the requirements of social life.

Other sects, "less pernicious," and especially the Old Believers, will, it is believed, be permitted to meet together at their houses, chapels, and cemeteries for prayer and religious service; the seals closing their sacred edifices will be removed and necessary repairs allowed; only the public celebration of their worship and the erection of new churches will remain prohibited. The Raskolnik priests and readers, even their bishops, consecrated by the pontiff at Belo-Krinitsa, will be exempted from pursuit, and, as a matter of fact, they already freely exercise their pastoral and clerical duties. They must, however, and the rule applies to all religious denominations in Russia, whether foreign or domestic, refrain from making proselytes among members of the Orthodox communion. This is not only a sin against the Church, but is a crime against the law.

INDEX.

A.

Absolution, 182, 200.
Absorption of Unia by Orthodoxy, 131; of Popovtsism, 231.
Academy of Kiev, 82; of Moscow, 120, 133; of St. Petersburg, 178.
Adaschef, Alexis, 49, 51.
Adrian, Patriarch, 83, 115, 116, 118.
Ahkmet, 42, 43.
Aix-la-Chapelle, 3.
Akoulina Ivanovna, 268, 285, 286.
Albasin, 116.
Aleppo, Paul of, 91, 92.
Alexis, Metropolitan, 28–30.
Alexis Romanoff, Tsar, *see* Romanoff.
Alexis the Judaizer, 184.
Alexis, Tsarevitch, 123.
Alexander I., 222, 223, 259, 261, 269, 273.
Alexander II., 206, 228, 296.
Alexander Nevski, St., 26, 165; Monastery of, 167.
Alexander of Lithuania, 44.
Alexandria, 63, 101.
Alexandrov, 51, 52, 55.
Ambrosius, 227, 228.
America, 206, 286.
Amoor, 116.
Amurat II., 34.
Anabaptists, 291.
Anastasia, *see* Romanoff.
Anastasius, Metropolitan, 51, 52.
Andrew, St., the Apostle, 12, 13.
Anglo-Saxon, 206, 257.
Anna, Princess, 18; Ivanovna, Empress, 217, 236, 239.
Anthony of the Petcherski, St., 22, 23, 29.
Anthony of Solovetsk, 74.
Anthony the Roman, St., 13.
Antichrist, 193, 202–204, 230, 236–238, 242.
Antioch, 60, 63, 94, 101.

Apocalypse, 189, 193, 204, 266.
Arcadius, 1.
Archangel, Church of, 184, 215.
Arius, 2.
Armenian Churches, 132.
Armenians, 212.
Ascension, Convent of, 78.
Asia, 31, 64, 140.
Asia Minor, 13, 218.
Assumption, Cathedral of, 36, 100, 184, 272.
Assur (Assour), 194.
Astracan, 50, 79.
Atheism, 137.
Athos, Mt., 46, 57, 186.
Attorney-General of the Holy Synod, 157.
Augustus of Poland, 129.
Austria, 117, 139, 218, 227, 228.
Azov, 121.

B.

Babylon, 192, 194.
Baikal, Lake, 205.
Bajazet, 33.
Baptism, 85, 86, 96, 127, 145, 147, 182, 200; of Skoptsi, 266; of Molokani, 276.
Barlaam of the Petcherski, 23.
Barlaam, Metropolitan, 46.
Basil I., 14, 15.
Basil II., 18.
Basil, Heretic, 277, *note*.
Basil, St., 162.
Batory, Stephen, 55, 66.
Beast of the Apocalypse, 193, 194, 244.
Beglopopovtsi, the, 219.
Begouni, the, *see* Stranniki.
Belevski, 289.
Believers, Old, 189, 193, 195, 198, 206, 211, 213, 215, 217, 225–232, 239, 248, 254, 265, 272, 288, 294, 297; their aspirations, 233.
Bellerophon, legend on statue of, 18.

INDEX.

Belo-Krinitsa, 227, 229, 230, 297.
Bethlehem, Council of, 126; village, 253.
Bezpopovtsi, the, 199, 200, 222, 236, 237, 239–241, 247, 248, 274, 275, 294; extravagances, 201–203; distribution, 215, 216, 219, 221; organization, 234; ceremonies, 235.
Bezpopovtsism, 219, 243.
Bezslovestnie, the, 289.
Bible, the, 15, 19, 84, 140, 182, 189, 194, 214, 216, 234, 235, 240, 244, 254, 255, 262, 268, 275–278, 282, 283, 287, 289.
Bishops, 19, 25, 33, 37, 40, 62, 63, 67, 74, 80–82, 86, 96, 99, 100, 106, 157–159, 175, 178, 198, 199, 224, 227, 297.
Blacherne, Church of, 14.
Black Clergy, see Clergy.
Black Sea, 284.
Boehm, Jacob, 253, 276.
Bogoloubsky, Andrew, 181.
Bogomiles, the, 277, and *note*.
Boretsky, Job of Kiev, 81, 82, 86.
Bosnia, 227.
Bosphorus, The, 18, 61, 139, 190.
Brahmins, the, 254.
Bread in the Eucharist, 5, 6, 35, 146.
Brethren of the Sword, the, 25.
Brodiagi, the, see Stranniki.
Budget, the clerical, 177.
Bukovina, 218, 227.
Bulgaria, Bulgarians, 4, 17, 277.
Burners, the, see Sojigateli.
Burnet, Gilbert, 117.
Busurmani, the, 69.
Byzantine theologians, 8, 216.
Byzantium, Empire of, 33, 37, 56, 163, 187.

C.

Calvinists, 115, 126, 277.
Capitation tax, 192.
Casimir, of Poland, 37.
Catherine II., 120, 130, 134, 135, 191, 217, 218, 220, 223, 231, 232, 268, 272, 293.
Catholic clergy, priests, 10, 34, 73, 117, 130, 150; communities, 215.
Catholics, in Russia, 57, 72, 115; in Poland, 70, 80, 81, 128–130, 217; and Peter the Great, 117.
Catholicism, 139, 152, 277.
Caucasus, the, 217, 271, 281, 292.
Celibacy, 149, 150, 160; among Bezpopovtsi, 201, 242.

Census, the, 192.
Centralization of Church government, 158, 159.
Ceremonies of the Church, 86, 145–151, 185, 288, 290, 291; of the Bezpopovtsi, 200, 235; of the Khlysti, 258, 259; of the Shakouni, 261–263; of the Skoptsi, 267, 272, 273; of the Rationalistic sects, 274, 275.
Cerularius, Michael, 5.
Champions of the Spirit, the, see Doukhobortsi.
Charlemagne, 3.
Chersonesus, the, 15.
Child-killers, the, see Dieto-oubiisti.
Children of priests, 170, 171, 176; of Raskolniks, 246; of Skoptsi, 266.
China, 116.
Chrism, The Holy, 4, 147.
Christ, Jesus, 2, 36, 43, 55, 84, 85, 95, 133, 141, 190, 198, 202, 204, 205, 230, 254, 255, 260, 262, 268, 269, 275–279, 281, 283, 285, 288, 289.
Christianity in Russia, 12, 19, 24, 139, 152.
Chrysostom, St., 59.
Church books, correction of, 45–47, 50, 78, 94, 186, 187; errors in, 185.
Church of Rome, 4, 34, 127, 131, 140, 151, 188, 190, 289; Eastern, 58, 59; of Little Russia, 68; government of the, 158, 159; see Unia, Uniates.
Church, Orthodox Greek, 3, 4, 9, 15–21, 24, 33, 61, 63, 94, 95, 140, 235, 250; union with Rome, 34–36; degradation, 58–60.
Church, Orthodox Polish; united with Russian, 32, 111, 112; separated from, 33; accepts Unia, 37; persecuted, 44–46, 66, 80, 81, 86, 128, 129; rejects Unia, 44; depends on Constantinople, 44, 112; reforms, 67; divided, Unia and Orthodoxy, 68; dissensions, 81; tranquil, 82; tolerated, 130.
Church, Orthodox Russian, 7, 235, 237–239, 260, 267, 268, 274, 275, 277, 283, 288, 289, 291, 293–295, 297; national character of, 19, 22, 24, 25–28, 42, 55, 139, 143; missions of, see Missions; under Tatars, 26, 27, 40, 41; reforms in, see Reforms, Church books; increase of, 29, 39, 65, 78; dissensions in, 28, 30, 31, 107, 112, 180; connection of, with Polish, 32, 33; rejects union with Roman, 36, 56, 123; with

INDEX.

English, 124, 126; corruption of, 31, 41, 52, 54; independent of Constantinople, 37, 38, 58; heresies in, *see* Heresies, Raskol, Dissent; struggle of, with State, 44, 87, 98, 105; martyrs of, 16, 53, 54, 74, 75; patriarchate of, 60–64; loyalty of, 70, 71–76; rebaptism in, 79, 127; doctrines of, 83–86, 116; differences of, from Greek Church, 94–96; from Catholic and Protestant, 144–152; Nikon's career in, *see* Nikon; Polotsky's scheme for, 108; persecutes Dissent, 122, 127, 132, 188; change of government in, 124, 125; synod of, *see* Synod; sacraments of, 85, 86, 145–151; marriage with non-Orthodox, 127; subjection of, to State, 128, 135, 136, 193; toleration in, 130; absorbs Unia, 131, 132; its property sequestered, 118–120, 134; influence of, on civilization, 140, immutability of, 140, 152; characteristics of, 142; isolation of, 143; historic development of, 153–155; Edinovertsism, 231–233; absorption of Popovtsism, 231; clergy of, *see* Clergy; monasteries of, *see* Monasticism, Monasteries, Nunneries; Dissent in, *see* Raskol, Dissent.
Churches, Eastern and Western, 2, 6–11.
Circularists, 230.
Claudio Rangoni, 70.
Clement, Metropolitan, 25.
Clement VII., Pope, 46, 70.
Clement VIII., Pope, 67.
Clergy, the, of the Russian Church, 31, 39, 113, 143, 165, 173–178, 182, 185, 210, 234, 237, 293; ignorance of, 31, 41, 88, 104, 106, 107, 120, 133, 175, 177, 182; effect of Tatar rule upon, 40, 42; entrance to, 119; morals of, 133, 144; poverty of, 149, 150; regular or monastic, secular, married, or parish, 159; black and white, 160, 161; restrictions, 166; a caste, 170, 171; numbers of, 172; English, 124, 126; of the Popovtsi, 199, 210, 219; of the Edinovertsi, 233, 247, 259.
Clerical life in Russia, 160; caste, 170.
Cocas, Joasaph of Constantinople, 59.
Code, the Russian, 148, 284, 297.
Colleges, of Peter the Great, 124; the Spiritual, 125.
Commission, the Economical, 134.

Communion, 127, 145, *see* Eucharist; the first, 147, 149; of the Khlysti, 255; Shakouni, 262, 263; Skoptsi, 271; Molokani, 276.
Comparison of East and West, 6; of America and Russia, 206, 207.
Confession of Peter Mogila, 82, 83, 94, 116, 126; auricular, 146–149, 182, 200, 276.
Confirmation, 86, 147.
Constantine the Great, 16.
Constantine VII., Emperor, 5, 15.
Constantine II., Metropolitan of Kiev, 181.
Constantinople, 1, 3–5, 7, 14, 16–18, 20, 22, 23, 27, 30, 36–38, 43–46, 56, 58, 59, 63, 67, 80, 82, 83, 94, 96, 111–113, 142, 145, 153, 154, 180, 186, 227, 277, 278.
Conversion of the Russian people, 14, 19, 185.
Cornelius of Novgorod, 110.
Cossacks, the, 68, 71, 73, 80, 81, 86, 97, 116, 214, 215, 226.
Councils: sixth, 2; of Aix-la-Chapelle, 3; seventh, 3; of Constantinople, 3, 4; of Florence, 34–36, 42, 44, 56; of the Hundred Chapters, 49, 106, 186; general, 85, 86; for Nikon's trial, 101; of Bethlehem, 126.
Counters, the, *see* Tchislenniki.
Court, the patriarchal, 78, 87, 106, 118; of the Great Palace, 79; the monastery court, 87, 98, 106.
Cracow, 130.
Crescent, the, 96.
Crimea, the, 135, 228.
Cross, the sign of the, 95, 188, 235, 274; Russian form of the, 95, 96, 188.
Cypharas, Constantine, 95.
Cyprian, Metropolitan, 30–32.
Cyprian, of Polotsk, 128.
Cyprus, 72.
Cyril Lucar, 59, 82, 83.
Cyril, Metropolitan, 26, 27.
Cyril, Metropolitan of the Popovtsi, 228, 229.
Cyril, St., 15, 19.

D.

Dacia, 15.
Dancers, the. *see* Pliasouni.
Dancing, 257–259, 261.
Daniel, Metropolitan, 46, 47, 186.
Daniel, Prophet, 202.

INDEX.

Danube, the, 15.
Deacons, 44, 86, 172, 236.
Debauchery of the Bezpopovtsi, 201; of Mystic Sects, 261.
Decentralization of Orthodox Church, 142.
Denisoff, 219, 236.
Department of the Monasteries, 118, 119.
Dependency of Church on State, 152; opinions of the Popovtsi, 233.
Development, historical, of the Russian Church, 153.
Diaconate, the, 173.
Dieto-oubiisti, the, 204.
Differences, between the Eastern and Western Churches, 2, 6–11; between the Russian and other Greek Churches, 94, 188; in rites and ceremonies, 144–150; between Greek and Latin Churches, 140–142, 150.
Dimitri, Archimandrite, and St., 120.
Dimitri II., 29.
Dimitri III., Donskoï, 29–31.
Dimitri, Pretenders, 73–75.
Dimitri, the False, 70–72, 75.
Dimitri, Tsarevitch, 65, 70.
Dionysius, Archimandrite, 74, 75, 79.
Dionysius, Metropolitan, 57, 58.
Dionysius of Constantinople, 59.
Dionysius, the Judaizer, 183, 184.
Dir, 14.
Dissent and Dissenters, 106, 107, 111, 113–115, 165, 179, 180, 248, 281, 293–295; persecution of, 121, 122, 127, 132; toleration of, 127, 133, 134. *See* Raskol; Raskolniks; Old Believers; Old Ritualists; Strigolniks; Judaizers; Popovtsi; Bezpopovtsi, etc.
Division, of the Raskol, 190, 198, 199; among the Popovtsi, 229, 230.
Divorce, 150, 158.
Dnieper, the, 13, 14, 19, 28, 153, 163, 164.
Dobrutscha, the, 226.
Doctrines of the Russian Church, 83–86.
Dodecalogue of the Khlysti, 256.
Don, Battle of the, 30, 31, 71, 122.
Don, Cossacks of the, 68, 71, 215.
Donskoï, the, 30, 31; Monastery of, 163, 164.
Dositheus, Patriarch, 83, 126.
Double Procession of the Holy Ghost, *see* Ghost.
Doukhobortsi, the, 273, 274, 277, 278, 280, 281, 294.

Doushilstchiki, the, 204.
Drunkenness of priests, 91, 133, 175.
Dumb, the, *see* Bezslovestnie.
Dwellers by the Sea Shore, *see* Pomortsi.

E.

East and West, comparison of, 6–11.
Easter, 2, 127, 288; Easter of the Skoptsi, 263, 271.
Eastern Church, *see* Orthodox Greek Church.
Eastern Patriarchs, 2, 8, 14, 36, 37, 43, 61, 63, 64, 80, 86, 94, 100, 101, 103, 110, 123, 126, 181, 188, 199, 216, 227; *see* Patriarch; Patriarchate.
Ecclesiastical authority, 141.
Economical Commission, the, 134.
Edinovertsi, the, 231, 245.
Edinovertsism, 233.
Education of White Clergy, 172, 173.
Efim, 243.
Ekaterinoslav, 291.
Elders, of the Bezpopovtsi, 200, 234, 235, 239; of the Khlysti, 258, 259; of the Molokani, 275, 281; of the Shakouni, 261; of the Strigolniki, 182.
Elia, St., 15, 138.
Elinski, 269.
Elizabeth, Empress, 129, 132, 285.
End of the World, the, 39, 202, 285.
England, 117, 206, 215, 217, 286.
English Clergy, the, 124, 126; Church, 126.
Epiphany, the, 181.
Episcopate, the, 160, 178.
Errors, in ritual and Church books, *see* Church Books.
Eucharist, the, 5, 6, 35, 85, 86, 145–149, 182, 188, 200, 276.
Eugenius IV., Pope, 34–36.
Eunuchs, the, *see* Stranniki.

F.

Faith, Peter Mogila's Confession of, *see* Confession.
Fasting, 4.
Fellers, the, *see* Doushilstchiki.
Feodoceï of the Petcherski, 23; of the Bezpopovtsi, 221, 236, 239.
Feodocians, the, 221, 222, 237, 239, 241–243, 265.
Feodor I., 57, 60–62, 65, 72, 73, 293.
Feodor III., 108–111.
Feodor, Martyr at Kiev, 16.
Ferrara, 35.

Filioque, 3, 4.
Flagellants, the, see Khlysti.
Florence, 35, 42, 44, 56.
Foreigners, Russian jealousy and hatred of, 22, 24, 25, 69, 113, 115, 116, 188, 193.
Formalism, of Russian Church, 145; of people and clergy, 185, 188, 274; of the Raskol, 189.
France, 3, 44, 160, 215.
Freedom of worship, 81; of conscience, 129, 130, 134, 210; of interpretation, 141, 151, 180, 189, 190, 197, 206, 214, 218, 219, 234.
Free Love, 201, 206, 240.
Free-masonry, 260, 272.
Fugitives, the, see Stranniki.

G.

Gallicia, 227.
Gapers, the, 200.
Gaul, 163.
Gelaktion of Souzdal, 74.
Genghis Khan, 31.
Gennadius of Novgorod, 74, 184.
George, St., 138.
Georgia, 157.
Germanus, 52.
Germany and the Germans, 17, 24, 115, 117, 163, 290, 291.
Gerontius, Metropolitan, 42, 184.
Ghost, the Holy, 2-4, 6, 36, 83-86, 256, 260, 277.
Godounov, Boris, 58, 61, 62, 65, 66, 68-73, 77, 154.
Gorodine, Mt., 254.
Gospel, the, see Bible.
Greece, 7, 156.
Greek Church, the, see Church; doctors, 17; empire, 4; people, 34.
Gregory, Metropolitan of Kiev, 37, 44.
Gregory Nanzianzen, 8.
Gregory of Constantinople, 59.
Gregory VII., Pope, 24.
Gregory XIII., Pope, 55, 56.
Gumbinnen, 218.

H.

Halleluia, 95, 188.
Head of the Church, 105, 141, 142, 156, 157.
Hegel, 278.
Helena, Daughter-in-law of Ivan III., 184.
Helena, Daughter of Ivan III., 44, 45.
Helena, St., 16.
Helena, Wife of Vassili IV., 47.
Henry of Germany, 117.
Heresies: of Arius, 2; of the Roman Church, 4; in the Russian Church, 43, 180-184, 266, 273, 277, 282; Gnostic, 251, 252; of Kullman, 254.
Hermitages, 162, 220, 235.
Hermogenes, Patriarch, 73-75.
Hierarchy, of the Church, 63, 101; of Popovtsism, 227; of Polish Church, 81; of Uniate Church, 232.
Hilarion, Metropolitan, 22, 23.
Holland, 117.
Holy, see Chrism; Ghost; Spirit; Synod; Thursday.
Honorius, 1.
Horde, the, 27; Golden, 50; beyond the Falls, 86.
Hospitallers, the, see Stranniki.
Hundred Chapters, Council of the, see Councils.

I.

Iberia, our Lady of, 169.
Icons, see Pictures.
Ignatius, Patriarch of Constantinople, 3-5.
Ignatius, Patriarch of Moscow, 72, 75-77.
Igur of Kiev, 15, 16.
Iissous, 95, 230.
Illyria, 33.
Ilmen, Lake, 13.
Ilyne, Nicholas, 282.
Image Worship, 2, 144.
Immutability of the Church, 9, 140, 141, 151, 152, 159.
Imperator, title of, 194.
Independence of Church of Russia, 37, 153, 159; of Church from State, 152, 233.
India, 212, 254.
Infants and Infanticide, 147, **241**.
Innocent IV., Pope, 26.
Inspiration, 256, 260, 268.
Irene, Tsarina, 58, 66.
Irkutsk, 116, 268.
Isiaslav, 23, 24, 117.
Isidore, Metropolitan, 33-37, 56; of Novgorod, 74.
Isolation of Russian Church, 140, 143; of the peasantry, 216.
Issous, 95, 230.
Italy, 34, 215.
Ivan I., "Kalita," 27-29.

INDEX.

Ivan III., 41–45. 79, 87, 183.
Ivan IV., the "Terrible," 47–57, 70, 113, 186, 277.
Ivan, Martyr at Kiev, 16.
Ivan, Tsarevitch, 55.
Ivan V., 111.
Ivanovitch, Simon, 82.
Iverski Convent, the, 89, 99, 164.

J.

Japhet, 12.
Jassy, 83.
Jehosaphat of Polotsk, 81.
Jeremiah I. of Constantinople, 59.
Jeremiah II. of Constantinople, 59–63, 67.
Jerusalem, 13, 24, 43, 63, 77, 81, 83, 126, 190.
Jesuits, the, 67, 72, 82, 115, 123, 127, 129, 130, 260.
Jesus, 95, 188.
Jews, the, 17, 43, 121, 132, 174, 183, 193, 205, 212, 270, 281, 282.
Joachim of Antioch, 60, 61.
Joachim of Constantinople, 59.
Joachim of Moscow, 107–111, 115.
Joasaph Cocas of Constantinople, 59.
Joasaph II. of Constantinople, 59.
Joasaph II. of Moscow, 106, 107.
Job of Novgorod, 121.
Job, Patriarch of Moscow, 58, 62, 71, 73.
John Palæologus, 33, 34, 36.
John the Apostle, St., 189, 193, 287.
Jonah II. of Kiev, 66.
Jonah, Metropolitan of the Steeps, 76, 100.
Jonah, Monk (Ivan IV.), 57.
Jonah of Riazan, 28, 33, 37.
Jonah of Rostov, 100.
Joseph, Hegumen, 184.
Joseph of Kolomna, 74.
Judæa, 252.
Judaizers, the, 43, 183, 184, 282.
Jumpers, the, *see* Shakouni.

K.

Kalouga, 290.
Kapoustine, 279, 281.
Karp, 181, 182.
Kasan, 50, 63, 79, 116.
Kherson, 18, 291.
Khlysti, the, 267, 268, 273, 283, 289, 294; origin of, 253, 254; deities, 255; moral law, 256; practices, 257–261; prophesying, 259, 285.

Khoutinsk, Convent of, 58.
Khrystovschina, 253.
Kiev, 13–15, 23, 24, 30, 41, 45, 56, 62, 120, 130, 153, 157, 162, 163, 165, 167, 180, 181, 190, 277, 291; martyrs of, 16; conversion of, 19, 20; primacy removed from, 27; conquered, 28; its see independent, 33; adopts Unia, 37; becomes Orthodox, 66; persecuted, joins Rome, 67, 68; revived, 80; bloody struggles, 81; Peter Mogila, Metropolitan of, 82, 83, 86; ceded to Russia, 112.
Kojeozersk, Monastery of, 88.
Kolisnikov, Sylvan, 279.
Kolomna, 50, 74, 96, 198.
Kominski, George, 129.
Kopeck, 255, *note*.
Kostroma, 243, 254, 255.
Koulchinsky, Innocentius, 116.
Kouritsin, Feodor, 184.
Koutchouk-Kaïrnadji, treaty of, 135.
Koveline, 219, 222.
Kremlin, the, 57, 66, 72, 101, 255.
Kroutitsk, 63.
Kullmann, 253, 254, 276.

L.

Lakes, the Great, 122, 215, 217, 221, 236.
Lapland, 45.
Larissa, 59.
Latin Church, the, 3, 25, 96.
Latin Doctors, 17.
Latin Language, the 143, 190.
Lavra, 162, 165, 167.
Lay Brethren, 165.
Lay element in Raskol, 215, 220.
Lay Sisters, 165, 169.
Lazarus, 189, 190.
Legends of the Russian Church, 12, 289.
Lent. 4, 55, 147, 274.
Leo IX., Pope, 5.
Leo X., Pope, 46.
Leon, Bishop, 180.
Leontius, St., Metropolitan, 20.
Leroy-Beaulieu, Anatole, iii, 209 *note*.
Lesbos, 60.
Lindsay, Rev. T. M., 83 *note*.
Lioudi Bojii, the, *see* Khlysti.
Lissovsky, Heraclius, 131.
Lithuania, and Lithuanians, 25, 26, 28, 32, 37, 44–46, 67, 77, 79, 128, 163, 183.

INDEX.

Little Russia, Church of, 68, 97, 107, 111; people of, 191, 291.
Lives of the Saints, 120.
Livonia, 25, 55, 122.
Lord's Supper, the, *see* Eucharist.
Lot, 262.
Louis XI. of France, 44.
Louis XIV. of France, 128.
Loyalty, of Russians, iv., 51; of Russian Church, 154; of Old Believers, 228, 229; of Bezpopovtsi, 238, 239.
Lubetsch, 22.
Lupkin, Procopius, 276.
Luther, and Lutherans, 72, 115, 188, 277, 290.
Lyeshi, the, 138.

M.

Macarius, Patriarch of Antioch, 29, 91, 94; Metropolitan, 47, 51.
Mahometans, 17, 43, 134.
Mamai, 31.
Manifesto of Peter the Great, 121.
Marcellus, 116.
Marina, 72, 74.
Mark of Ephesus, 35.
Mark of Jerusalem, 47.
Mark Xylocarabœus, 59.
Marriage, 150, 158; of priests, 4, 86, 149, 150, 160, 161, 170, 171, 176; between Orthodox and others, 127; among Bezpopovtsi, 201, 240-242; among Raskolniks, 247, 248, 296; among Khlysti, 262, 265; among Skoptsi, 266.
Martha and Mary, 189.
Martyrdom, of Feodor and Ivan at Kiev, 16; of Philip, 53, 54; of Hermogenes, 74, 75.
Mary, the Virgin, 84, 200, 263, 285.
Materialism in Russia, 260.
Matrimony, 86.
Maximus, Metropolitan, 27, 28; the Greek, 46, 47, 186.
Meletius Striga, 83.
Mennonites, the, 291.
Messiah, the, 183, 204, 253, 266, 270, 280.
Metempsychosis, 279.
Methodius, 15, 19.
Methrophanes of Constantinople, 59.
Metrophanes of Voronege, 121.
Metropolitan, the, in Russia, 20, 22, 23, 25-30, 32-34, 37, 42-46, 53, 54, 56, 58, 62, 63, 74, 89, 108, 110, 153, 154, 157, 167, 184, 186; in Poland, 33, 37, 44, 45, 66, 67, 81, 82, 86, 112, 128, 131; of Popovtsi, 226-230, 297; of Greek Churches, 101.
Michael III., Emperor, 3, 15.
Michael, palace of, 259.
Michael Romanoff, *see* Romanoff.
Michael, Saint and Metropolitan, 20.
Milk Drinkers, the, *see* Molokani.
Millenium, the, 204, 266, 280.
Millerites, the, 206.
Minime, Kozma, 76.
Minor Clergy, the, 172, 178.
Missions, of the Greek Church, 4, 15, 19; of the Russian Church, 25, 32, 45, 116.
Mitai, 30,
Mitau, 118.
Mogila, Peter, 82, 83, 94, 116, 126.
Mogilev, 128, 217.
Moldavia, 82.
Molokani, The, 273-281, 288, 291, 294.
Molotchnaya, the, 274, 279, 281.
Moltchalniki, the, 289.
Monasteries, 5, 23, 29, 39, 40, 44, 54, 66, 68, 69, 82, 94, 108, 109, 134, 150, 154, 162, 260; in the East, 9; in the West, 10; Dominican, 68; Department of, 118-120; number, wealth, regulations, 119, 120; in Poland, 129; extent, history, veneration for, 163-165; resources, 166, 168, 169; classification and inmates, 167, 168. *See* Alexander Nevski; St. Anthony the Roman; Ascension; Donskoï; Iverski; Kojeozersk; Novospasski; Otroch; Petcherski; Potchaïef; Simonov; Solovetsk; Staritza; Studium; Therapontoff; Troïtsa; Volokamsk; Voskresensk.
Monastery Tribunal, the, 87, 98, 106.
Monastic Life, 9, 11, 119, 120, 161-163, 165, 166, 169; clergy, *see* Clergy.
Monasticism, in the East, 9; in the West, 10; in Russia, 161, 165, 169.
Monks, 10, 91, 133, 150, 160, 163, 165-167, 169, 170, 187, 260, 270; of the Bezpopovtsi, 235.
Montani, the, 251.
Morality among Mystics, 257.
Moravians, the, 280.
Mormons, the, 206.
Moscow, 27, 29, 31, 32, 48, 49, 55, 56, 65, 67, 71, 82, 83, 100, 119-122, 125, 128, 133, 157, 163-165, 167, 169, 232, 254, 260, 267, 276; becomes capital, 28; its see separates from Kiev, 33; Unia

INDEX.

repudiated, 36; metropolitan assumes title of, 37; glory of, 43, 45, 46; Ivan IV. leaves it, 51; patriarchate of, 61–64; captured, recovered, Romanoff dynasty established, 74–77; Nikon, 88, 89; Polish and Russian Churches united, 112; the Judaizers, 43, 183, 184; Praobrajenski and Rogojski, 220–223, 237.

Moujik, 149, and *note*.

Music in the Russian Church, 144.

Mussulmans, 69, 135, 217.

Mutilation, *see* Skoptsi.

Mystical Sects, 252, 259, 260, 263, 269, 273, 287, 289.

N.

Napoleon, 164, 205, 269, 270, 280.

Natalia, 114.

Nativity, the, 181.

Nazareth, 255.

Nestor, Chronicler, 13, 16, 23, 164.

Nestor of Rostov, 180, 181.

Neva, the, 26.

Nevski, the, 26, 165.

New England, 206.

Nicea, Council of, 3.

Nicholas, a Fanatic, 54.

Nicholas, Emperor, 131, 135, 224, 228, 245, 255, 259, 272, 281, 292, 295.

Nicholas I., Pope, 3, 4.

Nihilists, the, 239.

Nijni Novgorod, 76, 87, 122.

Nikita, a Deacon, 182.

Nikita, a Dissenter, 114.

Nikita, St., 13.

Nikon, 87, 107, 108, 113, 115, 155, 190–194, 198, 199, 231; is called to Moscow, 88; commences reforms, 89, 90; patriarch, 91; preaches, 91, 92; reforms pursued, 93, 94; differences between Churches, 94–96; opposition to him, 97, 98; resigns office, 98, 99; attempts reconciliation, 100; his trial, 101–103; his purpose, 104–106; his death, 109, 110; his reforms and the opposition to them, 187, 188.

Nineveh, 194.

Noah, 12.

Nomocanon, the, 20.

Novgorod, 12, 13, 28, 47, 49, 54, 63, 74, 80, 89, 90, 99, 110, 121, 165, 182–185, 282.

Novices, 165, 169.

Novodyevitchi Convent, the, 78, 260.

Novospasski Monastery, the, 88, 164.

Novozsheny, the, 242.

Nunneries, 44, 169, 260.

Nuns, 150, 165, 167, 169, 260; of Bezpopovtsi, 235.

Nyemolyaki, the, 289.

Nyemtsi, the, 69.

Nyphon of Constantinople, 59.

O.

Obstchii, the, 280.

Odessa, 290, 291.

Oka, the, 42, 253.

Okroujniki, the, 230.

Olga, 16–18.

Olonetz, 122, 243.

Onega, Lake, 236.

Onicephorus, Metropolitan, 67.

Opposition to progress, 192, 194, 196, 203. *See* Reforms.

Opritchnina, and Opritchniki, 52, 53.

Oskold, 14.

Osliab, 30.

Ordination, 150, 182, 198–200, 219, 224.

Organization, aptitude for, iv., 212, 218, 219, 221–223; of Popovtsi, 227–229; of Bezpopovtsi, 234.

Origen, 264.

Orscha, 46.

Otroch Monastery, the, 54.

Ouvarov, Count, 245.

P.

Pacome of Constantinople, 59.

Pacome of Lesbos, 60.

Paganism, 138, 139.

Paisius, Patriarch, 94.

Paisius Ligarides, 100.

Palestine, 94, 96, 164, 187.

Palitsin, Abram, 74.

Panov, 288.

Papal Nuncio, the, 70, 117, 129.

Papal supremacy, 1, 2, 6, 11, 24, 26, 34, 36, 42, 46, 56, 66, 71, 123, 141, 142.

Paris, 123.

Parsees, the, 212.

Parthenius, Patriarch, 83.

Passports, 192, 244, 271.

Parish, parishes, and parishioners, 171, 172, 174, 177.

Patriarch, the, 12, 24, 28, 30, 37, 71–73, 77–80, 92, 93, 100, 105, 107, 109, 111, 112, 114–118, 124, 125, 135, 142, 153, 154, 156, 167, 181, 227, 233; *see* Patriarchate; Eastern Patriarchs.

INDEX.

Patriarchal Court, the, 78, 106, 118.
Patriarchate, the Eastern, 58–60, 63, 153.
Patriarchate, the Russian, 61–64, 76, 77, 79, 91, 99, 100, 106, 108, 116, 119, 124, 153, 155, 156, 193.
Paul of Aleppo, 91, 92.
Paul of Kolomna, 96, 198.
Paul, the Apostle, 182, 276.
Paul, Tsar, 156, 268, 269, 272.
Pekin, 116.
Penance, 85, 86.
People, peasants, peasantry, 97, 121, 129, 137–139, 145, 146, 170, 174–176, 179, 185, 187, 188, 190, 192, 196, 197, 210, 211, 214–216, 221, 240, 245, 260, 263, 264, 273, 277, 278, 283–287, 293.
Peresvet, 30.
Perm, 122, 213, 215, 286.
Peroun, 16, 19.
Petcherski, the, 23, 24, 29, 82, 163–165, 167, 168.
Peter, Church of St., 34, 67.
Peter III., 133, 134, 268, 270, 273, 285.
Peter, Metropolitan, 28, 100.
Peter of Kiev, St., 14.
Peter, Pretender, 73.
Peter the Great, 111, 114–118, 120–124, 126–128, 132, 134, 135, 137, 155, 164, 166, 191–193, 195, 203, 254, 259, 292, 293.
Petersburg, St., 123, 157, 167, 178, 259, 261, 267, 269, 272.
Philaret, Metropolitan, 83.
Philaret Romanoff, see Romanoff.
Philip, Dissenter, 204.
Philip, Saint and Martyr, 28, 52–54, 104, 154.
Philipovitch, Daniel, 253–256.
Philipovtsi, the, 204, 238.
Photius, Metropolitan, 33.
Photius, Patriarch, 3–6, 14.
Pictures, the Sacred, 19, 72, 84, 90, 144, 164, 168, 169, 235, 244, 270, 274, 275, 278.
Pilgrims, the, see Stranniki.
Pimen, 30, 32.
Pitirim, 99, 107.
Pliasouni, the, 288.
Poissevin, Anthony, 55–57, 66.
Pojarsky, Dimitri, 76.
Pokloni, 235, 275.
Poland, Poles, 28, 30, 32, 37, 55, 65, 71–76, 82, 91–93, 97, 111, 117, 122, 130, 131, 163, 282; persecution in, 44, 45, 66–68, 70, 79–82, 86, 112, 128–130.

Polish Church, see Church.
Polish nationality, 226, 228, 229.
Polotsk, 81, 128, 131.
Polotsky, Simon, 108.
Pomortsi, the (Pomorians), 107, 221, 236.
Pope, the (of Rome), 2, 5, 10, 24, 34, 36, 46, 55, 72, 117, 123, 141, 142, 156, 227, 232.
Popes (priests) and priesthood, 7, 39, 44, 57, 85–87, 105, 143, 147–150, 160, 161, 170, 171, 176, 178, 216, 234, 237, 240, 248, 288, 289; education of, 172, 173; marriage of, 149, 160; number of, 172, 177; poverty of, 174; vices of, 182, 183; of Bezpopovtsi, 199, 200, 235; of Edinovertsi, 231, 233; of Popovtsi, 198–200, 215, 219, 220, 224, 227, 229, 297. See Clergy.
Popovtsi, the, and Popovtsism, 199, 203, 217, 219, 221, 222, 234, 237, 247; distribution of, 215; organization of, 224, 227–231; present aspect of, 233.
Potchaïef, 167.
Pougatchev, 134, 243, 268.
Pouschkine, 286.
Poustynia, 162.
Praobrajenski, 222–224, 237, 239, 241–243.
Prayerless, the, see Nyemolyaki.
Pretenders: Dimitri, 70–72; Peter, 73.
Printing, 50, 82, 187.
Procession, Double, of the Holy Ghost, see Ghost.
Procopovitch, Feofan, 123, 124, 126.
Prophets, Prophecies, etc., 193, 194, 202, 204, 206, 252, 258, 259, 262, 264, 266, 285, 289.
Protestant churches, 132, 151.
Protestant clergy, 149, 178.
Protestant countries, 124, 216.
Protestant preaching, 117.
Protestant provinces, 214.
Protestant sects, 127, 147, 273, 276.
Protestantism, Protestants, 140, 146, 147, 149, 152, 179, 189, 214, 217, 218, 252, 290, 291.
Provincial Synods, 158.
Prussia, 218.
Pskov, 28, 54, 73, 89, 116, 165, 182, 284.
Purgatory, 35.
Puritans, the, 206, 216, 217.

Q.

Quakers, 117, 235, 251, 280.
Quarrel, those who, see Razdorniki.

R.

Radenie, 267.
Radonegl, 29.
Ragosa, Michael, Metropolitan, 67.
Rangoni, Claudio, 70.
Raphael of Constantinople, 59.
Raskol, the, 179, 180, 184, 188–190, 203, 205, 236, 246, 259, 265, 293–295; socially and politically, 191–197, 208; danger to, 198; division of, 199; strength of, 210–212; distribution of, 214–217; organization of, 218–220, 222, 225, 227, 229; changes in, 230, 231, 233; sects apart from, 248–251.
Raskolniks, the, 134, 191, 194, 202, 220, 221, 223, 270, 274, 275, 282, 283, 295–297; numbers of, 208–210; morality of, 211, 212, 241; relaxation of, 213, 214; children of, 247, 248.
Rationalistic Sects, 252, 273, 276.
Ratuzhny, Michael, 290.
Ravenna, 1.
Razdorniki, the, 230.
Rebaptism, 79, 127.
Reconciliation of Dissenters, 203, 229, 230.
Redeemer, the, 289, 290.
Reform in Russian Church, 26, 32, 44, 49, 77–79, 87, 90, 91, 104, 111, 133, 178, 187, 188; in parish clergy, 177, 178; recent, 246–248, 292, 296; among the Khlysti, 268; by Nikon, 90, 91, 94, 187, 188, 192; by Peter the Great, 117–121, 124, 127, 133, 166, 192–194.
Regulation, the Spiritual, 125.
Religious element in Russia, the, iv., 19, 39, 68, 76, 113, 137–139, 143, 164, 175, 184, 185, 190, 194, 197, 206, 210, 273, 283, 286, 287, 293.
Remarrying, the, see Novozsheny.
Reorganization of the Church, the, under Vassili III., 37, 38; under Feodor I., 63, 64; under Peter the Great, 124–126.
Repnine, 130.
Rhodes, 60.
Riazan, 33, 37, 72, 118, 262.
Ritualists, Old, 188, 192, 232.
Rogojski, 222–224, 227–229, 237, 239.
Romanoff, Alexis, 68, 87–89, 91, 97, 98, 102, 103, 106–108, 155, 231, 236, 293.
Romanoff, Anastasia, 48, 70.
Romanoff Family, the, 70, 76.
Romanoff, Michael, 76–78, 86, 97, 155.
Romanoff, Philaret, 70, 71, 74, 77–80, 96.
Rome, 1–3, 5, 10, 13, 15, 25, 26, 28, 34, 36, 37, 42, 63, 117, 139, 140, 227, 232, 250.
Rostov, 42, 58, 63, 71, 74, 100, 119, 180.
Rouble, the, 174 and *note*, 223.
Ruric, 14, 19, 56, 68, 130.
Russians, Old, 192, 196, 211, 225.

S.

"Sabaoth," 254, 255, 258.
Sabbatarians, the, see Soubbotniki.
Sabbath, the, 4, 282.
Sacraments, the, 85, 86, 145, 149, 200, 237, 274–276, 288, 290.
Saints, lives of the, 120.
Salomina, 47.
Saltan, Joseph, Metropolitan of Kiev, 45, 66, 81.
Samuelovitch, 112.
Saratov, 288.
Sarmatia, 15.
Saviour, the, 189, 205, 265, 267, 268, 270, 279.
Scepticism, 139, 260.
Schism of A.D. 1054, 1, 4, 6, 24.
Schools, 20, 41, 43, 68, 80–83, 111, 121, 133, 134, 159; for white clergy, 170, 172, 173, 178; for Raskolniks, 213, 296.
Scriptures, the, see Bible.
Secularization of Church property, 44, 119, 134, 168.
Selivanov, Andreï, 267–270, 272, 273, 285, 286.
Senate, the, 124.
Sensual excitement, 257–259, 261, 262.
Seraphim, 284, 288.
Serfdom, 68, 155, 170, 205, 246, 286, 287, 292.
Sergius, Monk, 109.
Sergius, St., 29, 30, 74.
Shakers, the, 258, 286.
Shakouni, the, 261, 262, 288.
Shorn, the, see Strijenisti.
Shouesky, Vassili, Tsar, 73–75.
Siberia, 79, 91, 96, 116, 122, 177, 204, 205, 214, 215, 246, 268, 269, 271, 292.
Siemasko, Joseph, 131.
Sighing Ones, the, see Vozdoukhantsi.
Sigismund of Poland, 66, 67, 70, 80, 81.
Simeon of Constantinople, 59.
Simon Ivanovitch, 82.
Simon, Metropolitan, 44.
Simonov Monastery, the, 163.
Sinai, 57, 101.

INDEX. 309

Skeet, *see* Hermitages.
Skoptsi, the, 253, 264-273, 283, 285, 289, 294.
Slavs, Slavonic, 143, 173, 214, 243; conversion of, 15, 19; race, 139, 140; figures, 194, *note;* empires, 227.
Slovenie, the, 69.
Smolensk, 263.
Sobiesky, John, 112, 128.
Sojigateli, the, 204.
Solomon, 183, 262, 275.
Solovetsk, Convent of, 74, 88, 107, 163-165, 236, 282.
Soltyk of Cracow, 130.
Sophia, Church of St., 6.
Sophia, Cathedral of St., at Kiev, 81.
Sophia, Regent, 111, 114.
Sophia, Tsarina, 42, 45.
Sorbonne, the, 123.
Soubbotniki, the, 282, 294.
Souslov, Ivan Timofeievitch, 254, 255, 258, 285.
Souzdal, 74, 181, 269.
Spain, 2, 3.
Spirit, the Holy, 84, 190, 253, 271-273, 285.
Spiritual College, the, 125; Regulation, the, 125.
Stanislas of Poland, 129, 130.
Staradoub, 217.
Staritza, Monastery of, 71.
Staroë, 255.
Staroobriadtsi, the, 188.
Staroveri, the, *see* Old Ritualists.
Stavropigia, 162, 167.
Stephen, St., 32.
Stranglers, the, *see* Tioukalstchiki.
Stranniki, the, 195, 238, 242-246, 265, 294.
Strannopreeimtsi, the, *see* Stranniki.
Streltsi, the, 113, 114.
Strigolniki, the, 181-183.
Strijenisti, the, 284.
Studium Monastery, the, 23.
Stundists, the, 290, 291.
Sundays, 127, 282, 288.
Sviatoslav, 16.
Sweden, Swedes, 26, 66, 73, 74, 76, 90, 163, 164.
Sylvester, Monk, 49, 51.
Sylvester of Mogilev, 128.
Synod, General, 85; Most Holy: establishment of, 125, 126; receives back the Unia, 131, 132; is intolerant, 132; character of, 135; not infallible, 142; may cancel priests' vows, 150; final form of Church government, 153, 155; logical form of, 156; composition, duties, etc., of, 157-159; control by, 166, 167, 174; proto-popes, 172; condemned by Bezpopovtsi, 203; reports of, 209; conciliates Raskolniks, 230; Edinovertsi, 231; Provincial Synods, 158.

T.

Taciturn, the, *see* Moltchalniki.
Tambov, 288.
Tamerlane, 32.
Tatars, invasions of, 25, 153, 163, 164; protect the Church, 26, 27, 105, 154; set aside the dynasty of Ivan Kalita, 29; Dimitri Donskoï defeats the, 30, 31; under Mamai and Toktamuish, 31; under Tamerlane, 32, 33; liberation from the, 39; effect of their rule, 40, 41; Ivan III. defeats the, 42, 43; Godounov defeats the, 65, 70; Cross and Crescent, 96; mosques of the, 132.
Tchislenniki, the, 288.
Teutonic Knights, the, 25.
Theophanes of Jerusalem, 77, 78, 80, 81.
Theoptus of Constantinople, 60.
Therapontoff Monastery, the, 104.
Thessalonica, 33.
Thomas à Becket, 88.
Thursday, Holy, 200.
Tiber, the, 13.
Timothy, 178.
Tioukalstchiki, the, 204.
Tirkhanov, Ivan, 290.
Tobacco, 116, 191, 235.
Toktamuish, 31, 32.
Toleration: Peter the Great's manifesto, 121; under Peter III., 133; under Catherine II., 134; general, 238, 296.
Touschina, 74.
Transubstantiation, 85, 146.
Tribunal, *see* Court.
Trinity, the, 84; Monastery of the, *see* Troïtsa.
Troïtsa, Monastery of the, 79, 106; foundation and growth of the, 29, 30; patriotism of the, 74-76; placed under the patriarch, 78; protects Peter the Great, 114; wealth of the, 119; size of the, 163; veneration for the, 164, 165, 168, called Lavra, 167; holy picture in the, 289; Town of, 288.
Trophimovitch, Isaiah, 82.

INDEX.

Tsar, 269, 280, 284; title of, 48, 239; prayers for, 69, 236, 239.
Turkey, Turks, 34, 65, 82, 83, 112, 139, 218, 227, 228, 277.
Tvaritenev, Dimitri, 277.
Tver, 31, 73.

U.

Ukraine, the, 86, 97, 112, 134, 217.
Unclean food, 74, 191, 235.
Unction of the sick, 86.
Unia, the, 37, 70, 111, 131, 132, 190, 232.
Uniate Believers, *see* Edinovertsi.
Uniates, the, 68, 80, 81, 123, 128, 129, 131, 132, 167.
Union, act of, 35, 42; of Greek and Latin Churches, 56, 117, 123; of Polish and Roman Churches, 67; of English and Russian Churches, 124, 126; of Uniate and Orthodox Churches, 131, 132.
Unity of the Godhead, 268, 277, 283.
Ural Mountains, the, 32, 204, 213–215, 217; River, 215.
Uspenski, *see* Assumption.

V.

Valdai, Lake of, 89, 164.
Varagians, the, 14, 16.
Varvara, St., 287.
Vassian of Kolomna, 50.
Vassian of Rostov, 42, 43.
Vassili II., 32.
Vassili III., 33, 34, 36.
Vassili IV., 45–47, 94, 186.
Vassili Shouesky, 73–75.
Vassiliev, Ouliana, 255.
Veronica, St., 290.
Vetka, 217.
Vienna, 117.
Vishnu, 254.
Vitoft of Poland, 32, 33.
Vladimir, City of, 27, 29, 61, 62, 165.
Vladimir II., Monomachus, 24.
Vladimir, Province of, 254.
Vladimir the Great, 16–20, 22, 78, 105.
Vladislas IV., of Poland, 75, 76, 81, 82, 86.

Vlas, St., 138.
Volga, the, 26, 109, 122, 134, 215, 253.
Volhymnia, 167.
Volkov, the, 182.
Vologda, 215.
Volokamsk, Monastery of, 184.
Voltaire, 134, 230, 260.
Voronege, 121.
Voskresenski Monastery, the, 101, 109, 164.
Vozdoukhantsi, the, 290.
Vyg, the, 127, 215, 221, 236, 239.
Vygoretsk, Convent of, 215, 221, 236.

W.

Walachia, 60, 101.
Wanderers, the, *see* Stranniki.
Warsaw, Diet of, 82, 129, 130.
West and East, *see* East.
Whip, 253.
White Clergy, the, *see* Clergy.
White Doves, the, *see* Skoptsi.
White Lake, the, 104.
White Russia, 129, 131, 206.
White Sea, the, 88, 107, 122, 164, 215, 221, 236, 282.
White Tsar, the, 193, 269, 280.
Wilna, 67.
Wives of priests, 176.
Wolsey, 88.
Word, the, *see* Bible.

Y.

Yanovsky, Feodoceï, 126.
Yaroslav, City of, 109.
Yaroslav, Province of, 243.
Yaroslav the Great, 22–24.
Yavorsky, Stephen, 118, 120, 122-124, 126.
Yawners, the, 200.

Z.

Zachariah, Heretic, 183.
Zalüsski of Kiev, 130.
Zishka, Leo, 128.
Ziuzin, Nikita, 100.
Zlotooust, 288.
Zosimos, Metropolitan, 43, 44, 134.

THE END.

VALUABLE AND INTERESTING WORKS

FOR

PUBLIC & PRIVATE LIBRARIES,

PUBLISHED BY HARPER & BROTHERS, NEW YORK.

☞ *For a full List of Books suitable for Libraries published by* HARPER & BROTHERS, *see* HARPER'S CATALOGUE, *which may be had gratuitously on application to the publishers personally, or by letter enclosing Ten Cents in postage stamps.*

☞ HARPER & BROTHERS *will send their publications by mail, postage prepaid, on receipt of the price.*

MACAULAY'S ENGLAND. The History of England from the Accession of James II. By THOMAS BABINGTON MACAULAY. New Edition, from New Electrotype Plates. 5 vols., in a Box, 8vo, Cloth, with Paper Labels, Uncut Edges and Gilt Tops, $10 00; Sheep, $12 50; Half Calf, $21 25. Sold only in Sets. Cheap Edition, 5 vols., 12mo, Cloth, $2 50.

MACAULAY'S MISCELLANEOUS WORKS. The Miscellaneous Works of Lord Macaulay. From New Electrotype Plates. 5 vols., in a Box, 8vo, Cloth, with Paper Labels, Uncut Edges and Gilt Tops, $10 00; Sheep, $12 50; Half Calf, $21 25. Sold only in Sets.

HUME'S ENGLAND. History of England, from the Invasion of Julius Cæsar to the Abdication of James II., 1688. By DAVID HUME. New and Elegant Library Edition, from New Electrotype Plates. 6 vols., in a Box, 8vo, Cloth, with Paper Labels, Uncut Edges and Gilt Tops, $12 00; Sheep, $15 00; Half Calf, $25 50. Sold only in Sets. Popular Edition, 6 vols., in a Box, 12mo, Cloth, $3 00.

GIBBON'S ROME. The History of the Decline and Fall of the Roman Empire. By EDWARD GIBBON. With Notes by Dean MILMAN, M. GUIZOT, and Dr. WILLIAM SMITH. New Edition, from New Electrotype Plates. 6 vols., 8vo, Cloth, with Paper Labels, Uncut Edges and Gilt Tops, $12 00; Sheep, $15 00; Half Calf, $25 50. Sold only in Sets. Popular Edition, 6 vols., in a Box, 12mo, Cloth, $3 00; Sheep, $6 00.

GOLDSMITH'S WORKS. The Works of Oliver Goldsmith. Edited by PETER CUNNINGHAM, F.S.A. From New Electrotype Plates. 4 vols., 8vo, Cloth, Paper Labels, Uncut Edges and Gilt Tops, $8 00; Sheep, $10 00; Half Calf, $17 00.

MOTLEY'S DUTCH REPUBLIC. The Rise of the Dutch Republic. A History. By JOHN LOTHROP MOTLEY, LL.D., D.C.L. With a Portrait of William of Orange. Cheap Edition, 3 vols., in a Box. 8vo, Cloth, with Paper Labels, Uncut Edges and Gilt Tops, $6 00; Sheep, $7 50; Half Calf, $12 75. Sold only in Sets. Original Library Edition, 3 vols., 8vo, Cloth, $10 50.

MOTLEY'S UNITED NETHERLANDS. History of the United Netherlands: From the Death of William the Silent to the Twelve Years' Truce—1584-1609. With a full View of the English-Dutch Struggle against Spain, and of the Origin and Destruction of the Spanish Armada. By JOHN LOTHROP MOTLEY, LL.D., D.C.L. Portraits. Cheap Edition, 4 vols., in a Box, 8vo, Cloth, with Paper Labels, Uncut Edges and Gilt Tops, $8 00; Sheep, $10 00; Half Calf, $17 00. Sold only in Sets. Original Library Edition, 4 vols., 8vo, Cloth, $14 00.

MOTLEY'S JOHN OF BARNEVELD. The Life and Death of John of Barneveld, Advocate of Holland. With a View of the Primary Causes and Movements of the "Thirty Years' War." By JOHN LOTHROP MOTLEY, LL.D., D.C.L. Illustrated. Cheap Edition, 2 vols., in a Box, 8vo, Cloth, with Paper Labels, Uncut Edges and Gilt Tops, $4 00; Sheep, $5 00; Half Calf, $8 50. Sold only in Sets. Original Library Edition, 2 vols., 8vo, Cloth, $7 00.

HILDRETH'S UNITED STATES. History of the United States. FIRST SERIES: From the Discovery of the Continent to the Organization of the Government under the Federal Constitution. SECOND SERIES: From the Adoption of the Federal Constitution to the End of the Sixteenth Congress. By RICHARD HILDRETH. Popular Edition, 6 vols., in a Box, 8vo, Cloth, with Paper Labels, Uncut Edges and Gilt Tops, $12 00; Sheep, $15 00; Half Calf, $25 50. Sold only in Sets.

LODGE'S ENGLISH COLONIES IN AMERICA. English Colonies in America. A Short History of the English Colonies in America. By HENRY CABOT LODGE. New and Revised Edition. 8vo, Half Leather, $3 00.

TREVELYAN'S LIFE OF MACAULAY. The Life and Letters of Lord Macaulay. By his Nephew, G. OTTO TREVELYAN, M.P. With Portrait on Steel. 2 vols., 8vo, Cloth, Uncut Edges and Gilt Tops, $5 00; Sheep, $6 00; Half Calf, $9 50. Popular Edition, 2 vols. in one, 12mo, Cloth, $1 75.

TREVELYAN'S LIFE OF FOX. The Early History of Charles James Fox. By GEORGE OTTO TREVELYAN. 8vo, Cloth, Uncut Edges and Gilt Tops, $2 50; Half Calf, $4 75.

WRITINGS AND SPEECHES OF SAMUEL J. TILDEN. Edited by JOHN BIGELOW. 2 vols., 8vo, Cloth, Gilt Tops and Uncut Edges, $6 00 per set.

GENERAL DIX'S MEMOIRS. Memoirs of John Adams Dix. Compiled by his Son, MORGAN DIX. With Five Steel-plate Portraits. 2 vols., 8vo, Cloth, Gilt Tops and Uncut Edges, $5 00.

HUNT'S MEMOIR OF MRS. LIVINGSTON. A Memoir of Mrs. Edward Livingston. With Letters hitherto Unpublished. By LOUISE LIVINGSTON HUNT. 12mo, Cloth, $1 25.

GEORGE ELIOT'S LIFE. George Eliot's Life, Related in her Letters and Journals. Arranged and Edited by her Husband, J. W. CROSS. Portraits and Illustrations. In Three Volumes. 12mo, Cloth, $3 75. New Edition, with Fresh Matter. (Uniform with "Harper's Library Edition" of George Eliot's Works.)

PEARS'S FALL OF CONSTANTINOPLE. The Fall of Constantinople. Being the Story of the Fourth Crusade. By EDWIN PEARS, LL.B. 8vo, Cloth, $2 50.

RANKE'S UNIVERSAL HISTORY. The Oldest Historical Group of Nations and the Greeks. By LEOPOLD VON RANKE. Edited by G. W. PROTHERO, Fellow and Tutor of King's College, Cambridge. Vol. I. 8vo, Cloth, $2 50.

LIFE AND TIMES OF THE REV. SYDNEY SMITH. A Sketch of the Life and Times of the Rev. Sydney Smith. Based on Family Documents and the Recollections of Personal Friends. By STUART J. REID. With Steel-plate Portrait and Illustrations. 8vo, Cloth, $3 00.

STORMONTH'S ENGLISH DICTIONARY. A Dictionary of the English Language, Pronouncing, Etymological, and Explanatory: embracing Scientific and other Terms, Numerous Familiar Terms, and a Copious Selection of Old English Words. By the Rev. JAMES STORMONTH. The Pronunciation Revised by the Rev. P. H. PHELP, M.A. Imperial 8vo, Cloth, $6 00; Half Roan, $7 00; Full Sheep, $7 50. (New Edition.)

PARTON'S CARICATURE. Caricature and Other Comic Art, in All Times and Many Lands. By JAMES PARTON. 203 Illustrations. 8vo, Cloth, Uncut Edges and Gilt Tops, $5 00; Half Calf, $7 25.

DU CHAILLU'S LAND OF THE MIDNIGHT SUN. Summer and Winter Journeys in Sweden, Norway, Lapland, and Northern Finland. By PAUL B. DU CHAILLU. Illustrated. 2 vols., 8vo, Cloth, $7 50; Half Calf, $12 00.

LOSSING'S CYCLOPÆDIA OF UNITED STATES HISTORY. From the Aboriginal Period to 1876. By B. J. LOSSING, LL.D. Illustrated by 2 Steel Portraits and over 1000 Engravings. 2 vols., Royal 8vo, Cloth, $10 00; Sheep, $12 00; Half Morocco, $15 00. (*Sold by Subscription only.*)

LOSSING'S FIELD-BOOK OF THE REVOLUTION. Pictorial Field-Book of the Revolution; or, Illustrations by Pen and Pencil of the History, Biography, Scenery, Relics, and Traditions of the War for Independence. By BENSON J. LOSSING. 2 vols., 8vo, Cloth, $14 00; Sheep or Roan, $15 00; Half Calf, $18 00.

LOSSING'S FIELD-BOOK OF THE WAR OF 1812. Pictorial Field-Book of the War of 1812; or, Illustrations by Pen and Pencil of the History, Biography, Scenery, Relics, and Traditions of the last War for American Independence. By BENSON J. LOSSING. With several hundred Engravings. 1088 pages, 8vo, Cloth, $7 00; Sheep or Roan, $8 50; Half Calf, $10 00.

MÜLLER'S POLITICAL HISTORY OF RECENT TIMES (1816–1875). With Special Reference to Germany. By WILLIAM MÜLLER. Translated, with an Appendix covering the Period from 1876 to 1881, by the Rev. JOHN P. PETERS, Ph.D. 12mo, Cloth, $3 00.

STANLEY'S THROUGH THE DARK CONTINENT. Through the Dark Continent; or, The Sources of the Nile, Around the Great Lakes of Equatorial Africa, and Down the Livingstone River to the Atlantic Ocean. 149 Illustrations and 10 Maps. By H. M. STANLEY. 2 vols., 8vo, Cloth, $10 00; Sheep, $12 00; Half Morocco, $15 00.

STANLEY'S CONGO. The Congo and the Founding of its Free State, a Story of Work and Exploration. With over One Hundred Full-page and smaller Illustrations, Two Large Maps, and several smaller ones. By H. M. STANLEY. 2 vols., 8vo, Cloth, $10 00; Sheep, $12 00; Half Morocco, $15 00.

GREEN'S ENGLISH PEOPLE. History of the English People. By JOHN RICHARD GREEN, M.A. With Maps. 4 vols., 8vo, Cloth, $10 00; Sheep, $12 00; Half Calf, $19 00.

GREEN'S MAKING OF ENGLAND. The Making of England. By JOHN RICHARD GREEN. With Maps. 8vo, Cloth, $2 50; Sheep, $3 00; Half Calf, $3 75.

GREEN'S CONQUEST OF ENGLAND. The Conquest of England. By JOHN RICHARD GREEN. With Maps. 8vo, Cloth, $2 50; Sheep, $3 00; Half Calf, $3 75.

ENGLISH MEN OF LETTERS. Edited by JOHN MORLEY. The following volumes are now ready. Others will follow:

JOHNSON. By L. Stephen.—GIBBON. By J. C. Morison.—SCOTT. By R. H. Hutton.—SHELLEY. By J. A. Symonds.—GOLDSMITH. By W. Black.—HUME. By Professor Huxley.—DEFOE. By W. Minto.—BURNS. By Principal Shairp.—SPENSER. By R. W. Church.—THACKERAY. By A. Trollope.—BURKE. By J. Morley.—MILTON. By M. Pattison.—SOUTHEY. By E. Dowden.—CHAUCER. By A. W. Ward.—BUNYAN. By J. A. Froude.—COWPER. By G. Smith.—POPE. By L. Stephen.—BYRON. By J. Nichols.—LOCKE. By T. Fowler.—WORDSWORTH. By F. W. H. Myers.—HAWTHORNE. By Henry James, Jr.—DRYDEN. By G. Saintsbury.—LANDOR. By S. Colvin.—DE QUINCEY. By D. Masson.—LAMB. By A. Ainger.—BENTLEY. By R. C. Jebb.—DICKENS. By A. W. Ward.—GRAY. By E. W. Gosse.—SWIFT. By L. Stephen. —STERNE. By H. D. Traill.—MACAULAY. By J. C. Morison.—FIELDING. By A. Dobson.—SHERIDAN. By Mrs. Oliphant.—ADDISON. By W. J. Courthope.—BACON. By R. W. Church.—COLERIDGE. By H. D. Traill.—SIR PHILIP SIDNEY. By J. A. Symonds. 12mo, Cloth, 75 cents per volume.

REBER'S HISTORY OF ANCIENT ART. History of Ancient Art. By Dr. FRANZ VON REBER. Revised by the Author. Translated and Augmented by Joseph Thacher Clarke. With 310 Illustrations and a Glossary of Technical Terms. 8vo, Cloth, $3 50.

REBER'S MEDIÆVAL ART. History of Mediæval Art. By Dr. FRANZ VON REBER. Translated and Augmented by Joseph Thacher Clarke. With 422 Illustrations, and a Glossary of Technical Terms. 8vo, Cloth, $5 00.

NEWCOMB'S ASTRONOMY. Popular Astronomy. By SIMON NEWCOMB, LL.D. With 112 Engravings, and 5 Maps of the Stars. 8vo, Cloth, $2 50; School Edition, 12mo, Cloth, $1 30.

VAN-LENNEP'S BIBLE LANDS. Bible Lands: their Modern Customs and Manners Illustrative of Scripture. By HENRY J. VAN-LENNEP, D.D. 350 Engravings and 2 Colored Maps. 8vo, Cloth, $5 00; Sheep, $6 00; Half Morocco, $8 00.

CESNOLA'S CYPRUS. Cyprus: its Ancient Cities, Tombs, and Temples. A Narrative of Researches and Excavations during Ten Years' Residence in that Island. By L. P. DI CESNOLA. With Portrait, Maps, and 400 Illustrations. 8vo, Cloth, Extra, Uncut Edges and Gilt Tops, $7 50.

TENNYSON'S COMPLETE POEMS. The Complete Poetical Works of Alfred, Lord Tennyson. With an Introductory Sketch by Anne Thackeray Ritchie. With Portraits and Illustrations. 8vo, Extra Cloth, Bevelled, Gilt Edges, $2 50.

SHORT'S NORTH AMERICANS OF ANTIQUITY. The North Americans of Antiquity. Their Origin, Migrations, and Type of Civilization Considered. By JOHN T. SHORT. Illustrated. 8vo, Cloth, $3 00.

Valuable Works for Public and Private Libraries.

GROTE'S HISTORY OF GREECE. 12 vols., 12mo, Cloth, $18 00; Sheep, $22 80; Half Calf, $39 00.

FLAMMARION'S ATMOSPHERE. Translated from the French of CAMILLE FLAMMARION. With 10 Chromo-Lithographs and 86 Wood-cuts. 8vo, Cloth, $6 00; Half Calf, $8 25.

BAKER'S ISMAÏLIA: a Narrative of the Expedition to Central Africa for the Suppression of the Slave-trade, organized by Ismaïl, Khedive of Egypt. By Sir SAMUEL W. BAKER. With Maps, Portraits, and Illustrations. 8vo, Cloth, $5 00; Half Calf, $7 25.

LIVINGSTONE'S ZAMBESI. Narrative of an Expedition to the Zambesi and its Tributaries, and of the Discovery of the Lakes Shirwa and Nyassa, 1858 to 1864. By DAVID and CHARLES LIVINGSTONE. Illustrated. 8vo, Cloth, $5 00; Sheep, $5 50; Half Calf, $7 25.

LIVINGSTONE'S LAST JOURNALS. The Last Journals of David Livingstone, in Central Africa, from 1865 to his Death. Continued by a Narrative of his Last Moments, obtained from his Faithful Servants Chuma and Susi. By HORACE WALLER. With Portrait, Maps, and Illustrations. 8vo, Cloth, $5 00; Sheep, $6 00.

BLAIKIE'S LIFE OF DAVID LIVINGSTONE. Memoir of his Personal Life, from his Unpublished Journals and Correspondence. By W. G. BLAIKIE, D.D. With Portrait and Map. 8vo, Cloth, $2 25.

"THE FRIENDLY EDITION" of Shakespeare's Works. Edited by W. J. ROLFE. In 20 vols. Illustrated. 16mo, Gilt Tops and Uncut Edges, Sheets, $27 00; Cloth, $30 00; Half Calf, $60 per Set.

GIESELER'S ECCLESIASTICAL HISTORY. A Text-Book of Church History. By Dr. JOHN C. L. GIESELER. Translated from the Fourth Revised German Edition. Revised and Edited by Rev. HENRY B. SMITH, D.D. Vols. I., II., III., and IV., 8vo, Cloth, $2 25 each; Vol. V., 8vo, Cloth, $3 00. Complete Sets, 5 vols., Sheep, $14 50; Half Calf, $23 25.

CURTIS'S LIFE OF BUCHANAN. Life of James Buchanan, Fifteenth President of the United States. By GEORGE TICKNOR CURTIS. With Two Steel Plate Portraits. 2 vols., 8vo, Cloth, Uncut Edges and Gilt Tops, $6 00.

COLERIDGE'S WORKS. The Complete Works of Samuel Taylor Coleridge. With an Introductory Essay upon his Philosophical and Theological Opinions. Edited by Professor W. G. T. SHEDD. With Steel Portrait, and an Index. 7 vols., 12mo, Cloth, $2 00 per volume; $12 00 per set; Half Calf, $24 25.

GRIFFIS'S JAPAN. The Mikado's Empire: Book I. History of Japan, from 660 B.C. to 1872 A.D. Book II. Personal Experiences, Observations, and Studies in Japan, from 1870 to 1874. With Two Supplementary Chapters: Japan in 1883, and Japan in 1886. By W. E. GRIFFIS. Copiously Illustrated. 8vo, Cloth, $4 00; Half Calf, $6 25.

SMILES'S HISTORY OF THE HUGUENOTS. The Huguenots: their Settlements, Churches, and Industries in England and Ireland. By SAMUEL SMILES. With an Appendix relating to the Huguenots in America. Crown, 8vo, Cloth, $2 00.

SMILES'S HUGUENOTS AFTER THE REVOCATION. The Huguenots in France after the Revocation of the Edict of Nantes; with a Visit to the Country of the Vaudois. By SAMUEL SMILES. Crown 8vo, Cloth, $2 00.

SMILES'S LIFE OF THE STEPHENSONS. The Life of George Stephenson, and of his Son, Robert Stephenson; comprising, also, a History of the Invention and Introduction of the Railway Locomotive. By SAMUEL SMILES. Illustrated. 8vo, Cloth, $3 00.

THE POETS AND POETRY OF SCOTLAND: From the Earliest to the Present Time. Comprising Characteristic Selections from the Works of the more Noteworthy Scottish Poets, with Biographical and Critical Notices. By JAMES GRANT WILSON. With Portraits on Steel. 2 vols., 8vo, Cloth, $10 00; Gilt Edges, $11 00.

SCHLIEMANN'S ILIOS. Ilios, the City and Country of the Trojans. A Narrative of the Most Recent Discoveries and Researches made on the Plain of Troy. By Dr. HENRY SCHLIEMANN. Maps, Plans, and Illustrations. Imperial 8vo, Illuminated Cloth, $12 00; Half Morocco, $15 00.

SCHLIEMANN'S TROJA. Troja. Results of the Latest Researches and Discoveries on the Site of Homer's Troy, and in the Heroic Tumuli and other Sites, made in the Year 1882, and a Narrative of a Journey in the Troad in 1881. By Dr. HENRY SCHLIEMANN. Preface by Professor A. H. Sayce. With Wood-cuts, Maps, and Plans. 8vo, Cloth, $7 50; Half Morocco, $10 00.

SCHWEINFURTH'S HEART OF AFRICA. Three Years' Travels and Adventures in the Unexplored Regions of the Centre of Africa—from 1868 to 1871. By GEORG SCHWEINFURTH. Translated by ELLEN E. FREWER. Illustrated. 2 vols., 8vo, Cloth, $8 00.

NORTON'S STUDIES OF CHURCH-BUILDING. Historical Studies of Church-Building in the Middle Ages. Venice, Siena, Florence. By CHARLES ELIOT NORTON. 8vo, Cloth, $3 00.

THE VOYAGE OF THE "CHALLENGER." The Atlantic: an Account of the General Results of the Voyage during 1873, and the Early Part of 1876. By Sir WYVILLE THOMSON, K.C.B., F.R.S. Illustrated. 2 vols., 8vo, Cloth, $12 00.

THE STUDENT'S SERIES. Maps and Illustrations. 12mo, Cloth:
FRANCE.—GIBBON.—GREECE.—ROME (by LIDDELL).—OLD TESTAMENT HISTORY. — NEW TESTAMENT HISTORY. — STRICKLAND'S QUEENS OF ENGLAND.—ANCIENT HISTORY OF THE EAST.—HALLAM'S MIDDLE AGES. — HALLAM'S CONSTITUTIONAL HISTORY OF ENGLAND.— LYELL'S ELEMENTS OF GEOLOGY.— MERIVALE'S GENERAL HISTORY OF ROME.—COX'S GENERAL HISTORY OF GREECE. —CLASSICAL DICTIONARY.—SKEAT'S ETYMOLOGICAL DICTIONARY.— RAWLINSON'S ANCIENT HISTORY. $1 25 per volume.

LEWIS'S HISTORY OF GERMANY.—ECCLESIASTICAL HISTORY, Two Vols.—HUME'S ENGLAND.—MODERN EUROPE. $1 50 per volume.

WESTCOTT AND HORT'S GREEK TESTAMENT, $1 00.

THOMSON'S SOUTHERN PALESTINE AND JERUSALEM. Southern Palestine and Jerusalem. Biblical Illustrations drawn from the Manners and Customs, the Scenes and Scenery, of the Holy Land. By W. M. THOMSON, D.D. 140 Illustrations and Maps. Square 8vo, Cloth, $6 00; Sheep, $7 00; Half Morocco, $8 50; Full Morocco, Gilt Edges, $10 00.

THOMSON'S CENTRAL PALESTINE AND PHŒNICIA. Central Palestine and Phœnicia. Biblical Illustrations drawn from the Manners and Customs, the Scenes and Scenery, of the Holy Land. By W. M. THOMSON, D.D. 130 Illustrations and Maps. Square 8vo, Cloth, $6 00; Sheep, $7 00; Half Morocco, $8 50; Full Morocco, $10 00.

THOMSON'S LEBANON, DAMASCUS, AND BEYOND JORDAN. Lebanon, Damascus, and beyond Jordan. Biblical Illustrations drawn from the Manners and Customs, the Scenes and Scenery, of the Holy Land. By W. M. THOMSON, D.D. 147 Illustrations and Maps. Square 8vo, Cloth, $6 00; Sheep, $7 00; Half Morocco, $8 50; Full Morocco, $10 00.

Popular Edition of the above three volumes, 8vo, Ornamental Cloth, $9 00 per set.

CYCLOPÆDIA OF BRITISH AND AMERICAN POETRY. Edited by EPES SARGENT. Royal 8vo, Illuminated Cloth, Colored Edges, $4 50; Half Leather, $5 00.

EATON'S CIVIL SERVICE. Civil Service in Great Britain. A History of Abuses and Reforms, and their bearing upon American Politics. By DORMAN B. EATON. 8vo, Cloth, $2 50.

Valuable Works for Public and Private Libraries. 9

CAMERON'S ACROSS AFRICA. Across Africa. By VERNEY LOVETT CAMERON. Map and Illustrations. 8vo, Cloth, $5 00.

CARLYLE'S FREDERICK THE GREAT. History of Friedrich II., called Frederick the Great. By THOMAS CARLYLE. Portraits, Maps, Plans, &c. 6 vols., 12mo, Cloth, $7 50; Sheep, $9 90; Half Calf, $18 00.

CARLYLE'S FRENCH REVOLUTION. The French Revolution: a History. By THOMAS CARLYLE. 2 vols., 12mo, Cloth, $2 50; Sheep, $2 90; Half Calf, $4 25.

CARLYLE'S OLIVER CROMWELL. Oliver Cromwell's Letters and Speeches, including the Supplement to the First Edition. With Elucidations. By THOMAS CARLYLE. 2 vols., 12mo, Cloth, $2 50; Sheep, $2 90; Half Calf, $4 25.

PAST AND PRESENT, CHARTISM, AND SARTOR RESARTUS. By THOMAS CARLYLE. 12mo, Cloth, $1 25.

EARLY KINGS OF NORWAY, AND THE PORTRAITS OF JOHN KNOX. By THOMAS CARLYLE. 12mo, Cloth, $1 25.

REMINISCENCES BY THOMAS CARLYLE. Edited by J. A. FROUDE. 12mo, Cloth, with Copious Index, and with Thirteen Portraits, 50 cents.

FROUDE'S LIFE OF THOMAS CARLYLE. PART I. A History of the First Forty Years of Carlyle's Life (1795–1835). By JAMES ANTHONY FROUDE, M.A. With Portraits and Illustrations. 2 volumes in one, 12mo, Cloth, $1 00.

PART II. A History of Carlyle's Life in London (1834–1881). By JAMES ANTHONY FROUDE. Illustrated. 2 volumes in one. 12mo, Cloth, $1 00.

M'CARTHY'S HISTORY OF ENGLAND. A History of Our Own Times, from the Accession of Queen Victoria to the General Election of 1880. By JUSTIN M'CARTHY. 2 vols., 12mo, Cloth, $2 50; Half Calf, $6 00.

M'CARTHY'S SHORT HISTORY OF OUR OWN TIMES. A Short History of Our Own Times, from the Accession of Queen Victoria to the General Election of 1880. By JUSTIN M'CARTHY, M.P. 12mo, Cloth, $1 50.

M'CARTHY'S HISTORY OF THE FOUR GEORGES. A History of the Four Georges. By JUSTIN M'CARTHY, M.P. Vol. I. 12mo, Cloth, $1 25. (To be completed in Four Volumes.)

ABBOTT'S HISTORY OF THE FRENCH REVOLUTION. The French Revolution of 1789, as viewed in the Light of Republican Institutions. By JOHN S. C. ABBOTT. Illustrated. 8vo, Cloth, $5 00; Sheep, $5 50; Half Calf, $7 25.

ABBOTT'S NAPOLEON. The History of Napoleon Bonaparte. By JOHN S. C. ABBOTT. Maps, Illustrations, and Portraits. 2 vols., 8vo, Cloth, $10 00; Sheep, $11 00; Half Calf, $14 50.

ABBOTT'S NAPOLEON AT ST. HELENA. Napoleon at St. Helena; or, Anecdotes and Conversations of the Emperor during the Years of his Captivity. Collected from the Memorials of Las Casas, O'Meara, Montholon, Antommarchi, and others. By JOHN S. C. ABBOTT. Illustrated. 8vo, Cloth, $5 00; Sheep, $5 50; Half Calf, $7 25.

ABBOTT'S FREDERICK THE GREAT. The History of Frederick the Second, called Frederick the Great. By JOHN S. C. ABBOTT. Illustrated. 8vo, Cloth, $5 00; Half Calf, $7 25.

TROLLOPE'S AUTOBIOGRAPHY. An Autobiography. By ANTHONY TROLLOPE. With a Portrait. 12mo, Cloth, $1 25.

TROLLOPE'S CICERO. Life of Cicero. By ANTHONY TROLLOPE. 2 vols., 12mo, Cloth, $3 00.

FOLK-LORE OF SHAKESPEARE. By the Rev. T. F. THISELTON DYER, M.A., Oxon. 8vo, Cloth, $2 50.

WATSON'S MARCUS AURELIUS ANTONINUS. Marcus Aurelius Antoninus. By PAUL BARRON WATSON. Crown 8vo, Cloth, $2 50.

THOMSON'S THE GREAT ARGUMENT. The Great Argument; or, Jesus Christ in the Old Testament. By W. H. THOMSON, M.A., M.D. Crown 8vo, Cloth, $2 00.

HUDSON'S HISTORY OF JOURNALISM. Journalism in the United States, from 1690 to 1872. By FREDERIC HUDSON. 8vo, Cloth, $5 00; Half Calf, $7 25.

SHELDON'S HISTORY OF CHRISTIAN DOCTRINE. History of Christian Doctrine. By H. C. SHELDON, Professor of Church History in Boston University. 2 vols., 8vo, Cloth, $3 50 per set.

DEXTER'S CONGREGATIONALISM. The Congregationalism of the Last Three Hundred Years, as Seen in its Literature: with Special Reference to certain Recondite, Neglected, or Disputed Passages. With a Bibliographical Appendix. By H. M. DEXTER. Large 8vo, Cloth, $6 00.